GESA

Gesar

Tantric Practices of the Tibetan Warrior King

Jamgön Mipham

TRANSLATED AND EDITED BY
Gyurme Avertin

WITH CONTRIBUTIONS BY
Chögyam Trungpa and Orgyen Tobgyal

FOREWORD BY
Dzongsar Jamyang Khyentse

SNOW LION

Snow Lion
An imprint of Shambhala Publications, Inc.
2129 13th Street
Boulder, Colorado 80302
www.shambhala.com

© 2023 by Gyurme Avertin

Cover art: Tara di Gesu
Cover design: Daniel Urban-Brown

9 8 7 6 5 4 3 2 1

First Edition
Printed in the United States of America

Shambhala Publications makes every effort to print
on acid-free, recycled paper.
Shambhala Publications is distributed worldwide by
Penguin Random House, Inc., and its subsidiaries.

LIBRARY OF CONGRESS CATALOGING-IN-PUBLICATION DATA
Names: Mi-pham-rgya-mtsho, 'Jam-mgon 'Ju, 1846–1912, author. | Avertin,
Gyurme, translator. | Trungpa, Chögyam, 1939–1987, author. | Orgyen
Tobgyal, author.
Title: Gesar: Tantric practices of the Tibetan warrior king / Jamgön
Mipham; translated and edited by Gyurme Avertin; with contributions by
Chögyam Trungpa and Orgyen Tobgyal; foreword by Dzongsar Jamyang
Khyentse.
Description: Boulder: Shambhala, 2023.
Identifiers: LCCN 2022043688 | ISBN 9781611809152 (trade paperback)
Subjects: LCSH: Gesar (Legendary character) | Gesar (Legendary
character)—Prayers and devotions. | Tantric Buddhism. | Buddhism—
China—Tibet Autonomous Region.
Classification: LCC PL3748.G4 M57 2023 | DDC 294.3/444—dc23/
eng/20221202
LC record available at https://lccn.loc.gov/2022043688

Page 297 constitutes an extension of this copyright page.

To my lamas, and to Gesar and his hordes who they revealed
   to me—
May their aspirations be fulfilled.
May people everywhere, and especially their leaders, be inspired
   by the dharma.
May peace and harmony prevail in the world.

PLEASE NOTE: The teachings and practices presented in this book are Secret Mantra Vajrayana teachings. As such, to benefit from this volume and the practices it contains, it is essential to first receive from a qualified master the Gesar Dorje Tsegyal empowerment or "entrustment with his life force," the reading transmission of the practice, and the associated instructions. If you have yet to receive the empowerment and reading transmission, it is best to keep this book on your shrine as an object of veneration until you receive them. The empowerment is a must, not an option.

CONTENTS

FOREWORD

Human beings with all their confusions, delusions, and self-righteous moralizing have relied to some extent on empirical research from time immemorial. Today, empiricism is the norm. If a phenomenon cannot be validated or legitimized by reputable academics—perhaps at an Oxbridge or Ivy League university—it is labeled with a carefully crafted literary term like *magical realism* or *legend* and relegated to a pile of quaint, old-fashioned, archaic beliefs. If it is validated—if a famous academic of scientific institution gives it their seal of approval—everyone else feels safer about using it and won't feel embarrassed about sharing it with others. But no matter what tools are applied during the process of legitimization, an "experiencer," "enjoyer," "decider" is a must. And the rather vague term we use to describe that experiencer is *mind*.

Curiously, empiricists don't appear to have noticed that no matter where mind is—with a shaman in a remote jungle in Peru or a nerdy scientist in a Cambridge lab—mind is necessarily an unstable, conditioned phenomenon that falls victim to causes and conditions at the drop of a hat. All it takes is an impatient word from a disgruntled spouse over breakfast or the wrong choice of salad dressing at lunch and mind flip-flops from happy to sad, kind to cruel, easygoing to outraged.

What is "true"? What is "right"? What is "legend"? What is "myth"? Historians have never been able to prove categorically that King Arthur ever lived, but that doesn't stop novelists, movie-makers, cartoonists, and so on from making fortunes from his legends. Where there is money to be made, even the communist Chinese, who habitually condemn all outdated, feudal systems and superstitions, don't hesitate to name a new business after a manifestation of the mythical first god of Chinese theology—the "Jade Emperor Restaurant."

With so many theories flying around and so much self-interest involved, the Himalayan legends, stories, and myths about a great spiritual warrior who may or may not have lived thousands of years ago might, at best, be designated "magical realism." As such, practitioners who long to become better acquainted with and even pray to and supplicate the great being, deity, guru, protector known as Gesar of Ling have little chance of avoiding ridicule.

Buddhism is firmly rooted in the teachings of the four seals: all compounded things are impermanent, all emotions are fundamentally unsatisfying, not one phenomenon truly exists, and the awakened state (enlightenment) is beyond extremes. Buddhist history is full of stories about practitioners and teachers who never deviated from the wisdom of selflessness and the compassion of skillful means. Thus, these great beings had the courage and wit to employ any number of skillful methods that were custom-made to suit the needs of those living at a specific time and in a specific culture—as is evident from skillful methods such as the creation of Zen gardens, Japanese tea ceremonies and flower arranging, the tradition of sitting cross-legged in meditation, and the use of the lotus (not poison ivy) in the Buddhist iconography of Japan, India, Tibet, and China.

But, of course, when we human beings come across anything that is not in tune with our own tastes, feelings, and cultural background, we either mock and make fun of it or denounce and condemn it. Imagine the number of blond, red, brown, and black eyebrows that would be raised if someone like me presented a systematic tea ceremony based on the English tradition of afternoon tea as a skillful method for developing mindfulness, discipline, and an appreciation of nowness.

The phenomenon of Gesar of Ling is just one of the many skillful means Himalayan peoples love to apply. Our songs are full of stories about courage, warriorship, respect for our elders, family loyalties, and the protection of the poor and needy. Sometimes we sing for joy because we love singing, but we also sing to cheer ourselves up, boost our confidence, inspire bravery, strengthen our resolve, and remind ourselves of our rich tradition of moving stories about the compassionate heroism of fathers, mothers, kings, queens, and masters of the past.

Pompous modern scholars tend to turn their noses up at Gesar's stories and chuck the entire tradition into the basket of myth and legend. But other more broad-minded beings see things differently. The great wisdom of many stouthearted, valiant, clever, compassionate teachers and practitioners has given them the courage to see and recognize the truth. For example, they can see that by placing a special mixture of dried leaves in a small, roughly formed cup, then swilling the mixture around the cup (for no scientific reason) and wiping the cup carefully with a cloth, the tea maker can be brought to the state of authentic presence and experience the joy of appreciating nowness. Mipham Rinpoche, who had himself invoked the spirit of profound brilliance, recognized that everything about Gesar of Ling had the potential to inspire authentic presence and an appreciation of nowness. And he didn't think twice about making use of any of it. But sadly, even the eyebrows of Tibetan Buddhist masters and scholars have twitched over Gesar, and many have chosen to dismiss him as a mere legend in the same way modern scientists do.

Today's world moves so fast. Joy, sadness, or simply reading a short email can open the door to emotional volatility and uncertainty more quickly and intensely than ever before—it's why the tsunami of human emotion is so out of control. Now more than ever before, we need to develop our ability to remain strong and kind within the fortress of who we really are. If someone like Mipham Rinpoche had no qualms about using Gesar—the king, the legend, the protector, the guide, and the guru—as a path to accomplishing authentic presence and emotional stability, why shouldn't we make use of this extraordinary path too?

Dzongsar Jamyang Khyentse Rinpoche

August 8, 2021

Translator's Introduction

Other than the general enemies of the Buddha's teachings,
I, Gesar, have no personal enemies.
Other than the general welfare of all beings,
I, Gesar, have no other personal aims.

—*The Epic of Gesar of Ling*[1]

King Gesar has piqued the curiosity of the West ever since missionaries and explorers first encountered Tibet. Today the legendary hero of days long gone is still very much alive in the Tibetan psyche. The vibrant bardic tradition of the Gesar epic continues to thrive; theatrical performances, operas, and lama dances continue to be played. A growing number of texts are being written about him, often transcriptions of bards' visionary performances but also prayers and invocations. Many Chinese academics are engaged in the studies of the Gesar legend under the patronage of the Chinese government, who considers Gesar a secular figure rather than a religious one—a recognition that has lent his name to many streets across East Tibet, not to mention a museum and an airport, and that has seen his statue appear in a burgeoning number of town squares. Early Tibetologists have written a great deal about Gesar, and his life and activities have been of sustained interest to the present day of academics and Buddhists alike. Gesar is mostly known as the hero of Tibet's national oral epic, but he is also the focus of Buddhist practices in which the enlightened form known as King Gesar the Jewel becomes one of the many spiritual methods offered by Tibetan Vajrayana Buddhism to progress toward buddhahood.

Although all Buddhist teachings and paths have but one goal, there are as many vehicles to reach awakening as there are dispositions and capacities of sentient beings. This is why the Buddha and all the accomplished masters who followed him taught a variety of methods to suit varying needs. Therefore one thing to bear in mind is that the teachings and practices presented in this book are Secret Mantra Vajrayana teachings. As such, to benefit from this volume and the practices it contains, it is essential to first receive from a qualified master the Gesar Dorje Tsegyal empowerment or "entrustment with his life force," the reading transmission of the practice, and the associated instructions. If you have yet to receive the empowerment and reading transmission, it is best to keep this book on your shrine as an object of veneration until you receive them. The empowerment is a must, not an option. The tantra called *Mirror of the Heart of Vajrasattva* makes it clear: "In the Secret Mantra Vehicle, there can be no accomplishment without empowerment; it is like a boatman with no oars." Kyabje Dilgo Khyentse Rinpoche explained that "as the Buddha Vajradhara said, 'Those who have not received empowerment are not allowed even to see the Secret Mantra texts.' If one looks at the texts without having received the empowerment, one cannot attain the ordinary and supreme siddhis. Receiving the empowerment and the accompanying oral transmission and secret instruction is like receiving a visa: it allows one to listen, meditate on, and accomplish the Secret Mantra teachings."[2]

Once we have decided to follow the fast track to buddhahood called Vajrayana and enthusiastically receive an empowerment, it is understood that we must guard the samayas, for they are the life force of the empowerment. Indeed, what could be the point of going through the trouble of getting a visa if we don't make the trip? Once we have received a Gesar empowerment, the samayas that guide us toward awakening are the specific samayas of Gesar mentioned in the original terma text on page 217 and the general samayas of Secret Mantra Vajrayana. The general samayas are taught in different ways, so you can refer to the teachings on the five root and twenty-five secondary samayas, or on the fourteen root downfalls, or on the samayas of enlightened body, speech, and mind.

The great Nyingma vidyadhara Jamgön Mipham wrote the most significant body of texts devoted to the wisdom deity Gesar, inspired by a treasure revealed by Lharik Dechen Yeshe Rölpa Tsal. Many other great masters—Do Khyentse, Chokgyur Lingpa, Dilgo Khyentse, Khamtrul Döngyu Nyima, Khenpo Jigme Phuntsok, and Yangtang Rinpoche, to name some of the most prolific ones—have composed or revealed Gesar practices. A compilation of Gesar prayers and practices published in Tibet in 2015 fills ten large volumes,[3] yet the hundred pages written by Mipham Rinpoche are universally regarded with the greatest respect and are the most widely practiced. That is why we chose to publish for the English reader all the texts that he wrote. They include the most famous supplications to the protector Gesar and sang practices and prayers to raise the windhorse, or lungta, as well as instructions on how to make prayer flags, a horsewhip, and a wealth pouch. There is also a text on how to consecrate a casket of abundance, a practice of Gesar's half-brother, Gyatsa Shelkar, and one of his own protector, Bernakchen.

What are these practices about? In one paragraph, Ling Gesar was the king of Tibet and an emanation of the lords of the three families and of Guru Rinpoche. Gesar practice increases the strength and speed of outer activities, as well as the power of the activities related to mind and rigpa. Mipham Rinpoche composed these practices, or rather they arose as mind termas, in such a way that anyone doing these practices will see an increase in auspicious circumstances, long life, wealth, fame, good reputation, good company, and so on. In particular, it is said that the experiences and realization in the practice, warmth of bliss, indications, and signs of practice will also progressively increase.

To unpack a little, Ling Gesar was the king of Ling, a country in the east of Tibet, and of several other regions that he conquered. But above all he was a warrior emanation of Guru Rinpoche who appeared in Tibet originally to tame what are known in the epic as the demon kings in the four directions. Not long after Guru Rinpoche helped King Trisong Detsen establish the dharma in Tibet, the royal dynasty fell, chaos followed, and the dharma all but disappeared. King Gesar rose at that time as a champion of the buddhadharma. Gesar personifies the ideal of the spiritual warrior, and he is the chief of the warlike gods and the tamer of demons. Gesar fights the maras. Maras are demons—the things that we are very afraid of and want to get rid of. Omniscient Longchenpa explained that, fundamentally, mara is deluded mind involved in dualistic clinging, which on the path is what prevents the practitioner from progressing in the right direction; it is the obstacle to liberation. We often hear about the four maras, he added, but in fact, their number is infinite because there is no end to thoughts, and through "the yoga of complete victory over the maras" we can realize the primordially free nature of thoughts. Eliminate mara and no more harm will ever come to you.

Many of us have been raised in countries and cultures that have grown on the legacy of overthrowing, even sometimes beheading, their kings, or in places that never gave rein to the monarchical system. So some of us might have a difficult time looking up to the warring king of Ling, who is far from our ideal of a great spiritual adept—unlike Milarepa, St. Francis of Assisi, or peaceful Thai monks who fit the bill far better. Gesar is not the one and only Buddhist teacher manifesting as a king, and as the anthropologist Daniel Miller explains:

> We need heroes in our lives: brave, courageous men and women who, through their valor or noble character, become legendary and inspire us. In Tibetan culture, some of the greatest heroes have come from nomad backgrounds. The exploits of Ling Gesar in the 11th Century are well known throughout Tibet and even Mongolia. Banished to the wilderness at a young age by a mean uncle, he cared for his mother, hunted wild yaks

and trained his horses. Returning home years later, he won a horse race and regained the right to rule his family's kingdom. Gesar fought many battles with enemy forces, upholding freedom over suppression. Even today among contemporary Tibetans, Gesar is used as a model of moral virtue.[4]

Gesar began as a minor king in eleventh-century eastern Tibet and then became the famous hero of the longest epic in the world, spanning more than 120 volumes that chronicle his exploits. So how did a Tibetan king, the hero of an epic poem, become a tantric deity? To answer the question, we must first realize that the form that Vajrayana's skillful means takes is not set in stone. We cannot say unequivocally that teachings that did not originate in India are de facto inauthentic. Think of the Guru Rinpoche practices in which he appears in a Tibetan brocade gown and wears Mongolian boots, or the practices invoking spirits endemic to Tibet as protectors. Hinayana teachings were all spoken by the historical Buddha Shakyamuni, so after he passed into parinirvana, the source of new teachings dried up. The fact that new teachings can appear doesn't mean that Gesar practices were simply added to the Vajrayana corpus by someone who felt it would be a good idea. Secret Mantra teachings explain that the buddha dharmakaya manifests in every possible way to help and guide sentient beings toward enlightenment. One such way is by teaching the tantras, for which it can manifest in the form of Shakyamuni, Samantabhadra, Vajradhara, and so on. So the tantras are not the teachings of ordinary individuals but the words of the Buddha, the Enlightened One who is free from all negative emotions and cognitive obscurations. Tantras cannot therefore be amended by ordinary people, unlike the Vinaya for which the Buddha said ordination rules can be changed should two hundred fifty bhikshus—who are also ordinary human beings—agree that it's necessary; this has never happened but is permissible. Mipham Rinpoche made clear in several colophons to his Gesar texts that he didn't "compose" the Gesar texts that he wrote; rather, they appeared to him from "mind's expressive power"—in other words, the wisdom of all the buddhas, a process Orgyen Tobgyal Rinpoche explains on pages 24–25.

In fact, tantric deities aren't invented. Specific circumstances call for an adequate enlightened manifestation. That is why each tantra begins with the circumstance that led to the appearance of the mandala that the tantra centers around, and how the deities accomplish their mission. These origin stories make clear the angle from which the particular deities weigh on the world of relative appearances. All enlightened manifestations are one in their wisdom mind and share the same enlightened qualities. As Atisha famously told Lotsawa Rinchen Zangpo, "Tibetans practice one hundred mandalas and realize none, whereas Indians practice one mandala and realize all." When the dharmakaya manifests in sambhogakaya forms—peaceful, wrathful, or in between—it can also very well manifest in human forms in our world, such as Buddha Shakyamuni and Guru Padmasambhava. And why not also a king, in a drala armor, by the name of Gesar?

Now that we know it is possible, who gives a deity permission to join the Vajrayana pantheon? This question must be answered from the Vajrayana perspective. Taking any other system of reference would be like trying to judge a football player's performance based on the rules of figure skating. Gesar was not a local feudal lord promoted to tantric deity. According to Mipham Rinpoche this would be a wrong apprehension, though not uncommon in the West. Buddhist understanding of reality is different from our ordinary view. Looking at Gesar through the prism of Western categories and concepts may have its own merit, yet the essence of the dharma is to reverse our ordinary human worldview because it is tainted by a fundamental misperception of reality. The reason why we practice the dharma, through Gesar or any other method, is to shake off our ordinary perspective and to reveal the vast, expansive view of reality that frees us from suffering and gives us the capacity to free others. Therefore, to try to squeeze dharma into the small conceptual boxes furnished by our education not only defeats the purpose but also annihilates the dharma's capacity to transform us. Instead, we have transformed the dharma to fit ourselves. To best relate to Gesar, we need to relax and open our minds. The question "How did Gesar become a tantric deity?" looks at the matter the wrong way. As all the prayers in this collection say, and as Orgyen Tobgyal Rinpoche explains on pages 18–19, Gesar is an enlightened manifestation appearing in the form of a human being to help human beings. The embodiment of the omniscient wisdom of all the buddhas is Manjushri; the embodiment of their compassion is Avalokiteshvara; and the embodiment of their power is Vajrapani. Manjushri, Avalokiteshvara, and Vajrapani are collectively known as the protectors or lords of the three families— "families" is a very loose translation of the Sanskrit *kula*, which has a wide range of meanings but here refers to the three enlightened qualities of wisdom, love, and power. All three qualities or protectors manifest as Guru Rinpoche, who in turn manifests in the form of a drala, Gesar Norbu Dradul, to help us raise our windhorse. This means that the Gesar we invoke in these practices is not an ordinary person but—and we must bear this in mind when we do these practices—the embodiment of all the wisdom, compassion, and power of the buddhas.

Basically, our fundamental nature and the nature of everything is shunyata endowed with all enlightened qualities. This nature manifests outwardly in the form of the world around us and the nirmanakayas, or tulkus, that we meet. These nirmanakayas are enlightened forms we can relate to. They manifest thanks to shunyata's inherent compassion, the aspirations made by bodhisattvas on their way to enlightenment and of course our own karma, which allows or prevents us from seeing them. Physically they might look very special, like Buddha Shakyamuni, who displayed the hundred and twelve physical marks and signs that he had reached enlightenment, or ordinary, like reincarnate lamas. Nirmanakayas can look like dralas, as in the case of King Gesar or Magyal Pomra, or like a waiter in Casablanca, buddha statues, or even roads, bridges, and so on. So we should not attempt to elevate a feudal king to the level of a god or buddha. Arguably, to do so is a very common but erroneous way many of us try to practice devotion. We are so in love with our Rinpoche that we see him or her as the best person in the world—much better than any other Rinpoche—and we try to imagine that he or she is the Buddha. Then our Rinpoche does something we don't like, something that doesn't fit our idea of how a sugata should behave, instantly tearing off the superhero costume we dressed them with, menacing the very existence of our devotion—or what we thought was devotion but is in fact infatuation, if we want to be honest with ourselves. The way to look at the guru, at Gesar or any other great being, is the opposite: it is actually the dharmakaya who dresses like us, in disguise . . . only to be recognized.

THE WORLD OF GESAR

Tibetan Buddhism is the marriage of Indian Vajrayana and Tibetan shamanism. Buddhism always adapted to the cultures that adopted it: Shakyamuni's disciples in Sri Lanka, Japan, China, or Tibet, to name a few, revere the same core teachings but have different ways of putting them into practice. Even before setting foot in the Land of Snows, Guru Rinpoche, who implanted Buddhism in Tibet, began to convert the gods and demons of the Himalayan plateau and to integrate local people's rites with Buddhist practices. He suggested, for example, that practitioners make various realist or symbolic shapes with tsampa and butter—the famous tormas—to replace sacrifices and for other purposes. He also transformed the local sang ritual into a Buddhist practice. So along with Vajrayana Buddhist understanding of how the universe and people's bodies and minds function, Gesar practices rely on the traditional Tibetan shamanic knowledge, in a combination designed to bring us closer to the attainment of enlightenment.

Gesar was born in Tibet, so his world is the Tibetan culture, which itself is based on both Bönpo and Buddhist lore. Tibet has managed to keep its vibrant spiritual and magical culture alive, in spite of the encroachment of modernity throughout the Himalayan plateau. In many other places, the spiritual and magical aspect of the culture has been obfuscated by centuries of clerical hostility and, more recently, extreme ratiocination. Nowadays, everything becomes a subject of academic study and must satisfy the conceptual matrix of academic paradigms. This tendency can also be seen in Buddhism as it enters the Western hemisphere with the flourishing of Buddhology and Tibetology. Yet every society, every culture has practiced magic and wrestled with the supernatural. Magic is a universal language. As Dzongsar Khyentse Rinpoche mentioned in his foreword, we must not dismiss the possibility that so-called magical practices could help us in our pursuit of bettering the human condition—and that of nonhuman beings. As we know, observations from different cultures and their sciences and bodies of knowledge can uncover unexpected properties of our world, properties that can only be expressed by radically foreign concepts (the nightmare of the translator). The following paragraphs discuss some of them.

In the Tibetan system, qualities such as good circumstances, wealth, charisma, and power are not the result of random luck or hard work alone but owe a great deal to specific causes and conditions. Of course the immediate external circumstances are essential, but, as we all know, such circumstances tend to come together for some people and not for others, no matter how hard they try. This is due to more profound aspects called "auspiciousness" for good circumstances; the "spirit of abundance" (or simply "abundance" in the following pages), which brings wealth; "authentic presence," which brings charisma and power; and "windhorse," which rules the success or failure of our activities. Mipham Rinpoche was an expert at understanding interdependence. That means he had a heightened knowledge of which cause produces which result. As Khenpo Jigme Phuntsok told us, he even knew how to hide a terma and how to reveal it. According to Jamgön Mipham's biography, most of the sadhanas and prayers he wrote were for his own use to accomplish a specific purpose, which points to their efficacy and shows that he knew clearly about the subtler levels of our reality and how to work with them.

Gesar practices also involve different beings or "spirits" and are sometimes based on rituals that have been traditionally used to propitiate them. Although by and large Bönpos consider Gesar to be a Buddhist figure who, if anything, is hostile to the Bön, the Tibetan Buddhist practice of Gesar is tinged with elements of Bön, such as his connection with the ancient warrior spirits—dralas, wermas, and zodors, for example. These spirits are active in Tibet and the rest of the world, and they have an important influence on all our life circumstances. Therefore, Vajrayana—the hallmark of which is skillful methods—has no reason to shun or avoid employing the Tibetan shamanic understanding of the world. Here, spirits are not "supernatural forces" as defined in English dictionaries but beings who are invisible to ordinary people and have a different relationship with the material world. This is the true world of Gesar and one of the levels at which he acts. It may be worth remembering that we are the offspring of the Enlightenment, which defined itself in opposition to myth and superstition. Which is why we often hear or ask the question "How can we as Westerners relate to these spirits?" The answer is quite simple: the way we always relate to everything. We don't need to change anything. We investigate and infer what we cannot see—like Eratosthenes of Cyrene in the fourth century B.C.E., who calculated the circumference of the earth using the great lighthouse of Alexandria where he lived. Unlike today's astronauts, Eratosthenes could not see that the earth is a globe, but he was able to deduce it is a sphere and calculate its circumference to within a couple hundred kilometers.

Generally Tibetans, Nepalese, and Bhutanese have no doubt about the existence and influence of auspicious interdependence, windhorse, dralas who enter our bodies and shape our interaction with the world, and all kinds of spirits and local deities. For modern people, this kind of perspective sounds quite alien. Not only have we never heard of these spirits and have no idea who they are but we have seldom heard about any spirit—at least not entities that we take seriously. They may pervade art, literature, movies, and music, but they are absent from our lives. We simply relate to them as creative expressions. Our education tells us that such beings do not exist and that most things in our lives are down to chance because we have no idea what causes them (which is the "antiscientific attitude par excellence"[5] for mathematician René Thom). The great logicians—such as Arthur Schopenhauer in the West and Dignaga in the East—explain that not seeing something that cannot be seen is not proof that it does not exist. What do rational people do? They use sensory observations to prove theories, and when they cannot see something, they use logical reasoning to work out what it is that they cannot see. Therefore, we have the tools necessary to establish whether spirits and protectors exist or not. We do practices to make them act, so we can observe whether these practices bring about the desired result. If they work, the principles on which the practices are based are true. Though it might be easier to check the effectiveness of the practice of a powerful yogi, you can see it from your own practice. If there is any truth to the practices devoted to Gesar, they must work and so there will be observable results, such as a shift in circumstance, but more obvious and important, the deepening of our meditation practice.

From its earliest beginnings, Buddhism has always acknowledged the existence of nonhuman "spirits" not normally perceptible to the physical senses—the Buddha's sutras are replete with mentions of nagas, yakshas, pishachas, bhutas, kumbhandas, kimnaras, and so on and so forth. In the Tibetan tradition especially, reference is often made to evil spirits, ghosts, and the like who are identified and categorized according to a complex demonology. They are explained in different ways and with varying degrees of subtlety according to context. Quite often, however, Buddhism also understands these evil spirits as personifications of psychic energies, perhaps more akin to the neuroses and complexes described by modern Western psychology—or, in other words, features of our own minds and manifestations of our own karma. Complementing Longchenpa's explanation above, Khenpo Ngawang

Pelzang has remarked, "What we call a demon is not something with a gaping mouth or staring eyes. It is that which creates all the troubles of samsara and prevents us from attaining the state beyond suffering that is liberation; it is, in short, whatever injures our body or mind."[6]

Dralas are omnipresent in the world of Gesar, who is Guru Rinpoche in the form of a drala and the king of dralas. *Drala* can have several meanings, but all dralas have in common that they protect the lives of those who invoke them and help them to overcome obstacles and defeat enemies. *Drala* is mainly used in three different ways: First, *drala* is used as a title for several protectors of the Tibetan pantheon. Second, *drala* is used as the name of a personal protective deity, one of the "five patron gods" who reside in a person's body and increase their well-being. The drala is said to be in the right shoulder next to the father-god, who is in the right armpit. They are the two most important personal guardian deities, and if they leave the body, all sorts of problems, including death, can befall the unprotected individual. *Spontaneous Success* (text #31 below) helps restore harmony with the father-god and the drala. Third, *drala* is used as the name of a whole group of warrior deities, such as the nine eminent drala brothers, the thirteen drala protectors, and the three drala brothers endowed with great power who are mentioned in *Spontaneous Success* (#31) and in *Sollo Chenmo* (#37).

In the following pages you will find two spellings—*drala* and *dralha*—reflecting the two spellings used in Tibetan. *Dralha* (*dgra lha*) is "enemy-deity," glossed as a warrior deity whose task is to fight the enemies of those who invoke them. Trungpa Rinpoche, however, strongly preferred the other spelling, *drala* (*dgra bla*), which he explained means literally "above the enemy," indicating that these forces are "beyond aggression." Mipham Rinpoche uses both, sometimes in the same prayer, and I have reflected his choice in the transcription, while we can appreciate the deeper meaning Trungpa Rinpoche's explanation brings out.[7]

Gesar is Guru Rinpoche taking the costume and temperament

of the dralas. Mipham Rinpoche describes Gesar Norbu Dradul's appearance briefly in *A Piece of My Heart: The Great Lion, King Gesar Secret Sadhana* (#6), referred to commonly and hereafter as *King Gesar Secret Sadhana*. Wermas are also an important category of protective deities. They are sometimes said to be a particular type of drala, and sometimes to be a different category of warrior spirit altogether. Trungpa Rinpoche explained that the term can refer to the retinue of one or more dralas, and that dralas and wermas are mostly synonymous. They are described as ferocious and fearless warriors who repel attacks and protect while traveling on the road, and they can also reside in weapons and enhance their power. In fact, dralas and wermas reside in all of Gesar's weapons and gears, as detailed in a terma by Do Khyentse Yeshe Dorje.[8]

Gesar's arena is the shamanic environment of Tibet, which is unlike the world of Indian tantras and poles apart from the real and imaginary Western universes. He is a warrior, and we invoke him to do what warriors do. Unlike India, the Tibetan highlands are ruled by a warrior culture of horse- and weapon-loving machos. They value courage. They fight, live in clans, and stage robberies. They have knife fights and take revenge for offenses that are remembered for generations. To understand Gesar and how he can help us get closer to enlightenment, we must learn how to relate to the principle of warriorship that Chögyam Trungpa Rinpoche presents with depth and clarity on pages 3–8. In his words, "We are not talking about learning how to handle lethal weapons and crank up our aggression and territoriality so that we can burst forth and conquer all our enemies. Warriorship here refers to realizing the power, dignity, and wakefulness that is inherent in all of us as human beings." Sogyal Rinpoche further explains:

> For the Tibetans, Gesar is not only a martial warrior but also a spiritual one. To be a spiritual warrior means to develop a special kind of courage, one that is innately intelligent, gentle, and fearless. Spiritual warriors can still be frightened, but even so they are courageous

enough to taste suffering, to relate clearly to their fundamental fear, and to draw out without evasion the lessons from difficulties. As Chögyam Trungpa Rinpoche tells us, becoming a warrior means that "we can trade our small-minded struggle for security for a much vaster vision, one of fearlessness, openness, and genuine heroism. . ." To enter the transforming field of that much vaster vision is to learn how to be at home in change, and how to make impermanence our friend.[9]

Practicing Gesar undeniably achieves this.

A TIMELY MANIFESTATION

For the Nyingmapas, Guru Padmasambhava is the chief guardian of Tibet who manifests in infinite ways because he is the fundamental nature. Lamas often say that Gesar is Guru Rinpoche for our time, and he is particularly potent for this period of degeneration. Apart from some rare exceptions, most Gesar prayers and practices have appeared from the nineteenth century onward. In Lharik Rölpa Tsal's terma revealed in 1808, Guru Rinpoche says that Gesar is the deity for these times. Mipham Rinpoche wrote, "In the past, the vidyadhara Padmasambhava; today the great lion, Norbu Dradul Tsal; in the future, Kalkin Rudra Chakrin."[10] According to Dudjom Rinpoche, Rudra Chakrin is the future king of Shambhala, who will lead its armies against the barbarians at the beginning of the Wood Male Monkey year in 2424.[11] Masters say that the present epoch is a "time of degeneration." But what does that mean? I always wondered if it was not yet another expression of the natural tendency many of us have to see the past more positively than the present, especially as we grow older—the "rosy retrospection" of the psychologist. But Buddha explained quite clearly what he meant. During such times, the so-called five degenerations are rampant. These five are the degeneration of negative emotions, which is the deterioration of moral values and the rise of sinful attitudes and behavior; the degeneration of beings, which means it is difficult to help them, as they won't hear about virtue and genuine dharma practice; the degeneration of times, as wars and famines proliferate; the degeneration of views, as false beliefs and "fake news" spread like wildfire; and the degeneration of life span, as, according to Buddhist cosmology, the hundred-year life span of present-day humans is slowly getting eroded. We have learned to think that thanks to science, technology, and the development of democracy, humans have made huge progress, particularly since the nineteenth century. Many of us, therefore, think that we live in a period that is the exact opposite of a time of degeneration. From the external, material point of view, we have unquestionably made huge leaps. On the other hand, the Buddha's perspective is concerned with spiritual development rather than with external, material circumstances, because, he explained, it is only by transforming our minds and changing the deluded way we look at the world that we will find true, lasting happiness. If we look a little more closely at the five degenerations from that angle, we will begin to notice that compared to human beings of ages past, spiritual practice is more difficult for us who live in a time when distraction is just one finger-swipe away. And the situation is not getting better; as we can see, we have increasingly greater difficulty to be moved by genuine spiritual teachings, to be interested in their practice, to make the decision to practice, and once all that has happened, to leave our mobile phones and get our minds to focus on the practice so that our time on the cushion bears fruit.

During the time of degeneration, the "windhorse" of all beings is low. The wind (*lung*) is like a mount upon which the mind rides, like a rider on a horse (*ta*), so it is called "windhorse" (*lungta*). All our experiences are the result of karma, and it is mind that creates karma. But we have no power or control over the mind at all. What really controls the mind is the wind that moves inside the body and determines the direction that the mind pursues. So it determines not only the karma that we accumulate but also the power of our dharma practice, our ability to liberate thoughts and to reach liberation. A thought can become a cause of staying in samsara if its nature is not recognized, but the same thought can become the wisdom of the Buddha if it is liberated within the expanse of the dharmakaya. Both come from the same "thought"; so it can go either way, and the direction it takes depends upon the windhorse. In other words, the merit of sentient beings and our capacity to practice and internalize the teachings are weaker than they were in the past, and we've been diagnosed with a general weak windhorse. Doing Gesar practices raises this windhorse, which increases the strength, effectiveness, and speed of our activities in general, and it also increases the inspiration and capacity to practice the dharma and the power of our meditation. Mipham Rinpoche has written these Gesar practices in such a way that anyone doing them will see their windhorse rise greatly.

GESAR, THE PROTECTORS, AND THE ACTIVITIES

In the following pages, Gesar mostly appears as a dharma protector. Tellingly, though, the text that Jamgön Mipham placed first in his collection is a guru yoga: in his view, Gesar was more than a protector; he was the lama—Guru Rinpoche—appearing in the form of a dharma protector. Dharma protectors can be manifestations of enlightenment, while other dharmapalas are worldly beings who pledged to obey the Buddha, Guru Rinpoche, and other great beings. Unlike deity sadhanas, during dharmapala practices, we rarely become the protector. Instead, we bring to mind the complete confidence of being our yidam—that is, our main deity, the deity that we practice constantly and at all times try to remember we are—or the main deity of the mandala that we have been practicing on that occasion. This is because the dharmapalas have pledged themselves to the buddhas, not to us ordinary beings. Then we invite the protectors, make offerings to them to please them and to mend whatever we might have done that could displease them, and then ask them to carry out their activities. All this can be contained in four lines or in longer practices. In general, protector practices are important for Vajrayana yogis and yoginis; dharmapalas have been appointed to protect the teachings that we use and practice. So, the moment we receive an empowerment and begin to practice these teachings we are in business with them. We perform the dharmapala practices to maintain a good relationship with these powerful beings and to ask them to help us on our dharma path. We request that they do what is necessary to support the dharma with the four types of activities: pacifying, enriching, magnetizing, and subjugating. After, once things have worked out, it is customary to go through the protector's practice again with large offerings and a ganachakra feast to thank the protectors and the dralas for accomplishing the activities we requested of them. Mipham Rinpoche lays out clearly the activities that we request of Gesar and protectors in general in one short paragraph, in the Request of Wishes and Entrustment with Activities section from *Instant Fortune* (#4) on pages 64–65.

Whatever their nature, the activities we ask them to carry out are to serve, protect, and spread the teachings, which are the true source of the happiness and well-being of sentient beings. We request the protectors to act on two fronts: external circumstances and our inner spiritual development, bearing in mind that the first is solely for the purpose of the second. As the Theravadin monk Walpola Rahula said, "Buddhism does not consider material welfare as an end in itself: it is only a means to an end—a higher and nobler end. But it is a means which is indispensable, indispensable in achieving a higher purpose for man's happiness. So Buddhism recognizes the need of certain minimum material conditions favourable to spiritual success—even that of a monk engaged in meditation in some solitary place."[12]

Once, shortly after Tibetans went into exile in India, a young monk at Khenpo Tsöndru's monastery had lost his shoelaces. He was devastated because, in those days, shoelaces were a very rare and precious commodity. So the poor little monk decided to make an offering to the protectors to ask them to bring back his priceless shoelaces. Khenpo Tsöndru heard about it, and he called up the monk. "The protectors' job and what they've pledged to do is to protect the dharma," he explained, "not to take care of your things. Of course, realized masters who see the protectors and can meet them, can ask what they need them to do, whatever it may be. But in our case, it would be very difficult to order the dharmapalas to drop what they are doing and to instead take care of our personal concerns. Their job is the protection of the dharma and of the people who hold the teachings and those who practice them." Selfishly asking protectors to bring us what we crave or to attack and harm our enemy on our behalf doesn't work. It goes against the basic principles of Buddhism that the protectors have pledged to follow. Entertaining such thoughts or making such requests will inevitably be the source of negative karma and the stream of unpleasant circumstances that goes with it.

The four types of activities are not exclusive to Vajrayana; it is simply a convenient way to categorize the things sentient beings do when interacting with their environment. What is specific to Vajrayana is the method: activities are accomplished through the power of deity, mantra, mudra, and samadhi. Mipham Rinpoche gave examples of what each of these four kinds of activities can be. He wrote in *Essence of Clear Light*, the overview of the *Secret Essence Tantra*, that pacifying activities include pacifying illness, malevolent forces, negativity, obscurations, enemies, fears, obstacles, black magic, and so on. Enriching activities increase life span, merit, wisdom, qualities, retinue, wealth, strength, prosperity, happiness, dharma, and so on. Magnetizing activities are used to attract something or someone. This may include humans, such as kings, ministers, queens, or learned teachers; nonhuman beings, such as gods, nagas, and malevolent spirits; positive qualities, such as experience, realization, and enlightened qualities; and material goods like food, drink, clothing, and wealth. Magnetizing activity draws the necessary circumstances that support spiritual development and ultimately lead to overcoming all confusion and superficial thought patterns and thus to awakening to our true nature. The fourth type, subjugating activity, can be of various natures, such as summoning, separating, binding, suppressing, averting, killing, expelling, destroying, and so on. Fundamentally, in the context of the dharma, subjugating activity is wrathful intervention to quickly cut through obstacles faced on the path and ultimately to annihilate all the ways we invest things with solidity.

Magnetizing and subjugating activities are not found in the Sutra teachings but only in Vajrayana, an approach characterized by the richness of skillful methods it offers. Vajrayana activities such as these are used to shift circumstances and the minds of beings that are impervious to peaceful methods. But, as Khenchen Pema Sherab mentioned, some of the practices in this book that involve such activities are for advanced practitioners; they are not for people like us, he says, because our realization is insufficient. Jamgön Kongtrul Lodrö Taye explained how we should go about the magnetizing activities—advice that can be applied to all activities:

> You might practice magnetizing activities for personal motives and even limited selfish purposes. However, if you do, these activities will not be accomplished, because of the key point that your mind would have then fallen under the influence of perceptions. They might only seem to have been accomplished superficially, but the greater result of accomplishing wisdom deity and mantra is wasted with minor purposes—like producing charcoal from sandalwood. You must understand this. When your realization is such that the time has come to accomplish the activities, you should accomplish them for the sake of the lamas or the teachings, detached from personal desires. If you practice like this, whatever you have begun will be quickly accomplished. These activities will also become accumulations for the attainment of enlightenment, which will in turn fulfill your own needs. However, nowadays, many people get all inspired when they hear about magnetizing activities, thinking they can allow them to gather wealth, attract people and

favorable circumstances, increase their magical powers, and the like. They treasure this kind of practice and make it the center of their dharma practice. But among them, I only see individuals who barely have enough to eat or clothes to wear, let alone being able to accomplish the benefit of self and others. Therefore, do not waste your body, speech, and mind in imitations of virtuous deeds.[13]

And, "The yogis who have attained warmth in the practice can serve the lamas and the teachings. When, free from selfish motive, they see important purposes such as leading others to enter the dharma or gathering financial means to support virtuous endeavors, [they can accomplish the different kinds of magnetizing activities]."[14]

As Alak Zenkar Rinpoche reminds us, "And in his [Gesar's] own words, 'Except for the enemies of the Buddha's doctrine and those who bring harm to sentient beings, I, Gesar, have no enemies.'"[15] This means that bodhichitta is at the heart of Gesar practice. We do these practices to contribute to the enlightenment of all sentient beings. That is the real reason. We ask Gesar to move circumstances in one way or another so that they be more conducive to the general good and support the ability of the teaching holders and practitioners—and our own realization and ability—to have a positive influence. To qualify as Vajrayana practice, any practice must involve: renunciation, the conviction that the normal dualistic way our mind functions doesn't work and only brings problems; bodhichitta, the acknowledgment of the possibility of complete enlightenment and our capacity to help others reach it; and pure perception, the way of perceiving the world and one's mind that is beyond the degenerating dualistic way. Vajrayana practices must always be performed out of this kind of motivation and outlook because then they work and are powerful tools that will draw us closer to enlightenment and give us the ability to help others gain buddhahood too. But, these teachings explain, if our mindset is ordinary, Vajrayana practice is just another ordinary, worldly activity, and as such, the source of positive and negative karma depending on our motivation. As the Buddha explained, our every thought and deed plants a seed that maintains us in samsara.

It is also important to remember that these practices are not without karmic consequences even for greatly accomplished masters. In *The Life and Teaching of Chokgyur Lingpa*, Orgyen Tobgyal Rinpoche tells the story of how Jamgön Kongtrul suffered from a leprosy-like disease because of something that happened in his past life as Vairotsana. Vairotsana had a problem with one of King Trisong Detsen's queens. At that time Vairotsana was passing on teachings to the king while the queen continually made obstacles. Vairotsana prayed to the dharma protectors for help in pacifying the queen. She subsequently suffered from headaches for six months, allowing Vairotsana to complete the transmission. However, there was still some residual karma, and when reincarnated as Jamgön Kongtrul, he was struck by this particular disease.[16]

GESAR PRACTICE

So how should we relate to Gesar practices? To begin with, they are Buddhist Vajrayana practices, and to become Buddhist means to change the way we look at the world. Of course, the word *Buddhist* is often applied to someone wearing a mala on their left wrist and who occasionally says some mantras or prayers. But a real Buddhist is someone who has taken refuge, for whom the fact that we have buddha nature and can therefore attain enlightenment is the keystone of their lives. Dzongsar Khyentse Rinpoche uses the example of a badly stained coffee cup. When we plunge it into hot, soapy water we think that we are washing this cup. "But are you?" he asks. "Are you washing the cup or removing the stains from the cup?" "Washing a cup" really means removing the stains from a cup that never is, never has been, and never will be anything other than clean. The cup and the dirt are two separate entities. We do not wash the cup; we wash the dirt. If we were to wash the cup, it would disappear completely. So, it is the dirt that is washable, and it has nothing at all to do with the cup. We all have the potential to become buddhas because we all have buddha nature. The problem is, we have yet to realize it.[17] Vajrayana goes further, and unless we have an understanding—if not a direct experience—of the view of Secret Mantra, a lot of practice won't bring the desired results. Rongzom Pandita explains that all appearances are nothing other than the buddha. Ordinary appearances that we experience are delusion; when delusion is removed, nothing else—no pure state—comes to exist in its place. So, delusion is simply the enlightened state, and therefore all appearances—in other words, all phenomena—are the deity, the Buddha. These Gesar practices, as all Vajrayana practices, are best performed within the expanse of that view. Again, thinking that there are existing enemies and evil spirits out there that we need to chase away, kill, or eliminate and real positive circumstances we want to acquire will greatly hamper the power of the practice and be the source of an accumulation of karma, mostly negative. There are evil and helpful spirits of all kinds that influence circumstances for us, those around us, and the dharma. But their existence, on different levels, is only relative, which means that they are simply delusory appearances that are in fact pure. This is how we must see them and all the rest—including ourselves and our lives.

Secret Mantra Vajrayana uses both recitation and meditation. So to do these practices, we recite the sadhana using our mouths while our minds actualize the meaning of the words. That's why Orgyen Tobgyal Rinpoche said that "simply mouthing empty words cannot be described as kyerim practice. But if you follow the words and try to actualize their meaning as you say them—even if your understanding of what you're saying is very limited—you are practicing kyerim."[18] If we practice in this way, the different aspects of the practice—such as the view, the deity, and the samadhi—will all come alive in our practice.

ABOUT GESAR'S LIFE

The prayers and practices written by Jamgön Mipham mention some events in the life of Gesar of Ling, his world, and his companions. So for the preparation of this book, I asked Orgyen Tobgyal Rinpoche to tell me the story of Gesar. As you will read in the following pages, Rinpoche replied that there are many versions of the events of his life but none are completely authentic and free from embellishment, which makes it difficult to tell the real story. He added that it would not help to include such stories in the book because the fanciful nature of some of them might undermine our trust and confidence in Gesar Norbu Dradul, the emanation of Guru Rinpoche in the form of a drala. We can also bring to mind that Jamyang Khyentse Chökyi Lodrö said that we'll discover more about Gesar and how he can help us reach enlightenment by reading Gesar texts such as the ones contained in this book.

We also must remember, as written at the beginning of Lelung Shepe Dorje's Gesar terma before it tells its unique version of the Gesar story, that even though there might be different versions of Gesar's life, they shouldn't be seen as contradicting each other—a well-known phenomenon in the case of Guru Rinpoche. According to some accounts of Padmasambhava's life, he was born from a lotus on Lake Dhanakosha; this is the "miraculous birth" account. In the Kama texts, he is said to have been born from a womb, and the Bönpos agree. One teaching says he manifested from a thunderbolt that struck the peak of Mount Malaya. But Vajrayana teachers insist that these stories are not contradictory. As Jamyang Khyentse Wangpo explains, every aspect of the vast and profound actions of Guru Rinpoche are only known to omniscient buddhas—they are way beyond the limited minds of ordinary beings. At the same time, ordinary beings are all so different, and he appears to each according to their normal perceptions. So all the apparently contradictory versions are true, because how he appears to each individual depends on that individual's unique perception and situation. The story of Asanga seeing Maitreya as a bitch crawling with maggots can also be helpful to understand this point.[19]

Still, for those who are interested, there is a lot of material in Western languages on the life of Gesar, such as Alexandra David-Neel's *The Superhuman Life of Gesar Ling*,[20] which gives a summary of the entire epic as written by Gyurme Thubten Jamyang Dragpa under the aegis of Jamgön Mipham. Jamyang Dragpa's version of the epic is being translated by the Light of Berotsana Translation Group, and the first two volumes of *The Epic of Gesar of Ling* have already been published by Shambhala Publications.[21] You can also consult *Gesar of Ling* by David Shapiro, a member of the translation team that works on *The Epic of Gesar of Ling*.[22] In his wonderful book, David retells the first three stories for a Western audience, for those who are not acquainted with the Gesar universe. Many academic papers discuss the dates and life of Gesar from a modern historian point of view; I'll leave it to the experts to debate about them.

GESAR'S FORMS

Throughout Mipham Rinpoche's practices, Gesar appears with several names and a few different forms. The qualities associated with each name are briefly presented in the Praise section from *Instant Fortune* (#4) on pages 65–66.

His name and form in Lharik's terma is Gesar Dorje Tsegyal, "Gesar King of Vajra Life." Gesar Dorje Tsegyal is described in greatest detail in *Instant Fortune* (#4). He is seated, white in color, smiling, shining light; he is so beautiful that we can never get enough of seeing him. He wears a robe of gray-blue brocade under a red gown, and his lower body is wrapped in the gray-blue skin of a beast of prey. His hair hangs loose, and rainbows and shining rays of light surround his head covered by a beautiful white, round felt hat with a spray of peacock feathers, a mirror, jewels, and a variety of silks on top. An enchanting smile radiates from his dignified face. He wears a gold locket, a mirror, a necklace of white and red jewels and a garland of various flowers around his neck. He holds a bow and an arrow in the left hand while the right changes according to the activities that we request of him, as indicated in *Instant Fortune* on page 58. (See the image of Dorje Tsegyal on page 56.)

Gesar's most common name is Gesar Norbu Dradul, "Gesar the Jewel, Tamer of Enemies" and its derivatives such as "Great Lion the Jewel," "Powerful Great Lion Jewel Tamer of Enemies," and "King Wish-Fulfilling Jewel." He can also bear other names such as Mara-Taming Drala Werma and Powerful Supreme Ornament of Jambudvipa. Gesar Norbu Dradul is described in *King Gesar Secret Sadhana* (#6). He wears armor and a helmet and holds the wish-granting horsewhip (described in text #7), which rains down gems and everything beings wish for and require. In the left hand, or in his armpit, he holds a spear that subdues all enemies throughout the three realms and bears the flag of the dralas. The left hand is holding the reins and can also hold a jewel depending on the practices. He rides his magical horse, who is the incarnation of Hayagriva and knows human languages, can fly through the sky, and travel the four continents of the world in an instant. (See the image of Gesar Norbu Dradul on page 74.)

The name Great Lion the Jewel is often, but not always, associated with his enriching form. As such, he is described in *The Jewel That Satisfies All Needs* (#8): sitting on a throne made of jewels and precious substances, his complexion is white with a tinge of red, youthful, and full of bliss and desire. He wears all the silk and jewel adornments. He holds a wish-fulfilling jewel in his right hand and an iron arrow and bow in his left. In *Sollo Chenmo* (#37), he holds the vase of inexhaustible treasure in the left hand. (See the image of Gesar Lion the Jewel on page 86.)

King Wish-Fulfilling Jewel is sometimes attributed to Gesar's pacifying form, who is also called All-Accomplishing White Werma or All-Accomplishing for short (Dondrup in Tibetan; Siddhartha in Sanskrit), King Dondrup, or Lord Dondrup Norbu. This form of Gesar also goes by the name of Akar Ökyi Werma— "Werma White Light A," as Trungpa Rinpoche sometimes translates it—which is Gesar's main form for divination. Texts #11 and #16 describe him as having the youthful charm of a sixteen-year-old boy and being white like pure crystal. In his right hand he holds a jeweled torch illuminating the three planes of existence. In his left hand he holds a precious mirror that lifts the veil on everything hidden. He wears a gown of white silk and clouds of rainbow lights. He stands majestically in a flower in full bloom, accompanied by the five secret goddesses who blaze with the five lights. Each holds a mirror and an excellent vase that satisfies all needs, and each looks passionately at him. (See the image of Akar Ökyi Werma on page 106.)

The name King Great Lion is also applied to a magnetizing form in both *King Gesar: Wangdu Practice* (#29) and in *Sollo Chenmo* (#37): he is brilliant red, full of bliss and desire, extremely handsome and blazing with a hundred beautiful expressions. His right hand forms the hook mudra or holds a hook, and the left pulls toward him a lasso made of red lotuses. He wears a brocade cloak and a head scarf of red silk, and necklaces of red stones and pearls. He sits in the half-lotus posture in an expanse of red lights. (See the image of Wangdu Gesar on page 162.)

These are the main forms Gesar displays but there are others, as well as variations in his hand implements according to the job at hand. Apparently a building has been erected on the site where Gesar's palace once stood in Golok; it houses magnificent statues of Gesar's different forms and of his retinue, as well as a small museum dedicated to the king of Ling.

LHARIK DECHEN YESHE ROLPE TSAL

The Gesar practices that Mipham Rinpoche wrote were inspired by a terma revealed by Lharik Dechen Yeshe Rölpa Tsal. Dzongsar Khyentse Rinpoche explained that rather than writing new Gesar texts, Mipham Rinpoche revealed more of Lharik's terma. You'll notice that some of the texts he wrote contain the terma mark—two circles, one above the other, with a short horizontal crescent between them (§) that tertöns add at the end of sentences or verses to indicate a terma. In other texts, Mipham Rinpoche did not add the terma punctuation but dakini script at the beginning, which also signals that the text is a terma. When tertöns write a text that isn't a terma, they do not include terma punctuation. Orgyen Tobgyal Rinpoche explained that Dilgo Khyentse Rinpoche would only add terma punctuation to the texts he wrote once he was absolutely certain that a teaching really was a mind terma. Most of the original terma that Lharik Dechen Yeshe Rölpa Tsal wrote down was included in Mipham Rinpoche's *Collected Works*, which is why it is sometimes attributed to him and also why we included this section of Lharik's terma in the book (#38).

We know next to nothing about Lharik Dechen Yeshe Rolpe Tsal except for a note Dilgo Khyentse Rinpoche inserted in the biography of Mipham Rinpoche. Kyabje Rinpoche wrote that Lharik Dechen Yeshe Rolpe Tsal was born in the Lhagyari area of Dakpo and that this tertön was the immediate incarnation of Gyalse Rinchen Namgyal (1694–1758), Minling Terchen's son.[23] The text of Lharik's terma tells us that it was revealed in the Earth Dragon year. In his vision, Lharik first saw Shepe Dorje, and then Gesar appeared to him in the form described in Shepe Dorje's pure vision. Lelung Shepe Dorje (1697–1740) was one of the first masters to reveal practices related to Gesar in 1729 at a place called Ölga in Lokha. In any case, since Lharik is the immediate incarnation of Gyalse Rinchen Namgyal who died in 1758, the Earth Dragon year of the pure vision must be 1808, at the beginning of nineteenth century when Gesar practices began to appear in earnest. It cannot be later because Mipham Rinpoche received the empowerment in 1864 or 1865 from Lap Kyapgön, before the following Earth Dragon year in 1868.

MIPHAM RINPOCHE

Mipham Rinpoche is widely considered to be among the greatest scholars and accomplished masters in the history of Tibetan

Buddhism, possibly the most influential teacher in the Nyingma school today. Despite this, until recently there were only short biographical sketches of him, available both in Tibetan and English. Mipham Rinpoche had a largely uneventful life, save for the visions and miracles. He wrote a one-volume autobiography that centered around accounts of these visions, but out of humility he decided to burn it. Until recently, the main source of Mipham Rinpoche's life has been Khenpo Kunpel's *Essential Hagiography*,[24] and to some extent Khenpo Jigme Phuntsok's compilation of stories that he collected from the people who knew him. But in 2010, Dilgo Khyentse Rinpoche's biography of Jamgön Mipham, composed in 1939, came to light. It was published in 2013 in India and was immediately—and beautifully—translated by the Padmakara Translation Group. I cannot but encourage you to read this translation, *Lion of Speech*, as well as Khenpo Jigme Phuntsok's booklet *Miracle Stories of Mipham Rinpoche*.[25] These short, eminently readable, and entertaining texts are a tremendous inspiration, and they shed light on why Mipham Rinpoche's teachings are so special and should be treasured.

Ju Mipham is often described as a polymath, sometimes even dubbed Tibet's Leonardo da Vinci. If such descriptions are helpful introductions of the great master, they, quite amazingly, fall short by a long way of who Jamgön Mipham really was. Apparently he was Manjushri in the flesh; and by his own reckoning, Mipham Rinpoche was a bodhisattva in the last life before enlightenment. This might sound like a self-aggrandizing remark, but the following story clarifies it. In Khenpo Jigme Phuntsok's collection of stories about Ju Mipham, he writes that the night before debating Lopsang Phuntsok, the Mongolian geshe whose scholarship stood out among the monks of Sera, Drepung, and Ganden, Manjushri appeared in front of Mipham Rinpoche. The sword and book that Manjushri held turned into five-colored spheres of light that dissolved into Jamgön Mipham's heart. From that moment on, he knew all the words of the Buddhist teachings in Tibet and understood their meaning[26]—a fact witnessed by many of his contemporaries and that his writings confirm. That is why he was far more than a polymath with vast knowledge and learning. He was someone whose realization was such that he could tap into buddhas' wisdom to teach, debate, and write teachings and practices. As Alak Zenkar Rinpoche wrote, "Even if hundreds of scholars were to discourse on his achievements for an entire kalpa, there would still be more to say."[27]

In many circles, particularly in the West, Ju Mipham is held to be a great philosopher. To be fair, one of Mipham Rinpoche's greatest contributions was to write the most influential shedra textbooks throughout the millennium-long history of the Nyingma tradition—which has also something to do with the relatively recent development of shedra institutions in Nyingma monasteries in the last two hundred years. Jamgön Mipham had a unique way of presenting the most profound topics clearly and without ever deviating from the Buddha's teaching, bringing out the depth and harmony of the different levels of teachings. Unlike philosophers, great masters such as Mipham Rinpoche do not present their own philosophical system but the Buddha's teachings in a way that makes it easier for students to understand and realize the path while limiting the pitfalls. Where the philosopher title falls distinctly short is that he was above all a great Vajrayana adept. Writing the shastra commentaries was simply an incidental task that his guru, Jamyang Khyentse Wangpo, asked him to perform. For most of his life he lived as a yogi alone in the wilderness, with the sole support of his lifelong attendant, Lama Ösel. He only allotted a couple of hours a day to writing. Yet with all the texts he produced dealing with ways to relate to the nature of things, it is understandable that non-Buddhists may look at him as a philosopher, someone who seeks to promote a new way of understanding reality or to improve on their peers' theories. But for Buddhists, particularly in the Nyingma tradition, Jamgön Mipham Namgyal Gyatso is understood to be a bodhisattva, someone whose only concern is helping others attain enlightenment. This is key to appreciating the teachings he left behind. As Orgyen Tobgyal Rinpoche explains in the following pages, because of Lama Mipham's profound realization, texts that he wrote do not express the deliberations and findings of an ordinary mind. Rather, they are the direct expression of the dharmakaya wisdom of the buddhas, and as such they have the same value as the great Indian texts—the sutras, tantras, and shastras. While his *Collected Works* contain many treasures, we are fortunate that an increasing number of excellent translations of Mipham Rinpoche's teachings are available for the English reader. They cover a wide range of subjects, from (mostly) shastra commentaries to Vajrayana explanations, from Dzogchen to the art of ruling a country.

The uninterrupted lineage of realized masters makes Tibetan Buddhism one of the most relevant spiritual teachings in the world today. When other religions have long struggled with the tension between scholars and mystics, Tibetan Buddhism has always valued the authority of realized masters as supreme, because they can see the truth directly, which is always better than mere theoretical knowledge, as we know from other fields of endeavor. This also explains that the culture so prevalent in our regions—in academia but also in religion—of acknowledging people who have made a significant contribution to a field of knowledge through their research, study, or writing (for example, Doctor of the Church) is totally foreign to Tibetan Buddhism. The dualistic mind of an ordinary person, however learned they may be in spiritual matters, doesn't have the ability to fully comprehend, let alone improve on, the Buddha's teaching. Buddhist siddhas have helped to preserve the authenticity of the Buddha's message: from time to time an enlightened being comes who straightens human intellectual drifting, and Mipham Rinpoche was such a guide.

Since this book contains tantric teachings, it is probably best to approach Mipham Rinpoche's life based on the tantric understanding of reality. So before we discuss his civil status, we must first look at the so-called ground of emanation. In other words, we must look at who Mipham Rinpoche really is.

The dharmakaya Samantabhadra, the original ground, is

beyond all discursive thought, yet it is endowed with self-arisen compassion that reaches out impartially to every being. Thanks to this compassion, effortless activities manifest, permanent and omnipresent, appearing in the three "families" of wisdom deities—wisdom, compassion, and ability. Mipham Rinpoche appeared in this way. He is a wisdom body, a manifestation of all the buddhas and inseparable from the expanse of the buddhas' primordial wisdom—Manjushri. So Mipham Rinpoche is Manjushri, and Manjushri is the state of ultimate reality, the experience of primordial wisdom, spontaneous and perfect. While never being separate from the dharmadhatu, Manjushri nevertheless acts on the relative level in harmony with the perceptions of beings to be trained. Manjushri's extraordinary feats and qualities would fill volumes. In short, Manjushri manifests as the foremost support of every buddha-to-be from the moment they first generate the mind of enlightenment until they at last attain buddhahood, assisting them in their accomplishment of the path. For all beings, he appears in the form of bodhisattvas, shravakas, and pratyekabuddhas who train beings on the path. He manifests as ordinary human beings, or as birds and other animals, both in animate and inanimate ways. In so doing, he works for the sake of beings throughout space and in accordance with their needs. In Tibet, Manjushri manifests continuously as a human in the form of the greatest masters, such as Thonmi Sambhota, Trisong Detsen, Vairotsana, Sakya Pandita, Longchen Rabjam and Tsongkhapa, to name but a few.

Thanks to his clear vision born of wisdom free from obscuration, Mipham Rinpoche remembered many of his past lives. But he constantly concealed such things, keeping them secret, so there is no certain record of what he said about them. We know that he was an extremely skillful carpenter in India, then Nup Sangye Yeshe and/or Chökrö Lui Gyaltsen, who were close disciples of Guru Rinpoche. He was the master Dothok Telpa Dorje Gyaltsen, a yogi of the Secret Mantra who became the principal spiritual preceptor of the Chinese emperor. When Jamyang Khyentse Wangpo was Rigdzin Jigme Lingpa, Mipham Rinpoche was Tsangtö Chöje

Trapukpa, the greatest of his heart sons. Given Ju Mipham's unrivaled knowledge, astonishing intellectual prowess and assurance, and everything he did to nurture the precious Buddha's teachings, it is obvious that he was no ordinary being. For Dilgo Khyentse Rinpoche, this proves without a doubt who Mipham Rinpoche really is. And, Khyentse Rinpoche noted, "In this life, his qualities of elimination and realization were immaculate—and this is something I find even more amazing than the record of his many hundreds of incarnations in times gone by."[28]

Ju Mipham was born to an aristocratic family in the kingdom of Derge in 1846. His mother, Sing Chungma, was a descendant of the Mukpo Dong clan, Gesar's family lineage. He began studying the dharma at an early age, and at twelve, a young Mipham took novice vows and entered Ju Mohor Sang Ngak Chöling, a branch of the great monastery of Shechen. By all accounts he was a child prodigy. His intellectual gifts were quickly recognized, and before long, he was known in the monastery as "the little scholar monk." Around 1861, Jamgön Mipham undertook an eighteen-month retreat on Manjushri at Junyung Hermitage. He later told his close disciples that from that time on he could understand any work on any subject without studying it simply by receiving a brief explanatory transmission.

Shortly after completing this retreat, Jamgön Mipham went on pilgrimage with his uncle to Central Tibet in order to flee the "Nyarong war" in Kham, which broke out in 1863 when Gompo Namgyal, the chieftain of Nyarong, invaded Derge. He was defeated in 1865, bringing an end to the constant war and famine that had plagued the region for the previous two years. During his journey to Central Tibet, Mipham Rinpoche studied Gelugpa teachings for a month at the famous Ganden Monastery. On his way back from Central Tibet, he met his two most important teachers, Dza Patrul Rinpoche and Jamyang Khyentse Wangpo, whom he considered his root teacher. During his life, Mipham Gyatso offered Jamyang Khyentse Wangpo all his belongings seven times. Mipham Rinpoche spent a lot of time at Dzongsar Monastery to be near his teacher. Quite soon, Jamyang Khyentse Wangpo asked him to write shedra textbooks on the different shastras from the point of view of the Nyingma tradition. These texts are now the basis of shedra studies in all Nyingma monasteries. Many of them are also now available in English translation. His writings encompass Sutra teachings, Vajrayana dharma, Great Perfection instructions, elaborate scholarly explanations, direct practical advice, practices that capture and essentialize the meaning of sutras and tantras, often in a novel and clear way. Perhaps less known to the Western audience, his writings also contain teachings on the traditional sciences, such as crafts, magic, medicine, divination, astrology, even a commentary on the *Kama Sutra* and a treatise for kings on ruling a country.[29] Jamgön Mipham thus offered many methods for dharma practitioners to bend interdependence and create circumstances that are more conducive to the path. In addition, he was known for his interest in the literary sciences and wrote authoritative texts on grammar, poetics, dramaturgy, and prosody. He also devised a great lama dance centered on Gesar that is performed over several days.

In his final days, Jamgön Mipham wrote about a debilitating illness that had plagued him for the last decade of his life, causing continuous intense suffering. At the end of his life he said that, in spite of the pain, he had chosen to remain in the world for the sake of others but that now there was no point in staying any longer. So, on Friday June 14, 1912, he sat up with his legs loosely crossed, one hand in the mudra of meditation and the other in the mudra of teaching. As the sun set, he became absorbed in the inner expanse of primordial luminosity and passed away at his hermitage in Ju. He remained in tukdam meditation for about twelve days.

Gesar was Mipham Rinpoche's chief protecting deity from early on. As Dilgo Khyentse Rinpoche wrote, "Quite beyond the way of ordinary children, he had no thought other than that of his yidam deity, Manjushri in peaceful and wrathful form, and of Gesar, his protector."[30] He received the transmission, "the entrustment of the life force" of Gesar Sengchen Dorje Tsegyal according to the pure vision of Lharik Dechen Yeshe Rölpa Tsal from Lap Kyapgön Gyerap Dorje on his way back from Central Tibet, in 1864 or 1865. The twelfth Lap Kyapgön (1832–1888) was the head of the Gelukpa monastery of Lapgön at Yushu in Kham. He was also one of the five chief disciples of Do Khyentse Yeshe Dorje and a teacher of Loter Wangpo. The young Mipham met Loter Wangpo at that time and became his disciple. After receiving the transmissions from Lap Kyapgön, Mipham Rinpoche went to stay at Loter Wangpo's hermitage, Pema Sangak Dechen Gakyil, where he accomplished the practice of White Manjushri and Hayagriva, showing signs of accomplishment. He also began to propitiate Gesar and took him as his chief protector. He wrote many marvelous teachings, profound and vast, related to Gesar, which are collected in this book. According to the colophons of these practices, Mipham Rinpoche wrote his first Gesar text in 1865, soon after having received the transmission of Lharik's terma.[31]

Before departing into parinirvana, he said decisively, "It is certain that I shall not remain and an incarnation will not appear because I am going to the pure realm of Shambhala in the north." God knows what he is doing there, but knowing him, there is no doubt that he continues to manifest for us in many ways, as human beings, roads or, why not, books...

CONTENT OF THE BOOK

In the foreword, Dzongsar Khyentse Rinpoche introduces Gesar practices by helping us navigate the difference of approach between East and West, and getting us into the mood for these very special writings. The book also republishes a wonderful piece that Chögyam Trungpa Rinpoche wrote as a foreword to *The Superhuman Life of Gesar of Ling*, the English edition of Alexandra David-Neel's retelling of Gesar's life that was published in 1981. The Vidyadhara, as his students respectfully call him, was known for his unique ability to transpose the ancient wisdom of Tibet for modern-day people. Thirty-five years after his much-too-early passing, he still remains the foremost translator of Buddhism, when translation is understood not simply as linguistic puzzle solving but more importantly as a complex art of transferring ideas and wisdom from one culture to another. His short text gives a very profound view of how best to relate to and benefit from practicing Gesar. In the next section, Orgyen Tobgyal Rinpoche leads us into the world of Gesar Norbu Dradul, the emanation of the Lotus-Born in the form of a drala. Rinpoche explains who Gesar is and the essential principles that we need to know in order to make Gesar practices meaningful and potent, putting in layperson's language the profound poems that Mipham Rinpoche wrote. Since many of these practices are sang offerings, Rinpoche also explains sang from the traditional Buddhist point of view. Finally, he presents briefly how to practice the longest text in Mipham Rinpoche's collection, *Sollo Chenmo*, to give readers a better idea of these practices and rituals.

These Gesar texts are based on the buddhadharma, and particularly on Vajrayana and the teachings of the Great Perfection. Explanations by Kyabje Dzongsar Khyentse Rinpoche, Vidyadhara Chögyam Trungpa Rinpoche and Tulku Orgyen Tobgyal provide important instructions but are not detailed commentaries of the practices. More specific instructions necessary to perform these practices effectively should be learned from one's teachers. It is important to ask teachers to teach, as it will fuel a deep connection with the dharma conferred as a result. In fact, receiving oral instructions is necessary if we are to follow the Vajrayana path successfully. As Rajiv Malhotra explains:

> The West tends to think of the oral tradition as a primitive and inefficient means for the transmission of knowledge, one that was wisely replaced by the invention of writing. Although writing did indeed revolutionize communication, the Indian tradition retains a sense (long gone from the West) that the spoken word carries spiritual energy and is filled with presence. This understanding is reflected not only in the mantra but

also in the *bhajan* or sacred songs. This emphasis on the spoken word also helps us understand why physical proximity to the guru is beneficial—because some knowledge or insight can be passed nonverbally. Such learning is *not* achievable via a hermeneutics of an inert external text, even when the external text provides a supportive framework.[32]

The main body of this book is made up of Jamgön Mipham's fifty-two Gesar texts from his *Collected Works*. "Collected works" compile texts that are gathered mostly after the passing of a master. During their lives, lamas write prayers when they are requested to and when they have paper, then they give them to the people who request them. Later, one or a few students take responsibility for visiting all the other students and people likely to have texts by their master and copy them. They can also be collected sometime later—such as Shabkar Tsokdruk Rangdröl's writings, which were assembled recently by Matthieu Ricard more than one hundred and fifty years after Shabkar passed into parinirvana in 1851. Mipham Rinpoche's *Collected Works* were mostly collected during his life, and he organized the texts in the order in which they arose in his mind and according to other criteria and intentions. To follow the author's wisdom intent, we present the prayers in the same sequence. Most of Mipham Rinpoche's Gesar practices are collected in volume *na* from the *om, ah, ra, pa, tsa, na,* and *dhih* volumes of his *Collected Works* issued by the Derge printery, the first edition of the compilation. Two texts, *The Great Werma Dance* (#5) and *A Piece of My Heart* (#6) were found later and added in the more recent editions of the *Collected Works* published in the twenty-first century. The translations assembled here end with eight texts, texts #45–52, which come from other parts of the *Collected Works*, namely the protector section (text #45) and the sang and lungta section (texts #46–52). I therefore chose to place them separately as part three.[33] Mipham Rinpoche authored five more texts on Gesar concerned with arrow divination that I did not include here. The texts are therefore not ordered thematically or even chronologically. The following list groups the texts by category:

One terma text (#38): Mipham Rinpoche included most of the terma that Lharik Dechen Yeshe Rölpa Tsal wrote down. Lharik's text tells us that he couldn't reveal the entire terma, and Mipham Rinpoche indicated in some of the colophons that his Gesar texts are further revelations of the same terma.

One guru yoga (#1): In this text, Gesar is not practiced as a dharma protector but as the lama, in a short and inspiring guru yoga practice.

One sadhana (#6): In this sadhana, which is probably the one mentioned in Lharik Dechen Yeshe Rölpa Tsal's terma, Gesar is practiced as the lama and adds the mantra to accomplish the deity and the mantras for the different activities.

Fourteen "offerings and supplications" (#2, #3, #18, #20, #21, #22, #23, #24, #25, #31, #34, #35, #37, #41, #45, #52): These are the most common forms of Gesar practice in which we invoke the presence of the dharmapala Gesar, make offerings to him and his retinue, praise them, and ask that they accomplish the activities we request. The supplications are as short as four lines (#45) or several pages long (#37) and include details about the offerings, the retinue, the invocation, and the activities. These practices are done as part of protector practices, or solka, after yidam meditation and recitation.

One fulfillment practice (#10): Fulfillment, or *kangwa* in Tibetan, is a practice of offering and purification of negativities, particularly impairments and breakages of samayas. Practitioners offer a vast wealth of sensual enjoyments, both real and imagined, to the deities of the mandala and confess their breaches. Offerings are made to support the confession as a show of good faith.

One fulfillment and request practice (#4): In a "fulfillment and request," we offer fulfillment as just explained and, once impairments and breakages have been remedied and promises fulfilled, we then request the protectors to accomplish their activities. This text is one of the longest in Mipham Rinpoche's Gesar collection. He based it on the terma revealed by Lharik Dechen Yeshe Rölpa Tsal (#38) in a practice arrangement that spells out the different phases of the practice of the protector Gesar, which makes this text a useful source to understand how to practice the shorter supplications in which some of these phases are only alluded to.

Five abundance practices (#8, #9, #19, #26, #44): In these practices we invoke Gesar, make offerings to him, praise him, and ask him to increase yang, or "enriching presence" as Trungpa Rinpoche called it, which is the capacity to attract abundance, well-being, and good circumstances. Text #8 is a ritual to consecrate a casket of abundance, which will then have the power to attract the yang quality. Practice texts #9 and #44 are to "summon" the quality of abundance from everywhere it exists in the universe and draw it into the practitioners and the practice articles, while #19 is an invocation and #26 a unique visualization to increase abundance.

Two magnetizing practices (#5, #29): As explained above, magnetizing activities are practiced to draw the necessary circumstances that will support spiritual development and ultimately overcome all confusion, and thus lead us to awaken to our true nature.

Seven sang offerings (#13, #14, #30, #33, #46, #47, #49): Several Gesar texts from Mipham Rinpoche are sang practices, while other liturgies simply suggest to add smoke offering to the other offerings prepared for the deity. These seven texts are of the first category—sang practices. Sang is the name of the Tibetan smoke offering. There are different types of sangs but, as Jamyang Khyentse Wangpo explains, they are all rituals during which offerings are made mostly using cleansing substances to purify all faults and problems for oneself and others while satisfying the recipients of the offerings.[34] Orgyen Tobgyal Rinpoche explains the general principles of Buddhist sang practice on pages 31–35. Sang, like lungta, is often associated with Gesar but can also be offered to many other deities. For example, volume 31 of Mipham Rinpoche's *Collected Works* contains general smoke offerings to the tathagatas. It also includes sang offerings to the bodhisattvas, to the lamas, to the yidams, and to the dakinis, and several smoke offerings each dedicated to one specific deity, such as Lhachen, Nyenchen Tanglha, Kurukulle, and so on. The seven sang practices included in this book are the ones that Mipham Rinpoche wrote as offerings to Gesar. If all the sang practices that he wrote would be translated, they would probably fill a volume like this one. Mipham Rinpoche even wrote a text on the signs of sang practice. For example: Smoke rising up well and the substances burning fast are both good signs that the practitioners' lungta will flourish and their hopes will be easily realized; if they burn with difficulty, they won't achieve their goal. White smoke is a sign that the gods are happy with the practitioners or the person they practice for. Auspicious shapes in the smoke or smoke speckled with blue patches are a good sign, while purple coloration in the smoke or inauspicious patterns are an indication that the gods are disturbed. Pleasant and pure scents and attractive shapes in the smoke mean the practitioners' wishes will be fulfilled; the opposite means negativity. If the signs are bad initially and become good later, this indicates that the practice is working, whereas good signs followed by bad ones means that practitioners or the person they practice for will face great obstacles and should be careful. If the smoke spirals in the direction of the local guardians and the practitioners and then rises up, this indicates that the gods protect them, so this is a good sign. Incense smoke can be interpreted in the same way. Mipham Rinpoche also says that we should pay attention to the sang burner, particularly the bottom where holes and breaches should be avoided. Ideally you would want a white painted sang burner of solid and thick build.

Seven practices for raising windhorse (#14, #15, #17, #32, #48, #49, #51): Although all Gesar practices have a positive impact on the windhorse, these seven practices are specifically devoted to raising it. They have a very similar impact to planting prayer flags on top of hills and mountains. Orgyen Tobgyal Rinpoche explains about windhorse on pages 13–19; he draws from text #48, which lays out the visualization for lungta prayers, and text #17, which goes into even greater detail concerning the visualization, the purpose of the different aspects, and the wisdom behind it all. Like sang practices, Gesar is not the sole recipient of windhorse prayers; they can also be dedicated to Hayagriva, Tara, and so on. Prayer flags can as well represent other deities than Gesar. The translations of all the lungta prayers that Mipham Rinpoche wrote for different deities could also fill a volume like this one.

Two practices for divination (#11, #16): In Buddhism, divinations are performed by asking a deity, such as Gesar, to tell us what they see about interdependence. Everything arises due to causes and conditions, and in their wisdom the deities are able to see what ordinary beings cannot; through divination, they communicate what interdependence is set to result. So before doing a divination, the diviner must meditate and invoke the deity. If their divination deity is Gesar, they could do these practices as instructed by their teacher.

Eight texts for the fabrication and consecration of blessed articles (#7, #8, #17, #23, #27, #38, #39, #40): As Mipham Rinpoche said, he was a skilled craftsman in one of his past lives in India. His collection of Gesar texts contains instructions for the fabrication and consecration of a Gesar horsewhip (#7), an abundance reliquary box (#8), how to draw life-force wheels (#27, #38), and how to sew a special wealth pouch (#39). In three texts (#17, #23, #40) Jamgön Mipham explains how to make Gesar prayer flags. We have designed a flag based on his instruction, which you can see on pages 228–29. Our flag is in English for, as Orgyen Tobgyal Rinpoche said, there is nothing wrong in not using the Tibetan. It might even be more suited in English-speaking countries.

Three prayers to Gesar's retinue (#28, #42, #43): Finally, the collection also contains three protector practices on members of Gesar's retinue: Little White Vulture, a protectress who is Gesar's maternal aunt; Gyatsa Shelkar, Gesar's elder half brother, who is a great warrior known for his courage, loyalty, and nobility; and Gabde Bernakchen, an emanation of Mahakala and Gesar's personal bodyguard.

The notes have been kept to a minimum. Deciding which note to include is never easy. In many cases, as Umberto Eco says, they are a sign of weakness on the part of a translator:[35] instead of writing an intelligible transposition of the original meaning, the translator uses an obscure formulation that requires a footnote to clarify. Another problem is that a note can become a random commentary. Expressions likely to elicit the curiosity of the reader are endless, owing to the great profundity of Vajrayana prayers and practices, which is not an empty laudatory formula but the acknowledgment that words have several levels of meaning—in fact, tantras are explained by means of four modes and six limits, which are the different levels at which each word must be understood. In this context, notes are not the appropriate tool to clarify Mipham Rinpoche's tantric poetry about Gesar. Only a living teacher with the qualities of a vajra master can explain them to a student. Since Mipham Rinpoche's texts mostly deal with Gesar as a dharma protector, this book is not intended for people completely new to Vajrayana but for practitioners with some prior knowledge and experience of basic Secret Mantra concepts and practice. Orgyen Tobgyal Rinpoche kindly agreed to introduce these Gesar practices by explaining the general context, who Gesar is, and some of the key concepts, to give an idea of what is happening, what we are trying to accomplish, and how to achieve it through these practices. The book however does not include an individual commentary of each of these practices for, as Rinpoche said, a commentary that would explain both the words and the underlying meaning of the three-page prayer called *Swift Accomplishment of Enlightened Activity* (#34), for example, would fill an entire book. However, a glossary at the end of the book presents some of the main characters, places, articles, and concepts that appear in these Gesar texts. The glossary also clarifies different word choices of the few translators who worked on this book to help readers connect them with other translations. Many notions—such as the seven traditional offerings, the eight auspicious symbols, or the seven emblems of royalty, for example—are probably known to them and are easily found on the internet, whereas explanations of the notion of abundance or the connection of the Ma valley with abundance are not so ubiquitous. In that spirit, the glossary presents terms that have a specific significance in the world of Gesar and that people with general tantric knowledge might not know about.

ABOUT THE TRANSLATIONS

As the most revered and one of the most prolific sources of Gesar practices, many of Jamgön Mipham Rinpoche's Gesar texts have been translated into English, some several times. However, people don't always know about these translations, and new translations are even sometimes unnecessarily commissioned. In general, the more translations of the same text the better, as it helps uncover the richness of a text's profound message. But sometimes also, new translations are produced without the knowledge of previous works, and people not quite as competent as the original translator pointlessly produce hapless new translations—once, I discovered that a Gesar supplication that I translated quite badly after much struggle, had already been masterfully translated years before by

Chögyam Trungpa Rinpoche with the Nalanda Translation Committee. Practitioners also are not always able to find the Gesar text they need. For these reasons it is perhaps timely to publish the complete collection of Mipham Rinpoche's Gesar practices.

But what would be the best way to publish these Gesar texts, which are no ordinary instructions and are meant for an informed readership? Should they be on a restricted website or publicly accessible? In a private publication or in a book? Several lamas and dharma friends I consulted about the project felt that since the objective is to further the Buddhist teachings that are the source of happiness in the world, and to support those who practice them, these highly esoteric practices should be reserved to Vajrayana practitioners who have received the proper transmissions. They should not be simply dropped on a website without explanations contextualizing and clarifying them, where search engines can harvest them and all and sundry can access them. A key practice for Vajrayana yogins is secrecy, not because the teachings contain anything kinky but because they can easily be misunderstood by those who lack the proper background or don't have the right mindset. Secrecy is the fourth of the five root samayas; it is therefore our responsibility as Vajrayana practitioners to avoid "revealing the secret," or at least to try our best to do so in this world dominated by internet. For all these reasons, a book appeared to be the lesser of two evils, even though anyone can buy it and that parts of it are likely to end up on the web.

This compilation includes translations from different translators. Several texts have been translated by the Nalanda Translation Committee, some under the guidance of Chögyam Trungpa Rinpoche. All the lhasang and windhorse chants (#12, #13, #14, #30, #49, #50, and #51) were translated with the Vidyadhara Chögyam Trungpa Rinpoche and Lama Ugyen Shenpen. The prayers #1, #34, #36, and #45 were done long after Trungpa Rinpoche's time, in consultation with other lamas. It's the same people, but in this book we use "Nalanda Translation Committee" to refer to translations with Trungpa Rinpoche and "Vajravairochana Translation Committee" for the others, which is the name they prefer for their Vajrayana publications.

The verses of the horse race supplication (text #2) was translated by Robin Kornman, Sangye Khandro, and Lama Chönam as part of their brilliant work on the first three parts of *The Epic of Gesar of Ling*[36] and which I have adapted for this book. The "enciphered" meaning of these verses is in part 3 of the *Epic* where Alak Zenkar Rinpoche interspersed them.

Adam Pearcey produced a remarkable translation of *Sollo Chenmo* (#37), nearly twenty years in the making, with the help of Alak Zenkar Rinpoche, Orgyen Tobgyal Rinpoche, Ian Maxwell, and Patrick Gaffney. Rigpa Translations translated some of the short supplications to Gesar (#24, #25, and #35) and produced the English version of *The Swift Fulfillment of All Wishes* (#48).

Despite lacking the qualities to translate such well-crafted, incredibly profound poems, we have done our best to attempt to write accurate and inspiring translations with the hope that in the future more apt translators will produce better versions. Our translations are doubtless not definitive, and every text we have translated will surely be reworked several times in the future. When I see that Latin classics such as *The Consolation of Philosophy* that Boethius wrote in the early sixth century was translated in Old English in the ninth century by King Alfred and later by many other translators such as Geoffrey Chaucer or Elizabeth I, and it is still being translated and retranslated at what seems to be an average of one new translation every ten years since the nineteenth century, I am wondering if there is even such thing as a satisfactory translation.

Since this publication is intended for a general Vajrayana audience, we haven't used Sanskrit diacritics, which many readers find difficult to read, especially in long mantras. Also, mantras in Gesar practices are often a combination of Sanskrit, Tibetan, and Shangshung words and onomatopes, so to write the mantras, I decided to try to reflect the Tibetan phonetization of all the syllables to emulate as close as possible the way Mipham Rinpoche intended them to be read by a Tibetan reader. Translations by the Nalanda/ Vajravairochana Translation Committee, such as *Invocation for Raising Windhorse* (#51), have largely been done with the full participation of Trungpa Rinpoche and all the conventions he established. In particular, the Vidyadhara insisted that mantras and Sanskrit words should be written according to the proper Sanskrit pronunciation, though the diacritics have been omitted in order to remain consistent with the approach adopted here. As you will see and as can be expected, the transfer to the Tibetan script and pronunciation leads to quite a different result. Trungpa Rinpoche was, of course, acutely aware of this difference, and he strongly preferred for his translators to correct any corruption of the spellings (which abound in Tibetan transcriptions) to proper classical Sanskrit whenever possible. We hope the reader finds it interesting to compare these differences, and we have provided the Tibetan phonetic rendering in the notes when the Sankrit has been used, especially for the sake of those who prefer to use that. Apparently, both are effective and lead to the accomplishment of the siddhis.

Many terms of the Gesar universe are unique to Tibetan culture. We retained some Tibetan terms (e.g., *chemar*), while others have been translated into Sanskrit (e.g., *garuda*). Linguistic creativity is an important tool for translators to render "stylistic values for which no means of expression have yet been evolved in the target literature."[37] While Tibetans made great efforts to translate every word from Sanskrit, they still sometimes use the Sanskrit of a term, such as *jagat* or *kalpa*; like every other language, Tibetan borrows from foreign lexicons. When English-speaking Christians use the Latin *cantor* and English-speaking Jews call their chant leader *hazzan*, why couldn't followers of Tibetan Buddhism use *umdze*? The book even uses—and I will probably be arrested by the "translation police" (as the more dogmatic among scholars of translation studies are known in mainstream translation) for this crime—both the Sanskrit and the Tibetan of terms (e.g., *naga* and *lu*). Trungpa Rinpoche chose *lu*. It works well in the rhythm of his translation, and I didn't want to change it in the name of a rigid notion of consistency. And maybe I should have followed Trungpa Rinpoche's use of *lu* instead of *naga* throughout the book for, as the great Tibetologist Rolf A. Stein noted, when researching Tibetan concepts and attempting to define them, we must pay close attention to the underlying Sanskrit equivalents; indeed Indian nagas are a little different from Tibetan lus. In any case, attempts at clarifying some of the terms can be found in the glossary.

Mipham Rinpoche was an expert astrologer, and he sometimes used very technical ways of expressing dates, which we have not always followed, preferring a simpler way that is more intelligible to anyone not familiar with Tibetan astrological systems.

ACKNOWLEDGMENTS

I must begin by expressing the tremendous sense of gratitude I feel for the teachers from whom I received the Gesar empowerment, for Kyabje Shechen Rabjam Rinpoche for the reading transmission, and Dzongsar Khyentse Rinpoche and Tulku Orgyen Tobgyal for the instructions.

My gratitude goes also to Yongzin Rinpoche Khenchen Yeshe Gyaltsen, Lama Chönam, Khenpo Yeshe Dorje, Professor Dorji Wangchuk, and Könchok Rinchen in helping me to make sense of the texts; to Tenzin Jamchen (Sean Price), Regina Marco, Janine Schulz, Jeremy Tattersall, Chris Jay, Tashi Coleman, Adam Pearcey, Philip Philippou, Daniella Vedelago, Peter Fry, Alessandra Belissario, Giuseppe Trubiani, Cher Sun, Ane Tsondru, Theresa Bachhuber, and Ann Alford and the Dzogchen Beara team for their help and support to see this project through. I would also like to thank Larry Mermelstein, Scott Wellenbach, Tingdzin Ötro and Pamela Bothwell of the Nalanda Translation Committee; Tara Di Gesu and Peter Fry for the illustrations; at Shambhala Publications, Nikko Odiseos for his immediate enthusiasm and support for the book, and Anna Wolcott Johnson and Emily Wichland for their editorial care; and the Khyentse Foundation for its generous financial support that allowed me to devote substantial amount of time to this book.

Gyurme Avertin
Dzogchen Beara, Ireland
May 2022

PART ONE

GESAR EXPLAINED

GESAR THE WARRIOR

CHÖGYAM TRUNGPA RINPOCHE

In order for us to understand Gesar of Ling, the great warrior king of Tibet, it is necessary first to understand the principle of warriorship itself. This concept has for centuries been the heart of the lineage of Gesar of Ling, whose Tibetan descendants still exist today. Although it has been somewhat influenced by Buddhism, as has virtually all of Tibetan culture, basically the principle of warriorship stands on its own.

By warriorship we are not particularly talking about the skills necessary to wage war in the conventional sense. We are not talking about learning how to handle lethal weapons and crank up our aggression and territoriality so that we can burst forth and conquer all our enemies. Warriorship here refers to realizing the power, dignity, and wakefulness that is inherent in all of us as human beings. It is awakening our basic human confidence, which allows us to cheer up, develop a sense of vision, and succeed in what we are doing.

Because warriorship is innate in human beings, the way to become a warrior—or the warrior's path—is to see who and what we are as human beings and cultivate that. If we look at ourselves directly, without hesitation or embarrassment, we find that we have a lot of strength and a lot of resources available constantly. From that point of view, if we feel we are without resources, if we feel incompetent or as if we were running out of ideas, it is said that we are being attacked by the enemy of warriorship: our own cowardice. The idea of warriorship is that because of our human potential we can go beyond that, step over the enemy of cowardly mind, and discover further banks of resources and inspiration within ourselves.

Cowardly mind is based on the fear of death. Ordinarily we try to ward off any reminders that we are going to die. We constantly produce artificial environments to shield ourselves from any harsh edges. We weave ourselves warm cocoons in which we can live and feel comfortable and sleepy all the time. We try to keep everything under control so that nothing unexpected will pop up and give us a nasty shock, reminding us of our impermanence, our mortality. By doing this, we are trying to defend ourselves from death, which we could say is the opposite of celebrating life. By maintaining our defensive attitude, we keep ourselves surrounded by a familiar fog. We wind up breeding depression and general unhappiness. In fact, that unceasing atmosphere of depression is what makes our little created environments feel so familiar and nestlike. But because it is based on struggle, this cowardly approach of ours is very far from the sense of real joy and playfulness that is associated with warriorship.

Becoming a warrior means that we can look directly at ourselves, see the nature of our cowardly mind, and step out of it. We can trade our small-minded struggle for security for a much vaster vision, one of fearlessness, openness, and genuine heroism. This doesn't happen all at once but is a gradual process. Our first inkling of that possibility comes when we begin to sense the claustrophobia and stuffiness of our self-imposed cocoon. At that point our safe home begins to feel like a trap, and we begin to sense that an alternative is possible. We begin to have tremendous longing for some kind of ventilation, and finally we actually experience a delightful breath of fresh air coming into our stale nest.

At this point we realize that it has been our choice all along to live in this restrictive, and by now somewhat revolting, mentality of defensiveness and cowardice. Simultaneously we realize that we could just as easily switch our allegiance. We could break out of our dark, stuffy prison into the fresh air where it is possible for us to stretch our legs, to walk, run, or even dance and play. We realize that we could drop the oppressive struggle it takes to maintain our cowardice, and relax instead in the greater space of confidence.

It is important to understand what we mean by the confidence of the warrior. The warrior is not developing confidence *in* anything. He is not simply learning one skill, such as swordsmanship, in which he feels he could always take refuge. Nor is he falling back on some mentality of choicelessness, a sense that if only he can hold out long enough and keep a stiff upper lip, then he is bound to come out all right. Those conventional ideas of confidence would simply be further cocoons, based once again on yet further styles of defensiveness and fundamental aggression.

In this case we say the warrior has self-existing confidence. This means that he remains in a *state* of confidence free from competition and any notion of struggle. The warrior's confidence is unconditional. In other words, because he is undistracted by any cowardly thoughts the warrior can rest in an unwavering and wakeful state of mind, which needs no reference points whatsoever.

On the other hand, we do not mean to say that once the warrior has uncovered his innate confidence there is nothing left for him to do. In many ways the path of the warrior is very similar to the Buddhist notion of the bodhisattva path of selfless action. The bodhisattva is a practitioner who isn't satisfied with the possibility of liberating himself from the pain of samsara, but heroically commits himself not to rest until he has helped save all sentient beings. In the same way the confident warrior does not simply feel proud of having seen the nature of his cocoon and stepped out of it. He cannot rest in any sense of smugness at his achievement, or even in the sense of freedom and relief itself. Rather his understanding and personal experience of the claustrophobia of cowardly mind serve as an inspiration for the warrior to free others as well as himself. He actually cannot ignore the suffering and depression he sees in those around him. So from his unconditional confidence, spontaneous compassion naturally arises.

The warrior's compassion manifests in different qualities, which all arise from the nature of his basic confidence. Because the warrior's confident state of mind is self-existing, unmanufactured by aggression, he is not bloated or arrogant. Instead he is humble, kind, and self-contained in relating with others. The warrior is not captured by doubts; therefore he is humorous, uplifted, and perky in his dealings. He is not trapped by the pettiness of hope and fear, so his vision becomes vast and he is not afraid of making mistakes. Finally his mind itself becomes as fathomless as space, so he attains complete mastery over the phenomenal world. With all of these qualities the warrior has a tremendous sense of forward vision. In other words, he is not deterred or depressed by obstacles, but with genuine inquisitiveness and cheerfulness he includes all of them as part of his path.

The confident warrior conducts himself with gentleness, fearlessness, and intelligence. Gentleness is the warm quality of the human heart. Because of the warmth of his heart, the warrior's confidence is not too hard or brittle. Rather it has a vulnerable, open, and soft quality. It is our gentleness that allows us to feel warmth and kindness and to fall in love. But at the same time we are not completely tender. We are tough as well as soft. We are fearless as well as gentle. The warrior meets the world with a slight sense of detachment, a sense of distance and precision. This aspect of confidence is the natural instinct of fearlessness, which allows the warrior to meet challenges without losing his integrity. Finally our confidence expresses itself as innate intelligence, which raises ordinary gentleness and fearlessness to the level of warriorship. In other words, it is intelligence that prevents gentleness from becoming cheap romanticism without any vision, and fearlessness from becoming purely macho. Intelligence is our sense of wakeful inquisitiveness toward the world. It is what allows us to appreciate and take delight in the vivid qualities of the world around us.

So what does all of this have to do with Gesar of Ling, the powerful warrior king who bore magic weapons, rode a marvelous winged steed, and slew numberless demons and other enemies of the sacred teachings? If we apply a more traditional language of warriorship to what we have discussed it will help make the connection.

We have already called cowardice the warrior's enemy. Cowardice is the seductive and distracting quality of our wandering or neurotic minds, which prevents us from resting in our natural state, the state of unwavering wakefulness, which we have called the warrior's confidence. Cowardice is actually the force of evil that obstructs what we could call our basic goodness, our inherent state of confidence, which is by nature devoid of cowardice and aggression, free from evil. From that point of view, the purpose of warriorship is to conquer the enemy, to subjugate the evil of our cowardly minds and uncover our basic goodness, our confidence.

When we talk here about conquering the enemy, it is important to understand that we are not talking about aggression. The genuine warrior does not become resentful or arrogant. Such ambition or arrogance would be simply another aspect of cowardly mind, another enemy of warriorship in itself. So it is absolutely necessary for the warrior to subjugate his own ambition to conquer at the same time that he is subjugating his other more obvious enemies. Thus the idea of warriorship altogether is that by facing all our enemies fearlessly, with gentleness and intelligence, we can develop ourselves and thereby attain self-realization.

With this understanding of warriorship we can go back and look at the history of Gesar of Ling. At this point we can regard the entire story as a display of how the warrior's mind works. Gesar represents the ideal warrior, the principle of all-victorious confidence. As the central force of sanity, he conquers all his enemies, the evil forces of the four directions, who turn people's minds away from the true teachings of Buddhism, the teachings that say it is possible to attain ultimate self-realization. These enemies of the four directions represent quite graphically the different manifestations of cowardly mind, which the ideal warrior subjugates through the power of his unconquerable confidence.

Gesar's magical weapons and his magnificent winged charger, Kyang Gö Karkar, are also important principles of energy in the warrior's world. Weapons are the symbol of warriorship itself. The warrior does not carry weapons because he is afraid of being attacked, but rather as an expression of who he is. Weapons actually magnetize the qualities of warriorship and inspire the warrior to be brave and very gentle. Gesar's winged horse symbolizes the warrior's confidence. He is the ideal image of something beautiful, romantic, energetic, and wild that the warrior can actually capture and ride. Such a horse could be very dangerous and unworkable, but the idea here is that when the warrior has challenged and conquered the enemies of the four directions, then he can ride the great winged horse of confidence and success with dignity and pride.

I was very pleased to be asked to write this foreword,* especially because I regard myself as a descendant of Gesar. I am proud to be a member of the tradition of warriorship and hope that clarifying these precious teachings will help others to bring the inspiration of Gesar's example of warriorship into their lives.

---

*This essay first appeared as a foreword to *The Superhuman Life of Gesar of Ling* by Alexandra David-Neel and Lama Yongden (Boulder: Prajna Press, 1981).

GESAR PRACTICES EXPLAINED

ORGYEN TOBGYAL RINPOCHE

INTRODUCTION

Generally speaking, all Nyingmapas have the greatest respect for Mipham Rinpoche and are very attached to him. He is considered to be a very great master in our tradition because, as all lamas will tell you, he wrote many shastras specifically for the Nyingma tradition. He championed the Nyingma tradition, so Nyingmapas are obviously really keen on him. Actually, among Nyingmapas, Mipham Rinpoche is even more popular than Omniscient Longchenpa and Jigme Lingpa. This very special master wrote a number of protector practices that we can read because they still exist.

There are many Gesar sadhanas. In some, Gesar is practiced as the lama, while in others, he is practiced as a yidam, protector, or wealth deity. But everyone agrees that Jamgön Mipham's approach of practicing Ling Gesar as a dharma protector is preeminent. Apart from one brief lama practice, the king of Ling appears as a dharma protector in all the practices Mipham Rinpoche wrote. This is the approach that I follow.

When you do these practices, you really must understand the main point. Those who ignore it end up practicing Gesar as if he were just a historical figure—a minor Tibetan king who lived in Kham and was little more than a local feudal lord who waged many wars. There's something not quite right about praying and making offerings to him based on that understanding. To be brutally honest, as far as I can see, that's how most Western people I have met think of him. What I want to tell you is this: Gesar is no mere feudal lord—he was not like that at all!

WHO THE PROTECTORS ARE

First, let's talk about the protectors. There are two kinds: wisdom protectors and worldly protectors. Who are the wisdom protectors? The wisdom protectors include the gönpo class of male protectors; the goddess, or lhamo, class of female guardians; and the maning class of epicene protectors. Essentially, the wisdom protectors are buddhas who take the form of those who protect. It works like this. The basic space of phenomena, or dharmadhatu, is "unborn" or "primordial purity." Sambhogakayas manifest from that unborn basic space to "tame" all the sentient beings it's possible to tame, and they are endowed with the infinite enlightened qualities of enlightened body, speech, and mind. A sambhogakaya's job is to benefit sentient beings; to do that, they must emanate the appropriate physical form, speak the appropriate words, and enter into the numerous samadhis that are the expressions of the enlightened body, speech, and mind. In other words, all the enlightened expressions exhibited by a sambhogakaya must suit and be appropriate to the situation and disposition of the sentient beings they wish to help.

Sentient beings cannot relate to enlightened body, speech, mind, qualities, and activities just as they are, but of course the buddhas can. So what has to happen? In the Highest Yoga Tantra, enlightened body, speech, mind, qualities, and activities are called "inexhaustible wheels of ornaments." Traditionally *wheel* is a metaphor for the quality of inexhaustibility—it can continue turning forever and the distance it covers is not limited by itself. The enlightened body, speech, mind, qualities, and activities are always benefiting sentient beings, constantly and endlessly. The "ornaments" are the display of these qualities. The inexhaustible wheel of the ornaments of enlightened speech, also called the "clouds of letters" in the *Secret Essence Tantra*, must manifest in the form of the tantras so sentient beings can benefit from all the enlightened qualities.

When the time comes to teach the tantras, this is what happens. The first buddha, dharmakaya Samantabhadra, is primordial purity free of elaboration, the aspect of emptiness. His consort, Samantabhadri, whose wisdom mind never wavers from Samantabhadra's wisdom mind, is the aspect of clarity. They are never not one, yet she appears as a separate being who asks Samantabhadra to teach the tantras. Out of compassion for sentient beings, Samantabhadra then sets out the "wheel of clouds of letters." In other words, he brings the tantras into the world by teaching them. When the tantras were first taught, both the root and supporting tantras were included. For example, the main Dzogchen teaching given was the root tantra known as the *Word-Transcending Tantra* (*Sgra thal 'gyur rtsa ba'i rgyud*), and it was accompanied by the other six million four hundred thousand tantras of Dzogpachenpo. The tantras contain sadhanas, which can be translated into English as "means for attaining accomplishment" and from which numerous deities appeared—for example, the buddhas of the five families and the hundred supreme peaceful and wrathful families. These deities include the protectors who own, care for, and protect these teachings. For instance, Samantabhadri herself sprang from a rock in the physical form of Ekazati, "the Protectress of Mantras." The teacher Samantabhadra, Samantabhadri, the deities of the hundred peaceful and wrathful families' supreme mandala, and the Protectress of Mantras are all simply different expressions of the same wisdom. In that sense they are the same. The various manifestations of this one wisdom are called "wisdom deities," and to be clear, they are not expressions of delusion but of cognizant clarity.

In addition to the wisdom deities, independently existing spirits like tsens and gyalpos appeared, but they had been under the influence of delusion for a long time. The masters eventually introduced them to their deluded condition to some extent and, as the traditional texts say, "established them as protectors of the teachings." In other words, these spirits promised masters like Guru Rinpoche that they would abide by their commands and protect the Buddhist teachings and the holders and practitioners of these teachings. There were also local deities. The spirits in Tibet were overpowered by Guru Rinpoche, who they then pledged to serve.

Therefore these local deities do whatever they can to help spread the teachings of the Buddha and to increase the well-being of sentient beings, who they do not harm, and cultivate the enlightened mind of bodhichitta. Some of these local deities were able to abide by Guru Rinpoche's words straight away and respect the pledges they had made to him, but it's likely that others weren't—at least to begin with. This is the first important point that you need to understand.

The next point is that to truly help sentient beings, it is important to manifest and act in ways that sentient beings can relate to. In fact, there's no other option. Even our teacher, Buddha Shakyamuni, entered the womb of King Shuddhodana's queen, Mayadevi, so that he could genuinely help sentient beings, fulfilling their expectations by enacting the twelve deeds. Guru Rinpoche also manifested for the benefit of sentient beings. A syllable HRIH emanated from the heart of Amitabha, descended onto a lotus in the middle of Lake Dhanakosha, and instantly transformed into Guru Rinpoche. This is how he appeared in this world through a miraculous birth. As he did not pass into parinirvana but instead attained rainbow body—the form he will remain in until samsara is empty—the methods he used to help sentient beings were the eleven deeds. When Manjushri, the embodiment of the wisdom of all the buddhas, had to teach sentient beings astrology, he first appeared on this earth in China and from the knot of a tree arose miraculously as a bird. In addition, Manjushri appeared in several other forms—for example, that of a golden tortoise. Accounts of the first time the teachings on astrology were given always start with this story of Manjushri's miraculous birth, the golden tortoise, and so on.

When the Tantra teachings were first brought to the world, Rudra Black Liberation appeared. To tame him, the power of all the buddhas' compassion and strength manifested in the forms of Hayagriva and Vajravarahi, who subdued him on the peak of Blazing Meteoritic Mount Malaya where he was residing. They "liberated" him and brought under their power all twenty-four sacred places, thirty-two sacred lands, and eight charnel grounds—the sixty-four places of power—which they then entrusted to the local dakas and dakinis. At the same location, the teachings of Secret Mantra Vajrayana were taught for the first time in this world, at which time all the tantras were taught. Twenty-four years after Buddha passed into parinirvana, the five great beings with exceptional qualities known as the Five Excellent Ones of Sublime Nobility (a god; a naga; a yaksha; a rakshasa; and a human being, Vimalakirti) gathered on Mount Malaya where Vajrasattva taught them the tantras exactly as they had been taught in Akanishtha. They received both the tantra and sadhana sections of the tantric teachings but did not keep them in this world for long. Instead, they concealed the tantras in space. When the right time came, all the tantra teachings descended to the roof of the palace of King Ja. The teachings of the sadhana section were hidden in the Dechen Tsekpa (Shankarakuta) stupa in the Cool Grove charnel ground, where they remained hidden until Guru Rinpoche and the eight great vidyadharas retrieved them. This was when the Vajrayana teachings started to spread in this world. In those days, every single man or woman exposed to the Vajrayana teachings became a mahasiddha. This is why we say that Mount Malaya is the source of the Vajrayana teachings. That's the second point you should know.

WHY WE NEED GESAR

You need to understand clearly these first two points—who the protectors are and that they manifest and act in ways that sentient beings can relate to—before we can discuss the third point, which is Gesar Norbu Dradul, "Gesar the Jewel Tamer of Enemies." Most importantly, you need to understand that incarnations who emanate to help sentient beings must manifest in a form that suits the dispositions and capacities of the sentient beings of that time and in which they can then help those beings. Of course, this isn't something that sentient beings themselves know; it's something only the buddhas know. Since the number of thoughts that arise in the mind are beyond measure, the antidotes are beyond measure. This is why we say that the Buddha in his great compassion is skilled in the use of many methods. You also need to know that the different aspects of deities, mantras, and samadhis were not created by the Buddha, nor thought out and produced by a conceptual mind: they are simply the qualities of the Buddha.

The times in which we live are thought of as "bad" times because the five degenerations are running rampant. Sentient beings are in a far worse state now than they were in ages past. So much so that they are unable to follow the path to liberation and omniscience. Why? Because their windhorse is weak and they can't understand teachings like Dzogpachenpo when they are presented to them because intense obscurations cloud their minds. This is how things are right now. Mipham Rinpoche explained that Gesar Norbu Dradul is important right now because the five degenerations are growing ever stronger, causing the lungta of all sentient beings to diminish. Sentient beings don't engage in positive activities, nor do they abandon negative ones. Their understanding of the laws of karma, cause and effect, is backward. When our windhorse is low, none of our worldly activities and worthwhile projects work out, whereas all our bad ideas and worthless projects are easily accomplished. Under such circumstances, no matter how much effort we put into trying to accomplish something positive, such as practicing the dharma, we face many obstacles; and however much we long to give up a negative activity, we are unable to do so. This is what happens when our lungta is low—it happens quite naturally. At the same time, raising our lungta prevents us from engaging in negative activities even if we don't try to avoid them by applying antidotes. The five poisons of desire, aversion, ignorance, jealousy, and pride are, by nature, suffering. When we are "unsuccessful"— that is, when our lungta is low—the five poisons lead us to experience pain in lower rebirths. But when we are successful, the five poisons are liberated as the five wisdoms—their true nature. This is why raising the lungta is extremely beneficial. You can therefore understand why the practices contained in this book are so important and why Guru Rinpoche needs to manifest in the form of a drala. It's all to do with the quality in beings that we term *lungta*, or "windhorse," which is increased by dralas.

There is something quite important in what I am saying, so pay attention. Samsaric beings fall into three categories: those born into the highest realms of samsara; those born into the lowest realms; and those who are born somewhere in between, where there is a mixture of positive and negative experiences. The minds of all these sentient beings are one. This oneness of mind is called "buddha nature." Nevertheless, the purity of beings' perceptions varies. As such, among the six realms of samsara, "gods" only experience happiness during their lifetime; their minds experience no suffering. Even so, when the moment of death comes, they still have to face the suffering of transference and falling into a lower rebirth. For humans, on the other hand, our experience is mixed. During our lifetime we experience states of joy and happiness, pain and suffering, and various positive and negative experiences mixed together. Hell beings in the lowest realms experience only suffering. All these experiences are the product of our mind, the essence of which is wisdom. Our mind is an expression of awareness. Buddhas and sentient beings are the magical manifestations of the same nature of mind: the impure aspects are sentient beings and the pure aspect is buddha. As it is said, "One instant distinction, one instant enlightened."[1] When an ordinary thought is liberated within the expanse of awareness, that is buddhahood. But when thoughts are not liberated and instead follow one after another, they become the cause for a being to fall into samsara. As long as that stream of thoughts continues, the being will not be liberated. The experiences of happiness, suffering, or a mix of happiness and suffering are the result of karma. Only mind is responsible for producing karma. Nothing and no one else does it. The mind, however, is such that under ordinary circumstances we have no power over it. Our mind may intend to do something virtuous, but if something changes, mind changes and can become quite negative. At the same time, we might experience states in which we are motivated by negativity but, again, something changes that makes mind more positive. In any case, the controlling factor is the mind, and mind is controlled by *lung*, the "wind" inside the body. At the moment, you are simply reading this text and you have no control over the thoughts that arise in your mind. When a thought arises, you act based on that thought, creating karma. *Lung*, or "wind," is responsible for providing the conditions for the thoughts to arise. The wind (*lung*) is a like a horse (*ta*) on which the mind rides, so this quality is called "windhorse."

When our windhorse is flourishing, the mind's "mount" increases in strength and our windhorse is high—even in a mind that arises from negative karma. Virtuous mindsets embrace attachment, aversion, ignorance, jealousy, and pride, then arise as the five wisdoms, which are their true nature. However, if your lungta is low, no matter how virtuous your motivation and how hard you try to follow the path of Buddha's teachings, as your mind is motivated by negative emotions, it will drag you down and you will not be able to liberate yourself from samsara. Needless to say, all the karma we create is based on activities driven by our likes and dislikes. And as we all know, "like" and "dislike" arise only in the mind.

An extremely profound point you need to know is that the border between samsara and nirvana beyond samsara—complete and perfect buddhahood—is very thin. A thought arises and naturally becomes a cause of remaining in samsara, but if it is liberated within the expanse of the dharmakaya, it is the wisdom of dharmakaya, the enlightened intent of a buddha. Both outcomes arise from an identical "thought." It can go either way: up to a state of freedom or down to a state of confusion. It all depends on the wind on which mind rides, the lungta. Mipham Rinpoche wrote in *A Vast Cloud of Jewels: Fulfillment Offering to the Wermas, Gesar's Treasure Guardians* (#10):

> Grant us the great good fortune of being able to travel freely
> From joy to joy to the jewel island of omniscience!

"From joy to joy": Mipham Rinpoche qualifies the kind of joy he means as "omniscient wisdom," which he compares to an island of jewels. The mind can go wherever it pleases, freely. When every thought is simultaneously experienced as realization and liberation, you can do whatever you want because the continuous stream of delusion has been stopped. Mipham Rinpoche's verse is a request that we accomplish the activities that enable us to perfect realization and liberation—that's what these prayers come down to.

Lungta is usually low and obscured in beings who live in the three realms of samsara, and it does not flourish at all. On top of which, the time of degeneration in which we live automatically corrupts the lungta of all beings, producing dull minds and thickening the obscurations to the wisdom of rigpa. When we pray to Guru Rinpoche and the dralas who make lungta flourish, the clarity aspect of mind and rigpa's capacity increase enormously. If the realization of primordial purity (*kadak*) becomes manifest, there is no more suffering—as it is said, even the name of suffering does not exist. This is not something you can understand immediately. However, if you take the time to contemplate and reflect on the logic of lungta again and again, the understanding you arrive at will make a big difference in your practice. But if you imagine that mind is a person of some kind and that lungta really is a horse, you will be making a grave mistake. This image is used to make it easier for us to understand, but it is only an example.

As the windhorse deity, Gesar Norbu Dradul, manifests in the form of a drala, everyone's lungta rises. Our minds become stronger and more powerful, and mind acquires the ability to liberate itself—this ability is explained in detail in the Dzogchen teachings. This is why Gesar practice is so important right now. In a nutshell, the strengthening and ultimate liberation of minds are the purpose of these practices. In earlier times, everyone was endowed with great merit, which meant their lungta was high. When the windhorse has been raised in a person, they have authentic presence, charisma, courage, and strength. They are capable of accomplishing exactly what they set out to accomplish. But now that the five degenerations dominate this time, people are weak and lack courage; the need to act virtuously doesn't even occur to them. We hardly ever think, "I should be meditating and resting in the nature of mind." However determined we are to try to meditate, we cannot. When all our attempts fail and we are unable to go directly to our destination, we are sidetracked by other paths. Sound familiar? In this case, Gesar practice ensures that we develop the capacity to follow the right path.

As I have just said, Guru Rinpoche manifests in the form of the drala Gesar Norbu Dradul to help us raise our low windhorse. When the Buddha appears to tame trainable beings, those beings must be able to relate to the form he takes. Gesar appeared at a time when beings were overcome by their own destructive emotions and spent their lives at war with one another. To tame birds, Buddha must manifest as a bird; to tame dogs, he must manifest as a dog; to tame bees, he must manifest as a bee; and to tame human beings, he must manifest in a human form, right? So, Buddha appeared as Gesar Norbu Dradul, the magical emanation of the Lotus-Born and of the lords of the three families. The lords of the three families are: Manjushri, who knows everything; Avalokiteshvara, who looks with the eye of compassion upon every single sentient being like a mother gazing on her only child; and Vajrapani, "the Lord of Secrets" and the embodiment of all the power, strength, and ability of all the buddhas. The embodiment of the omniscient wisdom of all the buddhas is Manjushri, the embodiment of their compassion is Avalokiteshvara, and the embodiment of their power is Vajrapani. All the "eight close sons" of the buddhas, the eight great bodhisattvas, are understood in the same way—as embodiments of specific enlightened qualities. You can read more about them in Mipham Rinpoche's *Garland of Jewels* in which each one is explained.[2] The lords of the three families are Manjushri, Avalokiteshvara, and Vajrapani; their magical manifestation is Guru Rinpoche; and his emanation is Gesar Norbu Dradul. As Gesar prayers often specify, the "emanation of Padma and the three families, Great Lion Gesar . . ."[3] This is entirely possible because

Guru Rinpoche can manifest as yidams, dharma protectors, and even wealth deities and treasure guardians, on top of which he said, "If you have faith in me, I am in front of you." Generally speaking, the Nyingma tradition says that the dynamic display of the nature of mind is Guru Rinpoche, and that Guru Rinpoche is the embodiment of all the lamas, yidams, dakinis, and dharmapalas. This is how we should think. We need to think about, contemplate, and practice these teachings. We shouldn't distinguish between Gesar and Guru Rinpoche and so on. Basically, the deity Gesar doesn't exist; he is simply Guru Rinpoche in the form of a drala—a form he takes to help raise the windhorse of sentient beings. Guru Rinpoche is also the embodiment of the enlightened qualities of all the buddhas. His enlightened activities are unfathomable, but a small fraction took place in the Land of Ling, "the awe-inspiring Ma valley" in Kham—this is what it's called in all the stories written about Gesar.

GESAR'S HISTORY

One point to clarify is that many stories are said to be historical accounts of Gesar's life, but, personally, I don't know how historically reliable these stories are. For example, there are several versions of when Gesar was born. Therefore, we can't be certain when that was, even though in *The Nyingma School of Tibetan Buddhism*, Kyabje Dudjom Rinpoche gives Ling Gesar Norbu Dradul's dates.[4] Nowadays, many stories are told about Gesar, and a few have even been written down. Some authors record information that is correct, while the scribbling of others is totally useless. International academics say that the Tibetan story about the individual known as Gesar Norbu Dradul is the longest epic in the world. But as I say, I doubt the veracity of most of it. Why? Because Drokpa Lharge, for example, whom I know, has written many books about Gesar, none of which have any basis in fact. Having said that, not every word we read about Gesar can be written off. Khamtrul Döngyu Nyima Rinpoche, for example, wrote a few books about Gesar that

Jamyang Khyentse Chökyi Lodrö and other great masters have described as "mind termas for this time." So I can't say that every word written is rubbish. However, it is impossible to establish with any certainty that any of the stories are based on fact merely by analyzing the texts. Neither is it possible to state with any confidence that no mistakes have been made.

What do the stories in this epic tell us about Gesar? The chapter called "The Events Leading to Gesar's Incarnation in the Land of Ling" describes how Gesar came into this world from a god realm. The chapter "Gesar's Birth and Childhood in the Land of Ling" describes his birth, his siblings, and how, based on the aspirations they made in past lives, different characters were born in Ling, Hor, Dü, and so on. It tells us that Gesar was a descendant of the Mukpo Dong clan (one of the six Mukpo tribes of Ombu), and it tells us about his father, Senglon—his patriarchal lineage is mentioned and his ancestors are listed. But the names quoted in these lists vary from one version to another. Senglon had three wives, and Gesar had two half brothers from different mothers: an elder half brother, Gyatsa Shelkar and a younger half brother, Rongtsa Marlep. Gesar's mother, a nagini called Gokza, became one of Senglön's wives when she first arrived in Ling, before she gave birth to Gesar.

Although I have yet to see an authentic version of this epic that is entirely beyond doubt, we cannot reject it out of hand as mere fantasy. We know that Lower Ma, the country of Ling, where many of the stories take place, is in the Golok area of eastern Tibet. We also know that the Array of Nine Peaks of Upper Ma is in Kham. The locations of these two areas have been passed down through generations from the time of Gesar until today. We know where the stories took place, but we cannot identify exactly when Gesar flourished on this earth.

In the epic, Ling sounds like a very big country, but nowadays all that's left is a minor king of the Lingtsang house who is said to have descended from Gesar himself—and no one can prove otherwise. In Chokgyur Lingpa's biography, the great tertön is said to have had a conversation with the ministers of Ling about the need to restore the old palace of Lingtsang. The ministers insisted that the palace was in good condition and so there was no need to restore it, to which Chokgyur Lingpa replied that they hadn't understood his point. "Come to the palace and see for yourselves," he said. When the panels above the doors that face each of the four directions were removed, they found large chang jars. These jars contained the heads of Gesar Norbu Dradul's great enemies, "the maras of the four directions," and had been hidden there after Gesar "liberated" them. When Chokgyur Lingpa went to Lower Ma, he saw Ma's Upper Dil-yag Tiger Plain where, in Gesar's time, the people of Ling would hold their assemblies. He also noticed that the local people were tall, brawny, and strong, which, he said, was exactly how they were described in the epic. Magyal Pomra, the local deity who protects Ling, appeared to Chokgyur Lingpa and said that Guru Rinpoche had given him the hat that he always wore when he commanded the local gods of the world. He then offered this hat to him. Later, Reting Rinpoche took it for the Tibetan government. I have seen the box that used to contain it. It is still in Kham.

When we hear accounts like these, we know that Ling Gesar cannot just be a figment of our imaginations—a legend. But as for the veracity of the stories themselves, it's probably fifty-fifty. This all makes telling Gesar's story quite difficult. And in any case, I don't think it is that useful. We could write something based on the many books that already exist, but I still don't think it will be helpful. If we bring Gesar down to the level of myth and fantasy, his spiritual stature would be lost altogether. There are many epics in this world (like those based on European lore) that all seem to have developed out of minimal provable fact.

In Nangchen, there is a Kagyupa monastery called Tana Gompa[5]—it was named after a nearby rock that looks like a horse's (*ta*) ear (*na*). It is said to have housed a number of Gesar's belongings, although very few are now left. Various old monasteries in Tibet, such as Katok Monastery, preserve several objects connected with Gesar.

This method of analysis is the modern scientific approach, right?

And it demonstrates that we cannot conclusively prove that Gesar never existed. But I don't know. I cannot say for sure whether he either did or didn't exist, and I cannot say that everything in the epic is true.

Many stories in the epic take place in Kham, which, it turns out, isn't as big as the epic makes it out to be. Tibet is not as vast a country as the Tibetans used to imagine, and Kham is only a small part of it. We may therefore wonder how, as it is said, "Gesar brought the whole world under his power." Khamtrul Döngyu Nyima Rinpoche wrote two volumes of stories describing Gesar's wars. One war is supposed to have taken place in Uyen in the East, which is said to be America; and the other in the country of Jar, which is said to be Germany. Khamtrul Rinpoche's texts also mention Ulang, or Australia, where Gesar hasn't fought yet—the war is only just beginning.

In general, the epic uses the term *foreign land* to describe all the other countries Gesar conquered. But with very little digging, you will discover that all the places mentioned fall within Tibet's cultural arena—for example, Hor, Jang, and Mön, which is Bhutan. We therefore don't know anything for sure. And this is why I don't think there's much benefit in writing anything here about the life of Gesar. I doubt it would support our practice of Lama Mipham's liturgies—in fact, quite the opposite as there are no verifiable sources.

Nowadays, Gesar is famous. For the Chinese, Gesar is not a religious figure but a political one. If they thought of him as Buddhist, he would not enjoy the popularity he has today. But not even the Chinese can say whether the epic's stories about Gesar are true or not. They have named the new airport on the road from Chengdu to Garze Gesar Airport in Derge, and large statues of Gesar have been erected in the major cities of Kham. The point here is that even though the stories cannot be verified, the Chinese government has no qualms about using Gesar's name.

Anyway, it is also impossible for me to tell you the story of Gesar's life right now because it fills so many volumes. But the practices that follow mention some of the people Gesar knew. For example, *Sollo Chenmo* (#37) says, "We invoke the elder brother Dungkhyung Karpo!" "We invoke the younger brother Ludrul Öjung!" and "We invoke the younger sister Tale Ökar!" So I'll say a few words about these people.

Gesar's father, Senglön, was from the Mukpo Dong lineage and was therefore a member of the patriarchal Mukpo clan. The Mukpo clan was made up of many smaller clans, including the Chöphen and Chölaphen lineages. His mother, Gokza, belonged to a clan called Gok, although she came from the land of the nagas and was actually a nagini. As Gesar entered his mother's womb, she dreamed about her five chakras—the chakra of great bliss on the top of her head, the chakra of enjoyment at her throat, the chakra of the dharma at her heart, the chakra of manifestation at her navel, and the secret chakra that holds bliss. All four of her children—three boys and one girl—entered her womb at the same time. The firstborn of these four nirmanakayas was the "elder brother," Dungkhyung Karpo. Gesar was born second, then his younger brother, Ludrul Öjung, and lastly his younger sister Tale Ökar. Gesar's three siblings took the forms of a human, a naga, and a goddess to support his activities. Gesar Norbu Dradul came out of his mother's secret place. As I mentioned above, Gesar also had two half brothers—they shared the same father, but Gyatsa Shelkar's mother was called Gyaza, and Rongtsa Marlep's mother was called Rongza. Some of Mipham Rinpoche's texts, such as *Warrior Song of Drala: Long Werma Lhasang* (#30), mention Minister Denma Changtra, his chief minister and most loyal supporter. Denma led the "thirty mighty wizard-warriors," Gesar's ministers, all of whom appeared at that time in the form of dralas. They were all nirmanakayas, which means they appeared in a form that sentient beings could relate to but were not sentient beings themselves. They could fly in the sky, live belowground, and display all sorts of miracles. Gesar's life is full of inconceivable stories. He was the kind of person to whom everything appeared as the natural expression of primordial wisdom, and he could magnetize and bring all appearances under his control. But he only remained on this earth for a short time.

Although Gesar had no direct descendants, the Mukpo Dong family, who are descended from the half brother Gyatsa Shelkar, still exists. Gyatsa means "Chinese" (*gya*) "grandson" (*tsa*). His mother, Gyaza, was the daughter of the emperor of China, and this is why his face was white, earning him the name Shelkar in Tibetan, which means "white face." The members of his lineage are, of course, all known, and it's also possible to identify a descendent after death by a large A syllable on their skull. It is also possible to identify them by the reddish color of their eyes.

GESAR PRACTICES AND MIND TERMAS

After Gesar's time, many tertöns revealed mind termas of Gesar practices, sadhanas, activity manuals, empowerments and so on, so today we have many volumes of Gesar practices. Jamyang Khyentse Wangpo and Jamgön Kongtrul revealed some, Mipham Rinpoche left many, Shechen Gyaltsap discovered a few, and so did Khenpo Jigme Phuntsok and Dilgo Khyentse Rinpoche—in the *Heart Essence of the Dralas* cycle, for example.

As I've already said, these teaching are mind termas. To reveal a mind terma, the tertön's wisdom mind must be indivisible from Guru Rinpoche's wisdom mind, which is indivisible from the wisdom mind of Gesar. This means that when these tertöns reveal their mind termas, their minds are the same as Gesar's wisdom mind. And there are no mistakes in an authentic terma because buddhas don't make mistakes! Mipham Rinpoche was the main revealer of mind termas based on Gesar, and both the literary style and meaning of his termas are flawless. Not only are his termas faultless, their power to accomplish activities and bring about a desired result can be witnessed to this very day. This is why I said earlier that you can practice Gesar as lama, yidam, or dharma protector—whichever you choose is fine and will be beneficial.

It is said that all Mipham Rinpoche's writings are mind termas.

This is quite possible given that "mind," in this context, does not move from the ground of the dharmata. For the great masters who can remain in that state of realization, everything that arises as the dynamic display of awareness is a terma. How does this work? There is no impurity as all that arises is the pure display of awareness. Since Guru Rinpoche's and Mipham Rinpoche's minds are the same, and as Guru Rinpoche didn't have any ordinary thoughts, everything that arose in Mipham Rinpoche's mind was a terma. We often hear that Mipham Rinpoche released the "eight brilliant treasures,"[6] which indicates he didn't have any ordinary thoughts—I believe he acknowledged that himself. He said that even when he wrote a short four-line prayer, the text came to him through the power of the blessings of the three roots and the infinite victorious ones. He never just wrote down his own thoughts.[7] The Nyingmapas say "through the blessing power" to indicate that all his writings are mind termas. But then, they do like to talk big. All the masters praise Mipham Rinpoche for many reasons, the most significant of which is that he revealed mind termas. Tertöns who discover earth termas are limited by circumstances—for example, they are often destined to discover a few termas and no others. Whereas mind termas are like the "treasury of space," inexhaustible, and everything required is there for the taking, it just needs to be revealed. Therefore, Mipham Rinpoche writes, "I have no earth or stone termas, only mind treasures." Mind termas leave no room for mistakes, but earth termas are vulnerable to inaccuracies in transcription. It's also possible that some parts of an earth terma are decoded, while others are not. On top of that, earth termas are hidden under many seals—the teachings mention thirteen seals: the seal of command, seal of concealment, seal of secrecy, personal seal, and so on—which make them difficult to reveal. This is why so many earth termas have not been revealed properly, and this point is often brought up when people heap praise on Mipham Rinpoche. To raise someone up, it's always necessary to bring someone else down, right?

DRALAS

I don't know what the Bönpos say about dralas, but in the Nyingma tradition, dralas are mentioned in the termas. *Dralha* literally means the "enemy" (*dra*) "deity" (*lha*). In other words, dralha is the deity that overcomes opposing enemies and ensures that our plans and activities develop and grow. The Nyingma teachings speak of thirteen dralas, forty wermas, and twenty zodors. Dralas also include the norlhas, or wealth deities. Gesar is Guru Rinpoche in the form of a drala, as described in the sadhanas on the thirteen dralas, such as the *Sang Offering to the Thirteen Dralas*[8] revealed by Rigdzin Gödem. "Arose in the form of a drala" is also a reference to Gesar's appearance as he manifests riding a horse, holding a whip and the horse's reins, as described in Mipham Rinpoche's *King Gesar Secret Sadhana* (#6).

Generally there are three categories: drala, werma, and zodor. There is a difference between the dralas and wermas, but clarifying the differences is difficult because so many texts say so many different things. Dralas and wermas are explained differently in different teachings. Identifying who's who is also difficult because detailed descriptions are not given. You can only trust the teachings given by very learned scholars because the less learned just make things up. One source says the dralas have a human form. Another source says the wermas protect the dralas. And yet another source says that the zodors are tigers, lions, garudas, snakes, bears, elephants, rabbits, and so on. I have read the descriptions given in many sources, and they all present each being quite differently, so I don't know for sure what they really look like. To give a detailed presentation about dralas, wermas, and so on, we first need precise descriptions, like the clear descriptions that exist for the thirty-two major marks and the eighty minor signs in the *Prajnaparamita*. But no such descriptions exist for dralas and wermas. In any case, the important thing to know is that all the dralas, wermas, and zodors are inside Gesar's body, "amassing as if in large clouds." Relate to them like that, and it will be easier for you.

These practices also mention the five patron gods—father-god, shoulder-god, and so on. Our bodies need these gods, which is why they take up residence in our bodies: the shoulder-god resides in the shoulder, and when a woman is pregnant, the mother-goddess resides in her belly. There's a father-god, a god of the maternal uncle, and so on. It's all too complicated for me; I don't know much about it. Even so, mention of these gods can be found in authentic sources such as the practices that talk about the thirteen dralas, so they're not outright inventions. There are even sadhanas that describe their color, hand implements, and so on. I have heard that the Bönpos have very detailed descriptions, but I have never read them.

ENLIGHTENED ACTIVITIES

We invoke and make offerings to the protector Gesar so that he will perform certain activities. Protector practices go into great detail about the specific benefits we should request from the dharmapalas, which always amount to protecting and furthering the dharma. Some of these practices focus on pacifying adverse circumstances, while others focus on increasing wisdom and the spirit of abundance (the quality in people that attracts prosperity). Some practices are about magnetizing people, other beings, and one's own mind, while others focus on more forceful activities to remove obstacles or to "liberate" harm-doers. Generally speaking, in Vajrayana, the root of blessings is the lama, the root of accomplishment is the yidam, and the roots of the enlightened activities are the dakini and dharmapala. Elaborate sadhana practices involve four stages: approach, close approach, accomplishment, and great accomplishment. These four stages can also be condensed into three: approach, accomplishment, and activity. The real benefit in practicing approach and accomplishment comes with the last stage, the accomplishment of the activities. There are four types of activity: pacifying, enriching, magnetizing, and subjugating. To accomplish these activities, we practice the dakinis and the dharma protectors. The *Lamrim Yeshe Nyingpo* describes the different practices associated with the four types of activity—for example, the purification ritual for the dead, consecration, and so on. Basically, these are all the practices lamas traditionally do to benefit others. None of the activities taught by the Buddha is harmful to beings. In the Vajrayana, it is necessary to accomplish the deity first in order to perform the enlightened activities of pacifying, enriching, magnetizing, and subjugating. Otherwise it doesn't work.

Pacifying activities are performed to pacify all obstacles— illness, malevolent forces, negativity, obscurations, enemies, fears, obstacles, black magic, and so on—on the path to enlightenment. Enriching activities are to increase merit, wisdom, qualities, and life span. Life span, as Guru Rinpoche said, is essential so that a practitioner has time to accomplish the practice. Enriching activities can also create the circumstances necessary—such as retinue, wealth, strength, prosperity, and happiness—to do one's own practice or for leading others on the path to liberation and omniscience.

Of the four types of activities, the magnetizing and subjugating activities are special features of Vajrayana, the vehicle that takes the fruition as the path, whereas the pacifying and enriching activities are also taught in the Causal Vehicle of Characteristics (the sutra teachings). In the sutras you find extensive teachings that explain how to pacify sentient beings and increase longevity, merit, wealth, wisdom, qualities, and so on. The enriching activities are naturally accomplished when we perfect the accumulations of merit and wisdom and remove obscurations. All sentient beings have buddha nature, and when accompanied by the white seed of faith and trust in the teachings, we are able to accomplish pacifying and enriching activities simply based on the sutra level of teachings. But sutra teachings cannot help people who don't have any faith, trust, or pure perception for the dharma. When you teach the sutras, you check whether the listeners hear what you say, and if they don't, all you can do is make prayers of aspiration for them. So the Sutrayana doesn't offer methods to reach those who lack faith and devotion. This is where the magnetizing and subjugating activities unique to Vajrayana apply. They can bring some beings under control through magnetizing and liberate other beings through violent or subjugating activities—all beings, even those who lack faith and pure perception.

The Buddha has the extraordinary quality of being able to accomplish infinite enlightened activities to help sentient beings, out of inconceivable compassion that looks with love and care upon every single sentient being without bias. So since he is accomplishing his activities constantly and spontaneously, to say that the Buddha is only able to help sentient beings who have faith and pure perception reduces and limits the Buddha's enlightened activities. When it comes to magnetizing and subjugating activities, no sentient being is unreachable, and the Buddha is able to care for all beings and lead them on the path to liberation.

Magnetizing activities (*wang dü*)—the activities to bring (*dü*) beings and circumstances under your control or power (*wang*)—have many aspects, but the most important is to bring your own mind under control. To look more deeply at magnetizing activity, the first question is: Who are the beings we magnetize? All sentient beings have buddha nature, but magnetizing activities are mainly concerned with gods, nagas, and humans. Of course, magnetizing activities can be applied to beings who have merit, faith, and pure perception, but typically magnetizing activities are intended for those without it.

The second question is: How do we perform magnetizing activity? It is not done by waging war or by forcing people. If the methods taught in the sutras of the bodhisattva vehicle (the "four means of attracting disciples": being generous, talking gently and kindly, giving helpful guidance, and practicing what you preach) are ineffective, then the special magnetizing methods taught in Secret Mantra Vajrayana are employed.

Performing this kind of activity is effective only when the practitioner is motivated by great compassion; it doesn't work when the motivation is attachment or desire. Whether the magnetizing activity focuses on a specific being or all beings in general, it must be motivated by compassion. What is the motivation of compassion? It is to realize that all beings want to be happy but do not know how to accumulate the causes of happiness—virtuous, positive actions. They do not want to suffer, yet everything they do leads them to more suffering because they do not know how to abandon the causes of suffering, the negative actions. Out of compassion for these beings we think, "I must magnetize them and bring their body, speech and mind under my power to lead them on the path to liberation and omniscience." That is the motivation with which you must perform such activities. You don't act out of desire, yet pure desire is the wisdom of discernment. So we bring forth the compassion that is the natural radiance of the wisdom of discernment and magnetize beings' body, speech, and mind by means of deity, mantra, mudra, and samadhi. Sentient beings are the "external objects" attracted by magnetizing activity. This is how to magnetize samsaric sentient beings.

Secret Mantra Vajrayana teachings are rich in skillful methods, and magnetizing activities are one of them. Basically we are allowed to do this kind of practice to further the teachings so they may reach more beings. But before you think about magnetizing some external sentient beings such as gods, spirits, or humans, you first need to bring under control or magnetize your own body, speech and mind, otherwise you won't be able to magnetize others. To reiterate, the most important aspect of the magnetizing activity is to bring one's mind under control.

Subjugating activities involve first protection, then averting, and lastly, if required, liberation. The example used to illustrate this is fighting a war. In the run-up to the confrontation you need to protect your land. So the protection is something you prepare beforehand. If you try to protect your territory when the battle has already started, you will lose your territory. Therefore, protection is the most important and comes first. Then the averting activity, which is turning away the opposing forces outside of your fortress. You carry out the averting activity, or dokpa, to accomplish this.

If we can't avert negative forces and obstacles through dokpa practice, what do we do? We annihilate them. How do we accomplish liberation or annihilating activity? As the root tantra of Vajrakilaya states, "Liberate through realization and annihilate through compassion." First you need a high realization and to have actualized the essence of shunyata. If this realization is not accompanied with the power of the yidam deity, annihilation cannot take place. If you use a phurba to carry out annihilation while you still hold on to "good" and "bad," the activity will be no different from using a weapon to kill somebody.

Directing the practice of liberating through visualization is not easy, and it is difficult to practice. However, if you must do this practice, you should know that all the harmful forces, all those who bring decline, all the instigators for every kind of problem are the gongpo demon of self-grasping—that's who you need to "kill." Consider that you have summoned the gongpo demon of self-grasping and that he actually comes. Imagine that all the mental poisons—desire, aversion, ignorance, and so on—are there within the gongpo of self-grasping. Then direct the practice through the emanation and reabsorption of rays of light and so on, and imagine that they are liberated in the basic space of dharmadhatu. There is nothing inappropriate about this visualization practice, even if it is practiced by a person who has no power in their practice and hasn't accomplished the approach and accomplishment. But if you don't practice in this way knowing that the only aim is self-grasping, if you don't have any power in your practice and do not actualize bodhichitta yet still actualize the visualization for the liberating activity, there will be very little benefit and great danger. All the lamas have taught that all three vows will instantly be torn into shreds. This is an important point to bear in mind.

SANG PRACTICE

Since this collection of Mipham Rinpoche's Gesar practices contains a number of sang offering texts, I will now explain the basic principles of sang practice.

In Tibet, the practice of sang predates the arrival of the Buddhist teachings. When Guru Rinpoche came to Tibet, he conducted the earth-taming practice to prepare the ground for the construction of the temple at Samye. On that occasion, he adapted the native sang and ngen (personalized gift) practices—which are slightly different practices—and serkyem offering, to make them part of the Buddhist path. The people, as well as the gods and spirits of Tibet, knew these practices and were familiar with them, so Guru Rinpoche retained some of these rites, which, by and large, did not need to be changed. Guru Rinpoche blessed them and adapted some aspects to make them Buddhist practices. In this way, Guru Rinpoche was able to ensure enormous benefit both for the people and for the nonhuman gods and spirits of that region.

In terms of the changes, it seems that in the pre-Buddhist tradition of sang offerings in Tibet, animals would sometimes be sacrificed in the fire. Guru Rinpoche resorted to skillful means to modify these practices: Instead of sacrificing animals, he established the tradition of making dough molds of various kinds. He also introduced the use of deity, mantra, mudra, and samadhi to bless the offerings so that local deities and spirits received an offering. He gave instructions about how to bless the offering substances for a sang ceremony—different kinds of grains, small pieces of fine silk, various powdered gems and so forth. The offerings are blessed as the "wealth of the space treasury"—in other words, they are transformed into an inexhaustible source of benefit and fulfillment of all one's goals from now until the end of the kalpa.

In general, the practices of Secret Mantra Vajrayana involve deity, mantra, mudra, and samadhi, whose qualities are inconceivable. It may be useful to tell you two short stories to help you understand their power. There was a very famous physician in Tibet, called Yutok Yönten Gönpo. He was a very effective doctor and extremely good at curing human beings, but he also treated local deities and spirits. One day he was invited to the palace of Nyenchen Tanglha, one of Tibet's main local deities, to treat his son. Nyenchen Tanglha showed the doctor all the treasures in his palace. In one chamber was a very special treasure that came from the "wealth of the treasury of space." Nyenchen Tanglha explained to Yutok Yönten Gönpo, "It was blessed by Guru Rinpoche who gave it to me. I never show it to anyone, but I will make an exception for you." The doctor saw a small, old torma (that looks like our sang tormas). Nyenchen Tanglha said, "Guru Rinpoche gave this torma to me. It's from the inexhaustible wealth of the treasury of space that gives you anything you wish for." Such was Guru Rinpoche's mastery of deity, mantra, mudra, and samadhi.

On one occasion, Jamyang Khyentse Wangpo and Jamgön Kongtrul Lodrö Taye went by Lake Sutrim in the Derge region. They pitched a tent and made a sang offering. A longish nugget of gold lay on the table in front of Jamyang Khyentse Wangpo. At one point, Jamyang Khyentse Wangpo handed the nugget to Jamgön Kongtrul, saying he had received it from Lake Sutrim's deity.

Jamgön Kongtrul rubbed the gold nugget for quite a while and said, "There still might be some very powerful mantra practitioners left. For instance, I can dissolve this lump of gold."

"Go ahead, dissolve it then," Jamyang Khyentse replied.

Jamgön Kongtrul Rinpoche said a few mantras as he rubbed the nugget in his hands, and it transformed slowly into a wooden stick, like the kinds of stick that are offered into the fire during a fire offering.

Blessing is only possible when a genuine mantra practitioner has gained complete mastery over deity, mantra, and samadhi. If someone tries to dissolve a lump of gold without this kind of realization, no dissolution will happen, even after resting in samadhi and directing the practice.

You must invite and make offerings to the "four types of guests" in a sang offering. Actually, the offerings of sang, torma, chöd or sur all require these four kinds of guest. The first type of guests, called "the three jewels invited out of respect," include all the enlightened beings who are beyond the world of ordinary individuals, such as the three jewels, lamas, yidams, dakinis, and dharma protectors. Guests of the second type are the "protectors invited for their qualities." They are the male, female, and epicene protectors—wisdom beings who manifest in the form of worldly beings to protect the Vajrayana teachings. It is said that it is also appropriate to make offerings of sang to a third type of guests, the "guests with whom we have karmic debts." They are those who constitute hindrances and obstacles, such as the eighteen great döns—the gyalgong male döns, and the dremo female döns. They arise from delusion and grasping at appearances—the natural self-manifestation of rigpa—as real. They are all included in the eight classes of gods and demons. The fourth type of guests corresponds to "the beings of the six classes invited out of compassion." These are the beings in the six states of samsaric existence, and especially the bardo beings who have abandoned the body of their former life and not yet found their next body and wander in the bardo regions, suffering from desire, aversion, and ignorance.

How is the sang offering made? When you offer sang, you must think that you are a yidam deity, such as Noble Avalokiteshvara or Guru Rinpoche. You meditate on the fire in front of you, into which you make the offering of sang, as the female deity Pandaravasini in nature. You meditate that from the heart center of you as the deity emanate the syllables RAM, YAM, and KHAM, which are the syllables of fire, wind, and water respectively. RAM produces fire that completely burns away all impurities; YAM blows wind that scatters them; and the water that comes from KHAM completely cleanses them away. Then the smoke of the fire and the fire itself are now in nature clouds of outer, inner, and secret offerings, multiplied billions of times over until they fill the whole of space, fulfilling every wish of the guests. This is, in short, how to offer sang.

The guests of the sang—the four types of guests we have just explained—are invited to the sang. They arrive instantly. The sang offering is offered to them on the spot, and immediately they are requested to depart.

What are the benefits of sang? By offering to the first kind of guests—the three jewels invited out of respect—you ensure that you and all beings in number as vast as space are brought under the protection of these sources of refuge and receive their blessings, and gain spiritual attainment. By making offerings to the second kind of guests—the protectors invited because of their qualities—they accomplish their activities to benefit sentient beings of overcoming any obstacles or hindrances to the practice of the holy dharma, so that ordinary and extraordinary spiritual attainments are achieved. By offering the sang to the third kind of guests—hindrances and negativity, invited because of our karmic debts—the precious mind of enlightenment arises in every one of them, they abandon their violent ways and harmful activities directed at any being, and instead turn their minds to the path of dharma and toward liberation. By making offerings to the fourth kind of guests—the beings of the six classes invited out of compassion—their karmic debts accumulated in the three realms from time without beginning are purified; suffering of attachment, aversion, and ignorance is pacified; and they make aspiration prayers to follow the path of happiness to higher states of rebirth.

SOLLO CHENMO

Introduction

Most Gesar practices are solka, or invocation of the protectors and offerings to them. To give you an idea of how these practices are done, I will now explain how to practice, visualize and direct the practice of Sollo Chenmo (#37). Sollo Chenmo is the longest and most detailed practice of fulfillment, offering, and invocation to the protector Gesar written by Mipham Rinpoche.

Background of the Practice

Mipham Rinpoche composed this sadhana—again, composed here means that it arose as a mind terma—in such a way that anyone doing this practice will see auspicious circumstances and long life increase, wealth rain down, and especially the continuous increase of fame and good repute, good company, and so on. More importantly, it is said that the experiences and realization in the practice—warmth of bliss, indications, and signs of practice—will also increase like the waxing moon. However, it is important to be aware that *Sollo Chenmo* is such a powerful practice that it is never done on a daily basis. My teacher, Dilgo Khyentse Rinpoche, would perform the practice only in exceptionally important situations, such as when the king of Bhutan went to visit the Indian prime minister.

How to Practice

Sollo Chenmo itself only contains offering and invocation, so it cannot be practiced on its own as it doesn't contain the stages of self-visualization and so on necessary for accomplishing such a practice of offering and invocation. It would be like organizing a reception in a wonderful place, with splendid decoration, the finest food, and so on but to forget to invite the guests. That is why Shechen Gyaltsap Pema Namgyal, who was one of Mipham Rinpoche's exceptionally gifted disciples, wrote guides to both *Sollo Chenmo* and *Instant Fortune: A Fulfillment and Request of Dorje Tsegyal* (#4). This was in response to several requests, particularly at the insistence of Shyape Chorampa, a high government official. These guides show how to combine several of Lama Mipham's Gesar prayers in an elaborate practice. They also add the yidam practice of Hayagriva and Pema Tötrengtsal from the Lama Sangdu. In Shechen Gyaltsap's guide for Mipham Rinpoche's Dorje Tsegyal sadhana, he clearly lays out all its stages—for example, self-visualization and tsok. He did the same for *Sollo Chenmo* in his *Sollo Chenmo Practice Guide*. In this text he explains how to do the practice and describes the prerequisite preliminaries that should be completed before approaching *Sollo Chenmo* itself. He also talks about the concluding sections that follow, such as offering the tsok. Here I will briefly explain the *Sollo Chenmo* practice manual by going over its structure.

Preliminaries from the Practice Manual

To start with, you take refuge, arouse bodhichitta, and make the seven-branch offering. Then you do the guru yoga of Gesar Dorje Tsegyal (#1) and bless the outer, inner, and secret offerings. Next, visualize yourself as a yidam deity, such as Tamdrin Yangsang.[9] By generating the visualization of the deity, you transform your body, your speech, and your mind into the three vajras—the enlightened body, speech and mind of the deity—and receive the empowerments of the five families transforming your five aggregates into the five wisdoms, and so on. Then you invite the deities of Tamdrin Yangsang; request that they be seated; present them with the outer, inner, and secret offerings; and praise them. After offering praise, recite the mantra for the self-visualization and continue the practice to the end of dissolution after which you arise again as the deity.

Then you practice the front visualization, following the text of *Instant Fortune* (#4). Imagine the front visualization—the manifestation of Gesar's pure land—in the space before you. Mount Meru appears, supported by the mandalas of the five elements,[10] on top of which are Gesar's five palaces: the central palace and palaces of the four activities (pacifying, enriching, magnetizing, and subjugating). Inside the central palace stands "Gesar who spontaneously accomplishes the four activities." This form of Gesar is portrayed in the secret sadhana, where he is described as being clad in armor and riding a wild warhorse as he wields a whip in his right hand and flourishes jewels in his left (see the drawing on page 74). He is surrounded by all the dralas and wermas.

Visualization and Offerings

How you should visualize the different forms of Gesar—pacifying, enriching, magnetizing, and wrathful—and details about the offerings themselves is quite clear in the *Sollo Chenmo* text. To the east of the central palace is the palace of pacifying activity, which is made of crystal. Inside this palace, visualize all the pacifying deities of Gesar's mandala as described in *Sollo Chenmo*. To the south is the mandala of enriching activity. Imagine the visualization as it is described in the text, including all the enriching dralas, wermas, and the rest. Meditate on all these deities. To the west are Gesar's magnetizing deities. Meditate on them as described in the text. To the north, in the palace of subjugating activity, is the subjugating Gesar. Again, actualize the visualization by following the text. Outside the palaces, all the armies of dralas, wermas, and so on are assembled; they are infinite in number. Visualize all these deities in front of you, just as they are described in the text.

Next, invite all the deities and ask them to remain, then chant praises and present the outer, inner, and secret offerings by following the *Sollo Chenmo* text. Once you have done all this, make the offerings specific to the four activities, as described in *Sollo Chenmo*. The special instruction about the offerings says that they should be inconceivable in quantity and quality. Start by presenting offerings in the central palace to the "Gesar who spontaneously accomplishes the four activities." This section begins with "*Ho!* Turn your attention toward us! *Ho!* Turn your attention toward us! *Ho!* Turn your attention toward us!" Next, give peaceful offering substances to both the pacifying Gesar, Akar Ökyi Werma, and to the assembly of pacifying deities. Then offer praise and entrust them with carrying out pacifying activities, as laid out in the *Sollo Chenmo* text. Similarly, present enriching offerings to Gesar and the deities of enriching activity, as described in the text. All the enriching activity deities accept your offerings and praise. As you recite the verses that begin "For us vidyadhara yogins...," entrust them with carrying out enriching activities. To the west is the magnetizing form of Gesar. Offer the deities magnetizing offerings and praise, and entrust them with carrying out all magnetizing activities. To the north, present the subjugating form of Gesar with offerings of subjugation—such as the vitality and breath of enemies—and offer praise, then entrust him with carrying out all subjugating activities. Make sure you actualize every word of the prayers associated with each of the four activities of pacifying, enriching, magnetizing, and subjugating. This is how to present offerings, offer praise, and entrust each deity with carrying out each of the four activities in their own way.

If there is no one to entrust the activities to—if you keep requesting activities, making offerings, and chanting praises to nobody at all—it will be like organizing a great banquet and forgetting to invite any guests! Therefore, you must meditate on the recipient of your offerings, as described in Shechen Gyaltsap's guide to the practice of *Sollo Chenmo*. If you don't have access to that guide and just rely on the *Sollo Chenmo* text, make sure you instantly invite the deities of the four activities into the space before you, one after the other. Having invited them, once they have arrived, present your offerings, offer praises, and request that they carry out their activities as laid out in the *Sollo Chenmo* text.

To recap, briefly:

- In the east, visualize the peaceful mandala and present its deities with pacifying offerings, then request the deities to perform the pacifying activities.
- Similarly, in the south, offer enriching offerings to the enriching form of Gesar and ocean of deities in his retinue, then offer them praise and request that they carry out the enriching activities.
- To the west, present the magnetizing form of Gesar with magnetizing offerings and request that he accomplish the magnetizing activities.
- To the north, present the subjugating form of Gesar with offerings of subjugation and request that he accomplish the wrathful activities.
- In the final part of the practice, make offerings to all the deities of the mandala together, praise them, then entrust them with carrying out their activities.

This is how you should practice.

Concluding Practice

Once all this has been fully accomplished and the offerings have been made, the manual guides through the steps of completing the mantra recitation and the fulfillment, entrusting the deities with the accomplishment of the activities, and requesting the dralas to stay in your body. At the end of the practice, all the drala and werma deities of *Sollo Chenmo* in the front visualization—to whom you have made offerings, praised, and so on, as I have explained— dissolve into your body. As a result, your body gains the dralas' power, well-being, glory, and goodness; your speech takes on the "qualities of the mighty voice of Brahma"; and empty bliss, the expression of awareness, is transferred to your mind. Basically, the body, speech, and mind of the dralas and wermas have penetrated your own body, speech, and mind, and you receive all their blessings. At this point, you should be utterly convinced that you are completely victorious over all opposition.

If you want to recite prayers to increase your lungta, do it at this point. Let your eyes pierce and penetrate the sky, then raise your gaze higher and higher as you merge your mind indivisibly with all of space. Finally, allow your mind to rest, free of reference, in the state of great simplicity devoid of conceptual elaboration. This is Mipham Rinpoche's instruction. After that, chant *The Prayer That Spontaneously Fulfills All Wishes* (*Sampa Lhundrupma* in Tibetan) and the vajra guru mantra very loudly, then shout out "Kiki so so lha gyalo!" and recite the heart of dependent origination mantra. At that point, if you rest your mind and focus on the meaning of the lines—"Empower us with the physical strength and might of the Great Lion Gesar and the dralas and wermas, and grant us all the siddhis of abundance here and now, this very instant!"—then everything you do will turn out well; even negative actions will only produce positive results.

SUMMARY

I have briefly presented the special practice instructions you need in order to do this sadhana, and it would be very good if you were to apply them whenever you practice *Sollo Chenmo*. To summarize, gather the offerings: offerings, sang, serkyems, prayer flags, and so on—whatever you can manage—then practice as follows. Instantly Gesar appears in the space in front of you as the king of the dralas surrounded by his retinue of all the armies of dralas and wermas. Invite them, make offerings to them, and offer praises—just follow the text. First, invite the pacifying deities, make offerings, and offer praises before you entrust them with their particular activity. Next, do the same for the other three deities and their activities: enriching, magnetizing, and subjugating. As you recite the text entrusting the deities to carry out their activities, make sure you actualize the words that you are saying. The glorious accomplisher of activity, the vajra dharma protector, Gesar Norbu Dradul, will then accept your request, and you should feel absolute confidence in the fact that he has agreed to do as you ask and will carry out his activities.

PART TWO
GESAR PRACTICES AND CRAFTS

BY TERTÖN LHARIK DECHEN YESHE RÖLPA TSAL
AND MIPHAM (THE INVINCIBLE)
who is also known as:
Mipham Nampar Gyalwa
(The Invincible, Completely Victorious)
Mipham Jamyang Namgyal
(Invincible Gentle Voice, the Completely Victorious One)
Mipham Jamyang Gyepa
(Invincible Gentle Voice, the Joyful One)
Rikpe Dorje
(Vajra of Awareness)
Seru Öden Karpo
Zilnön Gyepa Tsal
(Dazzling Joyful Energy)
Dhih
Jampal Dorje
(Manjugosha the Vajra)
Jampal Norbu
(Manjugosha the Jewel)
the tantric monk Padma

1. The Swift Entering of Blessings

The Guru Yoga of the Great Being of
*Unchanging Awareness Wisdom**

EMAHO

In the space in front, filled with rainbow light,
Amidst billowing clouds of dralas and deities of the three roots,
Sits the father, Great Being Norbu Dradul Tsal,
Radiant with blessings and smiling broadly.

Protector, compassionate embodiment of all the victorious
    ones,
Emanation of the great, glorious one of Oddiyana,
King Great Lion, embodiment of the lords of the three
    families,
O father, with overwhelming devotion and powerful
    longing,
We children supplicate you from our hearts.

Your unchanging, luminous mind
Is always filled with great clouds of love and compassion.
Compassionate one, you instantly bring down blessings
On disciples connected to you through karma and aspiration.
Glorious[1] drala, each one of your accoutrements
Contains countless mandalas of deities of the three roots.
Merely thinking of you, we receive great blessings and
    empowerments.

*Translated by the Vajravairochana Translation Committee.

The father warriors dance—TRAP SE TRAP.
The mother warriors sing—SHA RA RA.
The chief of steeds neighs—LHANG SE LHANG.
The warrior dralas laugh—CHEM SE CHEM.

For beings with devoted, yearning minds,
Now, don't be idle, don't be idle; grant your blessings.
Make this body the warrior fortress of the dralas.
Empower this voice with magical speech.
Ignite this mind with the display of awareness,
   bliss-emptiness.
Lord, may we be inseparable from you.

LAMA KHYEN NO*

Say that as much as you can.

LAMA KYE CHOK YISHIN NORBU KHYEN NO[†]

Say that.

OM AH HUM VAJRA MAHAGURU MANIRAJA
SARVA SIDDHI PHALA HUM

After reciting those, inseparable from Gesar, rest in the dharmakaya, beyond concept.

This *Swift Entering of Blessings* reveals the symbols and signs of
   the display of awareness.
If you supplicate for seven days, you will definitely be cared for.
Within self-arising awareness beyond concept,

---

*O lama, care for us!
[†]O lama, Great Being, Wish-Fulfilling Jewel, care for us!

Rikpe Dorje received the great blessings of Lord Great Lion and wrote this.

At the end of the session, with a pleasing melody, sing the supplications of "The Taming of Hor" and "The Horse Race."*

This was written on the twenty-third day of the third month of the year All-Victorious (1887). May there be virtue. Mangalam.

---

*These refer respectively to text #3, *The Warrior's Roar of Laughter: A Prayer to the Tamer of Hor* (pages 53–55), and text #2, *The Enciphered Mirror of Jewels: The Extraordinary Story of the Horse Race* (pages 49–51).

2. The Enciphered Mirror of Jewels

The Extraordinary Story of the Horse Race[*]

OM SVASTI
Within the play that accomplishes welfare and well-being in
   Jambudvipa,
Through the blazing glory of the garland of light rays of the
   wisdom jewel,
The great and powerful sorcerer has subjugated the enemy
   demons of the dark side—
Supreme being Great Lion King, grant auspiciousness!

At the moment the lotus emerges from the mud,
The garland of lightning dawns in the center of the red
   mirror.
Thanks to the roar of the dragon, the heroes ride the swift
   mounts of the wind.
I pray to the one who can bring everyone under his control!

It is Hayagriva who appears as the Sorrel Steed,
The four-legged miracle captured by the magical lasso.
From the illusory treasury, you amassed the treasures of the
   three.
I supplicate you who are respected by all the great ones.

---

[*]Adapted by Gyurme Avertin from a translation by Robin Kornman, Sangye
Khandro, and Lama Chönam and published in *the Epic of Gesar of Ling: Gesar's
Magical Birth, Early Years, and Coronation as King* (Boston: Shambhala, 2012).
The meaning of these verses is part 3, pages 315–17.

Racing like tigers, lions, dragons, garudas, and herds of
    elephants
All seeming madly intoxicated by the strongest of liquors,
The heroes appeared to be so splendid as they competed.
But the one lagging behind hidden by disguise, it is to you
    that I supplicate.

Just like the images projected by a flawless crystal,
Sung to so many, your myriad songs of experience
Have clarified the mind and desires of each individual—
I supplicate to the magical spectacle that you display.

In the presence of the hosts of beautiful youthful gods,
Like the movements of the sun, moon, planets, and stars,
The force of the mighty wind stirs
The waving banner of fame, to which I supplicate.

On the luminous shore of the brightly shining sun and
    moon of happiness and well-being,
Under the royal banner of victory in all directions,
The thunderous roar of your fame shakes the great earth—
I supplicate the one who holds the great throne of the
    kingdom.

Just as the sun appears from the clouds
Or a youthful lotus emerges from its casing of mud,
Your stainless, supreme body is favored by the gods and all
    who live—
I supplicate you who now truly appears in front of us.

No matter how arrogant they may have been made by their
    power,
In your presence, as one they bow their topknots to the ground,
And the great classes of maras bemoan their defeat—
I pray to the victor of the forces of good.

Then samsara and nirvana helplessly surrender their essence
To this wish-fulfilling kaya,
Who is permanent, stable, and naturally free from old age
    and decay—
I supplicate the one who propagates the well-being and
    benefit of the teachings and all beings.

By the karmic power of this prayer
To the king of the dralas, the manifestation of the Lotus-
    Born and the three protectors,
May you dwell in the center of the youthful utpala flower of
    my heart,
And may you bestow the siddhi that accomplishes whatever
    mind desires!

On the tenth day of the waning phase of the moon, the day the
    dakinis gather,
The twenty-fifth of the eleventh month of the Wood Dog year of
    the fifteenth sixty-year cycle (1874),
The yogi devoted to the Warrior of Ling,
Mipham Nampar Gyalwa, wrote this excellent prayer.

The happiness of a healthy body, like a tiny seed that grows into a
mighty banyan tree, grew from an imperceptible presence into a
vigorous force. In my mind, unaltered in these good circumstances,
I saw this prayer that arose repeatedly through mind's expressive
power. Filled with such joy that I felt like dancing, many words with
profound meaning arose from sleep's magical illusions. Examining
them, I found them the source of supremely auspicious interdependence. This supplication, which is like the victory drum of the
gods, is the story of the extraordinary horse race of Gesar Norbu
Dradul that is famous in every corner of the world. It is called *The
Enciphered Mirror of Jewels*. Sarva mangalam.

3. THE WARRIOR'S ROAR OF LAUGHTER

A Prayer to the Tamer of Hor

The natural state of the vajra wisdom of all the victorious
    ones
Blazes in the magical display of vajra wrath
That incinerates the dense thicket of maras with perverted
    intentions—
Victory to you, King Tamer of Enemies, supreme being
    Dradul!

From the mara-taming samadhi of great equality
Arise beautiful maidens who entreat you with dakini
    songs—
Amidst flashing red lightning bolts of compassion,
Gather the great clouds of your army of dralas, I pray!

May a powerful wind stir the master of the seven horses[2]
In the middle of the Awe-Inspiring Land of Ling—
May it magically increase his radiance a hundredfold
And bring the lotuses of joyful hopes and desires into
    blossom, I pray!

The jewel kayas display myriad maneuvers
To the thunderous sound of the dralas' flapping banners—
May your many skillful displays of peaceful and wrathful
    emanations
Tame all enemies encountered on the path, I pray!

Capture the hearts of maras with the hook of your
magnetism
And plunge them into the deepest darkness—
Let thousands of great magical displays
Unfold continuously for our constant satisfaction, I pray!

On the treasure lake replete with the jewel of great bliss,
May the lotus receive the sustained nourishment of a
thousand blazing lights of compassion,
And may vajra strength fill your supreme, concealed body—
Now let the astounding thunderclaps of your dragon's roar
sound, I pray!

As your hundred miracles smash your enemies' hearts to
pieces,
Compassion manifests naturally in the breast of evildoers—
May the power of your compassion, like the moon
illuminating darkness,
Bring light unceasingly, I pray!

The hook of your compassion inevitably attracts
All the maras whose heads blaze with the horrifying fire of
the five poisons,
And your wisdom sword decapitates them—
Display the wonder of your might, I pray!

The banners of the maras' northern forces have crumbled,
The drums celebrating the perfect dharma's victory resound
loudly—
You who are victorious over every enemy, like the bright
light of the sun and the moon,
Protect the kingdoms of virtue, I pray!

Through the auspicious coincidence created by these words,
May the might of the drala king fill my heart,

May all enemies—the obstacles to the development of my
    dharma and worldly activities,
And to positive circumstances—be tamed to the core by a
    mere thought!

Do not underestimate this prayer by thinking it is just a quick-
    fading spark.
Fanned by a timely wind, a small fire will devour a whole forest
As if the earth and the sky had opened like a mouth filled with
    red tongues of sharp flames,
So powerful that it roars louder than a thousand thunders.

On the fifteenth year of the present sixty-year cycle (1881),
Known as "the year of complete taming,"
On the twenty-fifth day of the second month,
In the Total Victory over Maras hermitage,
As my mind retained different powers
Such that my habitual tendency of devotion for the king of dralas
    took form
And appeared as distinctly as the moon reflected in a clear lake,
I, Mipham Nampar Gyalwa, wrote this down. Virtue.
Mangalam.

Gesar Dorje Tsegyal

4. INSTANT FORTUNE

A Fulfillment and Request for Dorje Tsegyal,
the Great Being Gesar*

To purify, say:

OM SAMBHAVA SHUDDHA SARVA DHARMA SAM-
BHAVA SHUDDHA HAM.

Then say:

I appear as Hayagriva Padma Maheshvara with Dorje
Tötrengtsal at the crown of my head. In the space in
front, amidst thick, white, rolling clouds of amrita, rises
the completely victorious palace, the pure mansion of
the deity. In its center, on a throne ornamented with
refined gold and jewels, is a seat of layered brocade and
silk, marked with a drawing of crossed vajras. On the
seat, in the center of a terrifying arrangement of skins of
maras and samaya demons, is Gesar, the king of dralas.
He is like the full moon and is so beautiful that one can
never get enough of seeing him. His youthful splendor
blazes, and he wears a robe of gray-blue brocade under
a red gown. His lower body is wrapped in the gray-blue
skin of a beast of prey. His hair hangs loose, and around
it are rainbows and shining rays of light. On his head is a

---

*Adapted by Gyurme Avertin from a translation by the Vajravairochana Trans-
lation Committee.

beautiful round felt hat, brilliant like the moon, its crest beautified by a spray of peacock feathers, a mirror, jewels, and a variety of silks. An enchanting smile radiates from his dignified face. He wears round lotus earrings made of precious substances. His neck is adorned with a gold locket and a mirror, and he wears a necklace of white and red jewels and a garland of various flowers. His right hand . . .

Then, adapt the visualization of the right hand according to the activity, such as:

. . . rests on a brocade cushion.

When practicing magnetizing activity, change "rests on a brocade cushion" to:

. . . holds a rope with a vajra for a handle and an iron hook on its end, and uses this miraculous device to stir and attract the vital essence of samsara and nirvana.

When practicing prosperity activity change it to:

. . . holds at his heart the king of wish-fulfilling jewels.*

When practicing arrow divination, change it to:

. . . is extended and holds a white lotus.

When practicing averting activity, change it to:

. . . holds a sword of meteoric iron with which he cuts off the heads of malicious rakshasas.

---

*Mipham Rinpoche indicated that this is the line that should be read by default.

Then, continue with:

> His left hand holds an iron bow and arrow. His two feet wear boots with turned-up tips, and he sits in the royal posture of enjoyment. On his right is the great being, youthful Dorje Lekpa, who wears a turban of white silk. He is beautifully adorned with flowers and is holding a dice. On his left is Mentsun Dorje Yudrönma, wearing a turquoise ornament in her hair. In her right hand she holds a ribboned arrow, and in her left hand, resting on her hip, she holds a kapala of amrita. Before him is the chief of the nine masang brothers, Great General Mikmar, who has a wrathful expression and wears a loose-sleeved red-and-green brocade cloak. He is measuring a magical red lasso into armlengths.
>
> In front of them are the four great secret consorts, youthful maidens of incomparable beauty, who are surrounded by a retinue of a hundred thousand female attendants. All around them is an army of gods ten million strong, arrogant tsens, yakshas, nagas, nyens, and so forth—the hosts of the eight classes of arrogant demons and innumerable troops of dralas and wermas. This retinue gathers like clouds over the whole of heaven, earth, and the space in between.

INVITATION

The three syllables OM AH HUNG mark the three centers of all the deities. Light rays emanate from them and from my heart to the places above, the abodes of the gods; to Oddiyana, the pure realm of the vidyadharas; to the lands of India, China, and Tibet; in particular, to Dokham's celestial Land of Ling, a place desired by all who see it; and all such places where Gesar and his retinue naturally abide. The light rays invite them, and they come to remain firmly in the samayasattvas in front of me.

OM TRIM SHIM KHYIM ME MUTRA BARRA HAM
A LA LI—merge!

Say this to invite the wisdom deities. Then, burn some incense, play music, and call out to them:

KYE
With faith and samaya,
Great Being Gesar, together with your retinue,
We invite you to this place; please come!
Remain firmly on this pleasing seat.
OM TRIM SHIM KHYIM ME MUTRA BARRA HAM
A LA LI LA MO
TUNGWA KHYE A HO YE SIDDHI HUM
TRAKSHER KHYEM §
SOK TUNG TUNG DZAH
SARVA SAMAYA TIP TIP DU DU TUNG TUNG YE YE
DZAH DZAH

At the end of the mantra say:

BENZA SAMAYA DZA
DZA HUM BAM HOH

With this mantra, the wisdom deities dissolve into the front visualization.

SAMAYA

Then, to unite your samayas say:

HUM
King of the dralas, think of us.

In the presence of Avalokiteshvara, Pema Tötrengtsal,
Their armies of powerful accomplishers of enlightened
    activities, and so on,
And all the other vidyadharas of the lineage,
You promised to help us yogins.
Do not forget your vows and commitments;
Until we attain enlightenment,
Perform all activities entrusted to you without exception.
VAJRASAMAYA RAKSHA HUM

Prostration and Offering

NAMO NAMAMI

Say this mantra to pay homage.

OM TRIM SHIM KHYIM SAPARIWARA OM BENZA
ARGHAM PADYAM PUSHPE DHUPE ALOKE
GENDHE NEWITE SHABTA ASHTA MANGALAM
DRACHAM LINGA SAPTA RATNA PENTSA KAMA
GUNA AMRITA RAKTA BALINGTA PUDZA PRA-
TITSA SOHA

Say this mantra to make offerings.

Confession

HUM
Embodiment of the three roots, wish-fulfilling jewel Gesar,
Please consider us with love and compassion.
Overpowered by ignorance and confusion,
We have gone against and corrupted
The samayas of body, speech, and mind, and the root and
    branch samayas.

We confess with regret all negative actions, obscurations,
  and faults
Accumulated from beginningless time.
Please grant us cleansing and purification,
And the supreme siddhi pure and free from obscuration.
BENZA SAMAYA AH

FULFILLMENT

HUM HRIH
Offering clouds from oceans of infinite buddha fields,
Flowers, incense, lamps, perfume water,
Food, music, the five sensual stimulants;
Wrathful substances such as the argham of blood and
  liquor, the flower of the sense organs,
The smell of burning grease, onion soup, lamps of great fat,
Great meat, thighbone trumpets, and skull drums;
Amrita medicine and the great red rakta,
Balim torma, and jagat, the warrior's select offering,
A hundred thousand consorts who arouse the four joys of
  great bliss,
Armor, weapons, countries, fortresses, food, clothing,
  ornaments, livestock,
Kingdoms, jewels, and a variety of precious possessions—
The sky is filled with an ocean of wealth from gods and humans.

Great battalions of fierce and awesome troops gather like clouds.
Supports such as yabdars, silks that adorn arrows, and other
  pieces of cloths snap like lightning.
The loud beating of drums thunders like dragons.
Weapons that destroy enemies strike like thunderbolts.

Life, prosperity, and wealth rain down—SI LI LI.
Incense clouds of rainbows, lights, and amrita waft—TA LA
  LA.

Red lights of love, joy, and power swirl—KHYUK SE
KHYUK.
Displays of bliss, heat, and awareness are vividly clear—
SHIK SE SHIK.

The great bindu of the wisdom that magics empty
appearances
And pervades the whole of samsara and nirvana
Appears spontaneously as offering clouds of sensual
stimulants we offer to you—
Life force of the three roots, dharmapalas, dralas, and wermas,
Great Lion Dorje Tsegyal,
Together with your beloved consorts, ministers, subjects,
and powerful troops,
With constant unwavering faith and devotion to be
inseparable from you,
We supplicate you, we offer to you; may your wishes be
fulfilled.
May violations and confusion be purified into dharmadhatu.
Through the secret vajra samaya of bliss and emptiness,
Within the state forever free from meeting and parting,
Swiftly bestow the splendor of the siddhis and all we desire.

GIVING THE OFFERINGS

Imagine that the great being Gesar and his retinue, through
tongues of tubes of light, draw up and consume the essence of the
torma. They are very pleased and satisfied.

OM TRIM SHIM KHYIM ME MUTRA BARRA HAM
A LA LI LA MO
TUNGWA KHYE A HO YE SIDDHI HUM
TRAKSHER KHYIM SAPARIWARA IDAM
BALINGTE KHA KHA KHAHI KHAHI

OM AKARO MUKHAM SARVA DHARMANAM
ADYA NUTPAN NATOTA OM AH HUM PE SOHA

Say this to offer the torma.

Then say:

OM TRIM SHIM KHYIM SAPARIWARA ARGHAM
PADYAM PUSHPE DHUPE ALOKE GENDHE
NEWITE SHAPTA PRATITSA HOH

Offer amrita with:

OM TRIM SHIM KHYIM ME MUTRA BARRA HAM
A LA LI LA MO
TUNGWA KHYE A HO YE SIDDHI HUM
TRAKSHER KHYEM ❂
OM AH HUM

REQUEST OF WISHES AND ENTRUSTMENT WITH ACTIVITIES

Gesar, great protector of the teachings, king of miracles, together with your secret consorts, ministers, retinue, dralas, wermas, and protectors, please accept this great and vast torma offering. Protect the teachings of the Buddha. Enhance the glory of the three jewels. Support the sangha and the kingdoms of dharma. Dispel the decline of the world. Increase the benefit and happiness of sentient beings. Be a friend to all yogins. Help all mantra practitioners to perform enlightened activity. Subjugate the enemy of aggression. Destroy all harmful obstructing spirits. In particular, for all the samaya holders gathered here, pacify outer, inner, and secret hindrances; increase and expand all conducive circumstances and excellent aspirations; and perform the enlightened activity that swiftly accomplishes all the supreme and ordinary siddhis.

With these requests for fulfilling wishes, encourage them to actions, both general and specific.

PRAISE

HUM
The embodiment of the victorious ones Pema Tötreng,
The three families and the magical emanations of peaceful
    and wrathful deities
All gathered in you, slayer of gyalpos, yamas, and damsis—
Gesar Norbu Dradul, we praise you!

Out of compassion, and thanks to the conditions offered by
    our pure karma and aspiration,
You manifest as the king of Tibet on Jambudvipa.
By simply remembering you, you bestow long life,
    abundance, and the most supreme of all that we desire—
Dorje Tsegyal, we praise you!

The moment fortunate ones have faith in you,
Power, glory, strength and ability blaze like the kalpa-
    ending fire,
And you pulverize the life force of enemies, döns, and
    spirits—
Great Lion, mara-taming warrior, we praise you!

As the crown of all mighty ones of the three worlds
You rule, victoriously achieving whatever you wish,
And cause the banner of fame to flourish throughout the
    ten directions—
All-Accomplishing White Werma, we praise you!

Today, thanks to our vidyadhara yogins'
Secret vajra samaya from which you never part,
Concentrate the essence of your life force,
Turn your attention toward us and swiftly accomplish our
intentions.

RECITATION

I am the yidam visualized clearly. My heart emanates
light rays that strike in the heart of the great being a
white A seated on a sun disk and surrounded by the
mantra garland. The syllables emanate rays of the
five colors that dissolve into me. I become capable of
accomplishing the four activities with a mere thought,
unobstructed.

Actualize this and focus one-pointedly on the visualization.

OM TRIM SHIM KHYIM ME MUTRA BARRA HAM
A LA LI LA MO
TUNGWA KHYE A HO YE SIDDHI HUM ⁞
TRAKSHER KHYIM SHANTIM PUSHTIM WASHAM
MARAYA SIDDHI HUM DZAH

Recite the mantra as much as you can.

End by reciting the vowels and consonants, the hundred-syllable
and heart-of-dependent-origination mantras. Then simply repeat
the offering above.*

---

*In other words, the mantra: OM TRIM SHIM KHYIM SAPARIWARA OM
BENZA ARGHAM PADYAM PUSHPE DHUPE ALOKE GENDHE NEWITE
SHABTA ASHTA MANGALAM DRACHAM LINGA SAPTA RATNA PENTSA
KAMA GUNA AMRITA RAKTA BALINGTA PUDZA PRATITSA SOHA.

ENTHRONMENT

To enthrone Gesar, sprinkle amrita and hoist various pennants, and with offerings, incense, and music, chant the following words:

HUM
Great warrior, the activity of all the victorious ones,
Nyen who overcomes all the dark forces that are difficult to
   tame,
Supreme victory banner for the forces of goodness,
Great Lion, you are the king of the dralas and wermas.

The unchanging source of our hope and trust, like a wish-
   fulfilling jewel,
A flag of victory raised in every direction,
Until we attain the essence of enlightenment,
We praise you! We enthrone you! We unite our vajra
   samayas!

In the palace of great bliss where all wishes are
   spontaneously accomplished,
You rule over the lives of all the arrogant demons of the
   phenomenal world.
Great vidyadhara, Powerful Supreme Ornament of
   Jambudvipa,
We yogins install you on the throne of our hearts.

Great warrior who subjugates the troops of inimical maras,
You wield the sword of prajna and a bow and arrow.
Merely thinking of you quells the warfare of samsara,
   confusion's appearance—
We enthrone you in the vajra space of equal taste.

You who rule unrivaled and with great majesty
On the crown of all beings of the three worlds,

Venerable warrior, you are enthroned as the ruler
Of the mandala of the dralas and wermas of the
  phenomenal world.

Like when hearing the sound of Indra's victory drum,
You swiftly bestow in our hearts
The incomparable amrita of fearless confidence.
Please perform without hindrance your activities, swift and
  accurate.

INVOKING AND ENJOINING

Invoke his sacred pledge and urge him to enlightened activity.
Sprinkle the select amrita again, and say:

HUM HUM
King of dralas, Dorje Tsegyal,
The time has come to fulfill your sacred vow from long ago.
Do not disappoint us yogins.
Without fail, bring about the fruition of our karma and
  aspirations.

When the legions of dark forces—elemental demons, maras,
  and rakshasas—multiply
And cause the power of the teachings of the supreme yana
  to diminish,
We unfortunate ones in the greatest depths of the dark age
  cry out to you:
Look on us with your eye of wisdom.

In the forest where the power of the enemy factions has spread
Due to the sudden influx of malicious armies of the four
  directions,
Be a vajra fire and a swift, voracious subjugator of enemy—
Warrior, remember your vow.

Pulverize all who harm us vidyadhara yogins
And all who oppose the teachings of the great secret.
Make our life and wealth an inexhaustible treasure.
Perform enlightened activity victoriously in all directions.

May the teaching and practice of the luminous vajra essence
Cover the whole extent of the earth.
May there be auspiciousness, may enlightened activities be
    powerful, and may the dharma lineage flourish.
Accomplish our dharmic wishes just as we desire.

From now until attaining enlightenment,
May we never be separated from you, like a body and its
    shadow.
Let us always meet with the good and avoid the bad.
Whatever activities have been entrusted to you, accomplish
    them without obstruction.

Bestow on us this very instant
All the power of the wondrous dralas and wermas
Who subjugate the three worlds
With the white banner, the renowned mark of virtue.

At this time, let us accomplish the activities of pacifying,
    enriching, magnetizing, and destroying without
    obstruction
By merely thinking of them.
Ultimately, in the primordial and fundamental expanse of
    your mind,
Let us attain the kaya of self-existing wisdom.

Without mistaking the vajra words and meaning of Lharik Dechen
Rölpa Tsal's mind terma, this text was written by Mipham Namgyal, one who has received a few signs of the blessings of the great

warrior. I wrote it at the age of twenty-eight, on the first day of the waxing moon of the month of Victory in the Water Bird year (1873), in the shrine room that is known as my place at Dzongsar Tashi Lhatse. May this cause the glory of the teachings of the great secret atiyoga and those who hold them to be elevated to the pinnacle of existence.

If you do this as an intensive practice, place a mandala on a shelf, just as it is described in the terma root text. The torma is a castle whose peak is ornamented with blazing jewels. It is surrounded by four subsidiary tormas and whatever offering materials you can assemble. Gather the tormas representing the three roots, the la stone and life-force diagram, and auspicious offerings. Do the recitation practice until you see a sign. You can modify the visualization according to whichever activity you are practicing. I have added these clarifications in the form of notes based on the terma text and oral instructions on subtle points of the abhisheka and the three phases of approach, accomplishment, and activities.

This practice is so auspicious that whoever practices it will experience long life and a torrential rain of wealth. In particular, they will become renowned, obtain fine clothes, and so on. In other words, their circumstances will become more and more excellent. Especially, experiences and realization, bliss and heat, and signs and indications will definitely arise. This is well known and has actually happened, so you can trust it to be so. This was also written by Mipham. Sarva mangalam.

5. THE GREAT WERMA DANCE

An Extremely Profound Practice to Perfect the Four Activities

---

I wrote this text for the magnetizing activity, even though each activity has its own related visualization and recitation. On an auspicious date, gather large gifts such as sang offerings, pieces of silks of different colors, serkyem, select portion, and so on. Offer them to the wermas and invoke them. After "Perform enlightened activity victoriously in all directions"* add:

> Armies of dralas and wermas who attract and magnetize, ξ
> Trample on the heart of the object of practice with steps of
> your riders' vajra dance. ξ
> Bring them irresistibly under my power and at my
> command. ξ
> Remember this task and bring it to completion! ξ

Say this prayer to urge the dralas and wermas to accomplish the
activity. As a result,
Gesar and all the armies of wermas ξ
Roar with the eight laughters,
Dance the riders' dance, and hoist flags and banners high in the
sky.
Phenomenal existence melts into red light,
And the world and beings vibrate like cymbals. ξ
With horse hooves adorned with red lotuses, ξ
The dance in the heart of the object of practice ξ

---

*See previous practice, page 69.

Ravishes them, stirs their mind, and crazes them. ⁑
They are brought under your power, and in your retinue at your
   command. Actualize this. ⁑
Chant the ten syllables of auspicious coincidence* with the eight
   laughters and "in such and such's heart HANA HANA RAGA
   DUN DUN WASHAM KURU HO" at the end. ⁑
Reciting this mantra will inescapably ⁑
Bring under your power the object of practice. ⁑
Even those who want to kill you will instead become your servant. ⁑
People will be attracted to you like insects by a flame ⁑
Or as if a hook driven in their heart was pulling them. ⁑

EMA Look at the power of the wermas! ⁑
They are behind everyone, capering around their crowns ⁑
In the wermas' dance. The vital point of the dance mantra ⁑
Spreads throughout sarvaloka³ and its purpose is fulfilled. ⁑
You become the king who has power over every excellence, ⁑
A universal monarch who turns the wheel of activities. ⁑
If those who don't pay respect to you create problems, ⁑
Take them as servants, as faithful as guard dogs, and their
   antagonism will be pacified. ⁑
You will establish yourself throughout the entire extent of the
   world. ⁑
Associate once with a person with the right qualities, ⁑
And from then on, things will be naturally taken care of ⁑
Without having to think about them. ⁑
People who need to prostrate to you will also come. ⁑
EMA Look at the power of the wermas! ⁑

This text arose from the center of Seru Öden Karpo's heart on
the twelfth day of the seventh month of the Fire Pig year (1887).
Mangalam.

*OM MAHA SENGHA MANI RADZAH HUM

Gesar Norbu Dradul

6. ༀ A Piece of My Heart ༃
The Great Lion, King Gesar Secret Sadhana ༃

Arrange elaborate offerings in front of the support for Gesar, and with the pride of being the deity, say and actualize the following:

In the space in front of me, in a vast tent of rainbow lights, primordial wisdom appears to itself as the celestial realm of the Awe-Inspiring Land of Ling. The immeasurable palace is complete with all its ornaments and perfect features. In the center, Gesar, the king of dralas, appears wearing the complete regalia of a drala, mounted on his skillful chestnut steed. White with a tinge of red, he holds a horsewhip in the right hand. His left hand pulls the reins while holding up a banner tied to a spear nestled in the crook of his left elbow. His retinue of mighty warriors, beautiful maidens, dralas, wermas, masangs, and zodors fills the whole of space, the entire surface of the earth and all space in between. From the three syllables at their three places and from my heart, light emanates and travels to Chamara and the Palace of Lotus Light, and the other buddha fields. The light rays attract the wisdom deities, who amass like huge rain clouds and then dissolve into the samayasattvas.

HUM
Wielder of the power of compassion, protector of every
  being,
Mighty tamer of maras, rakshasas, and damsis,

King of dralas who is the magical display of the three
   families and Padma—
Great king Gesar, please come here!
The mighty warriors, the beautiful maidens, and all who are
   at Gesar's command, please come here!
Hordes of dralas and wermas, please come here!
Masangs of the eight classes and zodors, please come here
And assemble in the sky like menacing rain clouds!
Amidst the thunder of the boisterous wermas,
Come here quickly and without delay
With the most amazing signs and auguries!
Out of love for us, supreme yogin practitioners,
Stay here, content and happy, and accept our offerings!

HUM
To the Great Lion and the armies of dralas and wermas
We offer the outer offerings that delight the five senses,
We offer the seven marvelous enjoyments,
We offer the priceless auspicious substances and symbols,
We offer the seven precious emblems of royalty,
We offer all the wealth of the gods, nagas, and humans,
We offer the sixteen vajra goddesses,
We offer the inner offerings of amrita, torma, and rakta,
We offer the secret offering, union's empty bliss,
We offer the annihilation of the fields of liberation,
We offer the great purity and equality of all phenomenal
   existence!
Accept and delight without duality in these offerings,
And grant us the supreme and ordinary siddhis!

HUM HRIH
Out of basic space, self-existing wakefulness, you arise as the
   supreme kaya,
King Padma, who rules all that appears and exists,

And manifest as the king of dralas to tame maras and
rakshasas—
Gesar Norbu Dradul, I rely on you!
Manifestation of wisdom, compassion, and great aspiration,
Whose blessings are particularly swift in these times of
degeneration,
Bless us, this very instant,
Fortunate ones who are longing for your presence!
Transform our bodies into the indestructible fortress of the
dralas;
Make our words blaze like fire with the power of truth;
Make our minds radiate with the energy of experiences,
realization, and primordial wisdom—
Bless us so that we may accomplish the supreme and
ordinary siddhis!

In the heart of the deity in front of me, on a moon,
A HUM and the mantra around it
Emanate light that brings offerings to the noble ones and
purifies the obscurations of beings.
The light gathers the strength and energy of all samsara and
nirvana,
And rays of light return and dissolve into his heart,
Which sends out a constant flow of white light that is
absorbed into my heart.

Once you have gathered the life force of the lord of all dralas,
You can accomplish all the activities.
If you recite the ten vajra syllables,
OM MAHA SENGHA MANI RADZAH HUM
One hundred thousand times,
Clear signs will appear.
Add DZAH when you call out to him,
And P'ET when you spur him on to activity.

During the accomplishment phase, and when receiving the
    siddhis,
Recite the innermost essence of the great being Dondrup, the
    All-Accomplishing.
It is the same as the main mantra for receiving the siddhis,
With SARVA ARTA SIDDHI HUM
And AH appended. Sixteen recitations
Will accomplish whatever you wish.

For the practice of the unhindered activities,
At the end of the sixteen syllables of the vajra mantra,
Add the boisterous wermas' roar of laughter,
"The essence and life force of a thousand braves,"
HA HAH HI HIH HE HEH HO HOH.
Then append to this life-force mantra known as the eight
    laughters,
The pacifying mantra or the mantra of the activity that you are
    performing.
It will accomplish whatever you want just as you intended.

For the invocation of the mantra recitation, say the following:

> Embodiment of all three root deities, Lord Sengchen
>   Dradul,
> All that appears and exists is perfect as the drala mandala
> And resounds with the chant of its life-force mantra.
> I recite the mantra without distraction and invoke your
>   wisdom and sacred vow—
> Show me signs and indications quickly
> And grant me the siddhi of victory in every direction!
> Bestow all the supreme and ordinary siddhis—
> Grant them to us yogins right now!

Rely on the life-force mantra and arouse devotion.
Guard the samayas and strive to supplicate and request Dondrup.

If you do that, your every intention
Will be accomplished as you wish, doubt not.
The strength of the great being Dondrup's blessing
Is like the light of one hundred suns.
Sitting in the center of the lotus of your heart,
He unfolds the vajras of the secret family.

The profound heart essence of Seru Öden Karpo. Ithi. Mangalam.

To pacify, AMUKA* SHANTIM KURU SOHA. To enrich, AMUKA
PUSHTIM KURU OM. To magnetize, AMUKA WASHAM KURU
HOH. To subjugate, AMUKA MARAYA P'ET. The four activities are accomplished through the unhindered recitation of their
mantras.

To clarify, you can also add AKA WERMA DU DU PRA POP for
a mirror divination, AMUKA STAM BHAYA NEN NEN for suppression, and so on.

By Mipham, on the third day of the eleventh month of the Fire
Monkey year (1896). Mangalam.

---

*In this and the following mantras, the Sanskrit term *amuka* means "so and so."
In other words, you can replace *amuka* with the name of the sickness or dön spirit
you want to pacify, and likewise in the other mantras what you wish to increase,
magnetize, or subjugate.

7. 𑀝 GESAR'S HORSEWHIP

The Consecration of a Horsewhip as a Wish-Fulfilling Jewel
through King Gesar Practice

---

i. Preparation

Take a beautiful, three-sectioned bamboo stick or some other kind of auspicious wood, and precious substances for the body of the whip. You will also need good-quality material for the whip's tails and to make a handle. Into the covered hollow cavity of the bamboo at the tip of the handle, or into a pommel made of silver or other precious material that's been attached to it, insert this mantra, written in a precious liquid, like gold or silver, or drawn in ink: 𑀝

OM AH HUM HRIH MAHARINISA RATSA HRIYA
SARVA KARMA SIDDHI HUM 𑀝 OM MAHA SINGHA
MANI RADZA SARVA ARTHA SIDDHI HUM
AH 𑀝 HA HAH HI HIH HE HEH HO HOH MAMA
BIDZEYE SIDDHI HUM 𑀝

You can also add the mantras of any lama, yidam, and dakini deities, and dharma protectors that you wish, as well as the heart of dependent origination mantra and a brief request to the deities; it is fine if you don't write those either. For the whip's tails, let silks of the five colors hang down for example, and beautify the horsewhip with any suited adornment. 𑀝

ii. Consecration

The first step is to make the whip, the physical support. Second, you consecrate it. For the consecration, arrange offerings around the whip, which is laid on a pile of white grains. Perform a washing ritual to purify it, or simply recite the Amrita mantra* and the Svabhava mantra.† ⸖

> From the natural state of emptiness, DROOM emerges and transforms into the whip. At the tip of the pommel is a five-pronged, diamond vajra marked with a syllable HUM. The central section is formed in the shape of an eight-faceted jewel made from the wood of the wish-fulfilling, wish-granting tree, and marked with a syllable AH. At the top of the vajra sits the fabulous wishing gem, a blazing jewel of lapis lazuli called "king of wish-fulfilling power" that is marked with the white syllable OM. The handle is made from woven threads of the five precious substances that radiate rainbow-colored lights and is marked with a yellow SVA syllable. The tail is woven from strands of the eight precious substances meshed together in a square shape, which shines with the eight colors and the mingled light rays of the different activities. The tail is marked with a green HA syllable. ⸖
>
> Merely thinking about this whip brings down a shower of all that we wish for. It is an excellent support, a la stone of the dralas and wermas, mamos and dakinis. It is a great blessing substance imbued with accomplishments. ⸖

Say these words, and the following mantra seven times: ⸖

---

*OM BENZA AMRITA KUNDALI HANA HANA HUM PHAT.
†OM SOBHAVA SHUDDAH SARVA DHARMAH SOBHAVA SHUDDHO HAM.

OM AH HUM SVA HAH 𑖪

Inside the horsewhip, a syllable DROOM manifests the infinite palace in which sit, in the middle of a perfect arrangement of everything that one may desire, every single deity of the three roots and samaya-bound dharma protector, and especially King Gesar and his entire court, including all the mighty warriors, the beautiful maidens, the dralas, and wermas, without one missing. The three syllables mark their three centers and send out rays of light that draw the wisdom beings back toward the horsewhip into which they dissolve. 𑖪

OM BENZA GURU DEWA DAKINI DHARMAPALA
MANI RADZA SAPARIWARA BENZA SAMAYA
DZAH | DZAH HUM BAM HO 𑖪

Say this mantra three times for the wisdom deities to dissolve into the horsewhip. Make offerings and offer praises. 𑖪

Think that the light rays emanating from the deities and the emissaries who accomplish the various activities leave the whip through the tail. They fill the whole universe and accomplish spontaneously the supreme pacifying, enriching, magnetizing, and subjugating activities according to your wishes. All is achieved perfectly, as we are given complete victory over all adversity. Recite successively and a hundred times each of the two composite mantras written above to bless the horsewhip. If you want to practice intensely, recite the mantras until you see signs—this means until the whip is moving, becomes warm, begins to smolder or burst into flame, forms clouds of rainbow lights, produces sounds, and so on. After this, simply holding the whip will bring the accomplishment of all wishes. 𑖪

At the end of the practice, deities and horsewhip are indivisible. The horsewhip is now the Great Lion Gesar appearing as the whip. Simply by holding and wielding it all your wishes are accomplished without obstacles. Actualize this, and say the Supratishtha mantra and the heart-of-dependent-origination mantra three times to consecrate the horsewhip and thus ensure that the blessings fully remain in the whip. Say words of auspiciousness.

iii. Use

Third is how to use the whip. If you hold it wherever you go and wherever you stay, it will protect you from all obstacles. Everything will become auspicious and all your wishes will be fulfilled. ៖

More specifically, when you want to avert any attempt to harm you, to be successful with whatever activity you are involved in, wave the whip in the direction that harm comes from, recite the mantra, and actualize the visualization. In case of heavy rainfall and strong winds, simply waving the whip will protect you from fear and from all enemies along the way. All inauspicious signs and conflicts will also be warded off. ៖

If you want to bring some lands or countries under your control, wield the whip while reciting the Gesar mantra, adding SARVA LOKA AKARSHAYA DZAH WASHAM KURU HO, and visualize that from the top of the whip an inconceivable number of dakas and dakinis of the four activities pour out, together with dralas and wermas and a host of emissaries. They radiate rays of red light that dissolve all lands and countries into red light that then melt into the soles of your feet—wield the whip in any direction you wish, and all the lands will be magnetized and brought under your control. ៖

If you have trouble with someone or get into a fight with an enemy and their armies, first wave the whip vigorously in their direction, using whichever magnetizing or subjugating visualizations you wish. ៖

If you enter into a debate with someone, or an argument or the like, wave the whip before you begin in your opponent's direction.

Return the whip to your pocket or bag [without anyone seeing it].
If you do this, you will be victorious. ﹡

In short, whatever the activity you require, if you wield the
horsewhip while reciting the mantra and maintaining the relevant
visualization, it will definitely be accomplished—guhya.

This instruction appeared suddenly in my mind on the eighteenth
day of the tenth month of Shubhakrit, the Water Tiger year (1902),
so I, Mipham, wrote it down. Anyone who has consecrated the
horsewhip will be successful. Mangalam.

﹡The important detail in square brackets is from Orgyen Tobgyal Rinpoche.
He also added, "In case of sickness, as you wield the whip, visualize a shower
of nectar cascading out of the whip and consider all illnesses cured. And if you
need to conduct enriching activities, raise the whip above your head and visualize
all the dralas and wermas, dakas and dakinis, and all the deities of wealth that
dwell inside the whip streaming out to gather the essence of the food, resources,
and wealth of the universe." http://all-otr.org/short-talks/5-gesar-s-horse-whip.

Gesar Great Lion the Jewel

8. The Jewel That Satisfies All Needs

King Gesar Consecration of a Casket of Abundance

NAMO PADMAKARAYA

The following is a method to increase wealth
Based on Gesar Norbu Dradul of Jambudvipa.
This most excellent and wish-fulfilling tree,
Heavily laden with a crop of jewels, I shall now present.

In a reliquary box made of precious substances, place the la stone and the life-force wheel described in the source text.[4] Fill it with a large array of substances that attract abundance, such as gold, silver, copper, iron, lapis, coral, and so on. Write the dharanis or the names of the wisdom, activity, and worldly wealth deities, and words of request in verses and prose. Roll up the paper on which you wrote them, insert it in a tube made of precious substances, and then put it in the reliquary, the practice support. Arrange clouds of all the clean offerings you can gather and follow the text of the yidam practice. Then:

> In front of me appears a golden syllable DROOM,
> "The universal monarch of the ushnisha."
> It melts into light and dissolves into the precious reliquary
> box,
> An unfathomable palace as vast as the dharmadhatu.
> Filled with cloud banks of desirable objects of all kinds,
> It embraces everything and has no inside and outside.

A throne made of a wealth of precious substances stands at
the center.
On the throne, the syllable A transforms into Great Lion
the Jewel.
His complexion is white with a tinge of red, youthful, and
full of bliss and desire.
He wears all the silk and jewel adornments.
He holds a wish-fulfilling jewel in his right hand
And an iron arrow and bow in the left.
His delightful consorts are the four great, secret consorts,
Beautiful and smiling, holding ribboned arrows and long-
life vases.
Dorje Lekpa and Yudrönma,
The great warlord Mikmar,
The wealth protector Magyal Pomra
And the other wermas who guard treasures
And grant our every wish assemble like clouds.
They are surrounded by the mighty warriors and beautiful
maidens
Who sing joyful songs and dance with great cheer.
The four gods of the miraculous windhorse,
The thirteen changsengs expert in covering long distances,
And all the others in their various magical displays
Move as fast as lightning, darting around like specks of
dust.
In a white cloud of nectar in the sky
Appear Gesar's elder brother, Dungkhyung Karpo,
And the other deities who rule over the prosperity and
abundance of the god realms.
Clouds of rainbow light, flowers and incense smoke
Pour down longevity and abundance—TO LO LO!
In midair, a tent of light
Houses Gerdzo and a hundred thousand nyen warriors
Who let loose the wondrous roar of their KI's and SO's—
SHA RA RA!

On the earth, younger brother Ludrul Öjung
And all the other guardians of the nagas' treasure
Dwell in the ocean Heavenly Luster of Prosperity
From which an abundant mist of riches wafts up—CHI LI
LI!
Above the ground, in a filigree of five-colored lights,
Aunt Gungmen Karmo,
Sister Tale Ökar,
And the other goddesses who own the five elements
Are all charming, looking joyful and swaying with delight.
Wisdom, activity, and worldly
Wealth deities, treasure guardians, and wermas
Arrive and assemble from every direction
Within an expanse of blazing golden light
That pervades everywhere in all directions.
They all appear fully and distinctly,
Clear and vivid in the great equality of appearance and
emptiness.

HUM
In the northwest of the land of Oddiyana,
In the heart of a lotus flower,
Endowed with the most marvelous attainments,
You are renowned as the Lotus-Born,
Surrounded by many hosts of dakinis
Following in your footsteps—
I pray to you: come, inspire me with your blessing!

Now, in these times of the five degenerations,
To quell the forces of evil that ignite dissention and strife
And the brutality of foreign invasions,
You arise in the form of a drala—
King Gesar, rain down your blessings!
Bless this auspicious secret relic box
And transform it into the immeasurable deity's palace.

Bless the jewels, la stones, and life-force wheel
Into wisdom deities.
Bless the various precious materials, jewels, and substances
that attract abundance
Into wish-fulfilling gems.
Make these supreme supports retain their qualities
And make the reliquary your permanent abode,
Increase my longevity, abundance, and wealth,
Spread my fame and repute in a hundred directions,
And grant me this very instant
The quality to increase the spirit of abundance that brings
victory over every adversity
And the peerless might to preside from the summit of the
universe!
Gather the happiness, well-being, wealth, fortune, and
abundance
Of the worlds of the gods, nagas, and humans—
Shower them down from above,
Gather them in thick clouds in between,
And let them arise from below like mist on a lake.
All prosperity and abundance from every location and
time—
Bring them here, gather them here, imbue these supports
with them!
Seal the amulet box of five-colored lights, which appears
while empty,
With the indestructible bindu.
The lights of vajra-life and abundance blaze forth,
Victory banners adorned with the jewel of auspiciousness
soar high.

I make offerings to you—
I offer you the symphony of all sensual pleasures
From the worlds of the gods, nagas, and humans
In their entirety.

Please accept them out of love for me.
Let the wish-fulfilling jewel, the wish-granting tree,
The treasury vase, the amrita, the bountiful cow,
And the clouds of pure gold
Bring down a great rain of everything I want and need,
Sound the thunder of praise and fame,
Make blaze the lightning of happiness, pleasure, and power.
Accept these offerings I give you
From within the dance of the magical net devoid of
    attachment
And the great equality of appearance and emptiness!
Amrita, torma, rakta, jagat, and select portion,
And the beautiful maidens' blissful and sensuous dance of
    appearance and existence,
The untainted pleasure of union,
Who stir you, attract you, embrace you and utterly satisfy
    you—
I offer them to the blossoming glorious knot of your heart.
In short, all that appears and exists
Blazes in the mudra of offering of blissful union in the
    indivisibility of emptiness and appearance,
Satisfying you within dharmadhatu.

A LA LA HO! Accept my offering!
Through auspicious coincidence, karma, aspirations,
And the dharmata's wisdom and compassion,
Ripen this very instant and without hindrance
The fruits of all the yogin's hopes
Into tangible experience—
May it never leave us until enlightenment,
And may the wish-granting tree and the wish-fulfilling
    jewel,
The excellent treasury vase and so on
Be always with us, as clearly as a person standing in front of
    us,

And fulfill our every need
Without anything going amiss—please grant us all this!
The sacred pledges of the vajra secret
Are not transgressed—samaya!
May the one taste within the expanse of secret enlightened
mind
Spontaneously accomplish the two purposes!

Then, for the recitation, rays of light sent from your heart reach the heart of the deities in front of you and invoke their wisdom mind. The light from their hearts summons the infinite array of wisdom, activity, and worldly wealth deities, who in turn emanate rays of light permeated with their strength, magical abilities, and powers. The light reaches all corners of space in the ten directions and moves as swiftly as lightning. The whole essence of vitality and wealth within samsara, nirvana, and the path appears in the form of bindus both large and small, each one marked with the auspicious signs and substances and so on. The bindus vibrate, pulsate, and shimmer. They dissolve one after the other into you and the practice articles that are now indivisible and forever inseparable from the deities, and into your precious secret reliquary box, the auspicious and immeasurable palace. As a result, like a clearing in the clouds that reveals the moon, all the strength and wealth, and all the essence of vitality and radiance increase hundreds and thousands of times. You become the great, almighty deity who grants spontaneously every want and need, and rules from the seat of the siddhi of incomparable splendor on the summit of samsara and nirvana. Think that it actually happens while you recite the mantra in the state of vajra-like equanimity:

OM TRIM ZHIM KHYIM ME MU TRA BARRA HAM
A LA LI LA MO TUNGPA KHYE A HO YE SIDDHI
HUM TRAK SHER KSHIM RARNA PALA SIDDHI
DROOM ŠNA NA KHA DE PUSHTIM SIDDHI HUM

Add the visualization for the secret recitation and recite the mantra in the proper way.

When you see signs of accomplishment in actuality, in meditative experience, or in dreams, receive the siddhis. To conclude, make offerings, chant praises, and fulfill samayas. Pray for food and wealth in general, and for your specific needs and whatever you desire, and summon abundance.

Always keep this support with you, and repeatedly make offerings and invocations. If you do this, just as when a pauper finds a great treasure of jewels, your every intention will be spontaneously accomplished without effort. Samaya.

I didn't invent this text; I took this jewel out of the treasury of wisdom, the pure vision of the great Lharik that accords with the tantras and the most excellent scriptures. Ithi.

The werma called Seru Öden Karpo wrote this instruction as it arose during the afternoon session of the twenty-fifth day of the third month of the Fire Bird year (1873) and again in the Iron Dragon year (1880). May virtue abound. Mangalam.

9. DISTILLING THE UNIVERSE

A Practice of King Gesar to Summon Abundance

HUM HRIH

From the expanse of the great equality that pervades all
  space and time,
From the indestructible bindu of blazing five-colored lights,
From the secret palace, permanent, immovable and
  indestructible,
The great vidyadhara Powerful Supreme Ornament of
  Jambudvipa emerges
Endowed with vajra wisdom's supreme power over life.
He is the great hero who overcomes the armies of all
  enemies
With the sword of wisdom, his bow and arrow.
He is King Wish-Fulfilling Jewel, the source of every
  goodness,
And All-Accomplishing White Werma who fulfills every
  purpose.

To you and your retinue, the armies of haughty spirits of the
  universe,
I make these offerings, chant your praise, and invoke the
  pledge you made!
Please bring here, with the light rays of unimpeded
  magnetizing activity,
Like iron attracted by a magnet,
The longevity, well-being, and strength of the worlds of
  gods, nagas, and humans

Who live in the realms in the ten directions, above and
below.

Also extract the positive essences of samsara, nirvana, and
the path
And pour down these blessings on the mandala of Secret
Mantra
In a rain of auspicious substances blazing with lights.

I invoke the sacred promise of the ocean of treasure
guardians and wealth deities
Who appear in limitless wisdom, activity, and worldly
forms,
The great displays of equality's joyful desire,
As appearance and existence melt within the expanse of
empty bliss.

Dance the dance of joy, move to the steps of elation,
Let blissful songs resound like a thousand thunderclaps,
Permeate every place with rays of light of magnetizing
blissful desire,
Let infinite appearance and existence vibrate, flicker, and
hum,
Extract from above the auspicious abundance and
prosperity of the gods,
Extract from below the abundance and prosperity of the
nagas that multiply naturally,
Extract from in between the positive abundance and
prosperity of humans,
Extract from basic space the wealth of blessings of the
buddhas and bodhisattvas,
Extract from the sacred places the wealth of joy of the
multitude of three root deities,
Extract from the sacred lands the wealth of power of the
dharma-protecting dralas,

Extract from every direction the wealth of jewels of the
treasure-keeping wermas,
Extract from the outer world the wealth of support of the
five elements such as space,
Extract from the inner world the wealth of the essence of
sentient beings of the universe,
And extract the wealth of increasing prosperity and
longevity from the buddha fields!

In short, let fall the heavy rain of the glorious essence
Of all auspiciousness, positivity, abundance, prosperity, and
the wealth
Of appearance and existence from every direction and
time—
Let it amass in vast oceans!
Extract it so that it collects in thick clouds and fog!

Gather everything
Into this auspicious and inalterable infinite palace of Secret
Mantra,
Lead us to victory in the great indestructible bindu,
Hoist the victory banner of vajra life, prosperity, and
abundance!
Pour down everything needed and desired in a wish-
fulfilling rain,
Let loose lightning bolts of a thousand joys, well-being, and
happiness,
And roar with the thunderous sound of complete victory
over all adversity!
Unceasingly gather the most extraordinary abundance and
prosperity,
And grant us, right now in the great equality of emptiness
and appearance,
The siddhi of accomplishment

Of the wealth of great self-arisen wisdom, ⁝
The perfect coincidence that matures the untainted
   rainbow body.

This wealth-gathering wish-fulfilling jewel
That extracts from everywhere without obstacle
The vital essence of samsara and nirvana
Remains forever within the ocean of the profound secret
   enlightened mind.

Zilnön Gyepa Tsal wrote this prayer on the ninth day of the fifth
month of the Fire Mouse year (1876). May it be the cause for the
teachings to prevail and the well-being of beings to increase!

10. A Vast Cloud of Jewels

Fulfillment Offering to the Wermas, Gesar's Treasure Guardians

---

Gather some fulfillment substances, bless them, and say:

HUM HRIH
The self-arising bindu of primordial purity
Has always been the wisdom of the sameness of appearances
    and emptiness;
Its self-occurring, spontaneously present power
Manifests as the Jewel Palace, the pure expression of the
    world and beings,
Vast as the expanse of dharmadhatu.
It is filled with excellent vases, wish-fulfilling trees,
    bountiful cows,
The various jewels of both gods and bodhisattvas,
Mountains of precious substances, oceans of nectar,
The grains that require no toil, siddhas' samaya substances,
Masses of possessions, treasuries of jewels,
Auspicious substances and symbols, precious emblems of
    royalty, and so on.
The extraordinary wealth of gods, nagas, and humans
Are piled everywhere and fill the whole of space.
In the sky above, from great clouds of pure gold,
A hundred thousand claps of thunder roar praise and
    homage
As golden bolts of lightnings flash, their forks dancing
    elegantly,

And a rain of jewels that satisfy every want and need pours
down.
Tens of thousands of magnificent fearless warriors throng
throughout the whole of space
Dancing delightful steps of elation,
And hundreds of thousands of ravishingly beautiful girls
Sing charming songs.
Samaya substances in oceans of amrita and rakta, and
mountains of tormas,
And clouds of sensory delights are amassed,
And a hundred thousand vajra consorts offer the pleasure of
their embrace.
In short, the magical net displays a vast profusion
Of outer, inner, secret, and worldly and transcendent
offerings,
All spontaneously present, inexhaustible, and fulfilling all
needs.
Appearance and existence arise naturally as great bliss
In a marvelous vajra array of immense offerings,
Wisdom's symphony of objects of desire,
A spontaneously present treasury of Samantabhadra's
everlasting, all-pervasive clouds of offering.

This great offering of supreme and glorious riches
Fulfills the noble wishes of the ocean of three jewel refuges,
Of the infinite deities of the three roots,
And of the dharma protectors, wealth deities, and treasure
guardians,
Especially the noble wishes of All-Accomplishing White
Werma,
Powerful Great Lion Jewel Tamer of Enemies,
The emperor who rules over vajra life, abundance, and
pleasure,
And the king of all the dralas of the universe.

It fulfills the noble wishes of the four dakinis, mothers of
the joys,
Of General Mikmar Chenpo,
Of Damchen Dorje Lekpa,
Of Mentsun Dorje Yudrönma,
Of Magyal Dorje Draktsal,
Of elder brother Dungkhyung Karpo,
Of the owners of the treasures of the gods above,
Of father Gerdzo Nyenpo,
Of the owners of the treasures of the nyens in the middle,
Of younger brother Ludrul Öjung,
Of the owners of the treasures of the nagas of the
underworld,
Of aunt Gungmen Gyalmo,
Of the assembly of mamos of phenomenal existence,
Of sister Tale Ökar,
Of the goddesses of the five elements,
Of the four gods of the miraculous windhorse,
Of the thirteen gods expert in covering long distances,
Of the wermas who live between sky and earth,
Of the dralas and wermas in Gesar's retinue,
Of the assembly of fair-maiden dakinis,
Of the assembly of fearless warriors,
Of the army of gods who obey him,
Of the haughty spirits of phenomenal existence who abide
by his command,
And of the dralas and wermas of appearance and existence.
In short, our offering fulfills the noble wishes
Of every single deity appearing in wisdom, action, or
worldly form
In the infinite assembly of wealth deities
Who abide joyfully in the mandala of Great Lion Jewel
Tamer of Enemies.

As you endlessly delight in the great bliss of purity and
    equality,
Please increase like the waxing moon
Our longevity, abundance, merit, prosperity, well-being,
    happiness, dharma, and force;
The vitality of our memory, confidence, eloquence,
    intelligence, charisma, brilliance, and radiance;
The vigor of our experience and realization, and our
    resourcefulness, strength, and power.
Constantly pour down the glory of abundance and
    prosperity from every corner of the universe
To fill ocean-like reservoirs! Let them gather like clouds!

In the natural state of vajra mind's empty bliss
Be always with us and never leave us without what we enjoy,
Grant us the great good fortune of being able to travel freely
From joy to joy to the jewel island of omniscience!
Bring the power of blessings to this place
And attract the abundance and prosperity
Of the mandala of the ocean of glorious wealth deities!
Bring the three planes of the three realms under our control
And grant us supreme victory over all!

Let our fame and good reputation fill every realm!
Show us auspiciousness and make it fill the whole region,
Let the praise of our rule and stature rise to the top of the
    world,
And bring about excellence and the fulfillment of wishes!

Let the prosperity of tens of thousands of resplendent
    auspicious signs
Shine constantly within the bindu of empty appearances!
Let the excellent vase, the indestructible source of everything,
Grant us the kingdom of siddhis, the source of supreme
    satisfaction!

For all beings, infinite in number,
May the brilliant light of the blazing jewel of wisdom,
The basis of inexhaustible, supreme benefit and happiness
Always spread like the dharmadhatu!

This abundance practice of Gesar, the king of wermas, is a wish-
fulfilling jewel that grants every desire.
Without letting anyone see you, practice the sadhana, the
summoning of abundance,
And add this fulfillment offering and request, as this is the most
excellent way to practice.
Combine these three and success will be easy.

After wondering whether longer or shorter practices were of any
use,
At the time of a virtuous conjunction of stars,
I wrote down the stages of this fulfillment practice
Just as they arose and appeared in my mind.

Through this merit may all beings
Have the good fortune to enjoy their every wish
In the jewel ocean of inexhaustible abundance and prosperity!

This fulfillment and request was written by Mipham at Dzongsar
Tashi Lhatse. Mangalam.

———

AH
In the bindu of the great equality of appearance and
emptiness,
The permanent, eternal, indestructible wisdom deity
Abides joyfully without transformation, change, or loss,
And offers prosperity, abundance, and signs of merit
spontaneously!

OM SUPRATISHTA BENZA YE SOHA
RAKSHA RAKSHA SHRI MANDALA DROOM

Say these words and rest evenly in their meaning.

Akar Ökyi Werma

11. The Scroll of Seru Öden Karpo's Profound and Secret Whispered Transmission

SO

The great equality of appearance and emptiness, the
   dharmadhatu, ⁸
The unchanging swastika, ⁸
The ultimate bindu, ⁸
Manifests naturally as the kaya of self-arising
   compassion— ⁸
Gesar the Jewel, Norbu Dradul Tsal! ⁸

Above Mount Magyal Pomra in the East, ⁸
In the celestial citadel fashioned from rainbow lights, ⁸
The palace where all that appears and exists is revealed
   clearly, ⁸
Akar Ökyi Werma, the magical deity of Chashen
   divination, presides. ⁸
He has the youthful charm of a sixteen-year-old boy, ⁸
Graced with a radiant complexion, white like pure crystal. ⁸
In his right hand he holds a jeweled torch, ⁸
Which brightly illuminates the three planes of existence. ⁸
In his left hand he holds a precious mirror ⁸
That lifts the veil on everything hidden. ⁸
Gowned in white silk, wearing clouds of rainbow lights, ⁸
He stands majestically in a flower in full bloom. ⁸
The five secret goddesses, his delightful consorts, ⁸
Blaze with the five lights. Each holds a mirror ⁸

And the excellent vase that satisfies all needs, ༔
And looks passionately at him. ༔
All around, the hundred thousand wermas who reveal
  everything clearly ༔
Perform vajra dances and sing songs. ༔
The heat of bliss blazes and irradiates—YA LA LA! ༔
Fragrant scents of medicinal incenses waft up—TU LU
  LU! ༔
Flowers rain down from clouds of rainbow lights—TO LO
  LO! ༔

Give your love and respect to the practitioners ༔
Who ask you to come here because of your samayas— ༔
Please come to this place without delay! ༔
We offer you clouds of smoke ༔
From the three aromatic woods and white incense. ༔
We offer you a drink of supreme taste, ༔
A cocktail of milk, water, rice beer, and the three sweets. ༔
We offer you the lamp that eliminates the darkness of
  ignorance, ༔
A ribboned arrow, mirror, chemar, select portion of
  offering, ༔
And the six sensory delights. ༔

As the self-appearing illusory deity ༔
Manifests from all-revealing space as the play of the moon's
  reflection in water, ༔
The vajra life force is upheld and samayas unite— ༔
Accomplish the very heart of the samaya of the mantra. ༔

Visualize a syllable A, white like the moon, at the heart of the
deity and the mantra garland revolving around it, as you recite the
mantra.

SO ༔ AKAR WERMA KHÖ DE DU ༔ SAL SALE PRA
POP SOHA ༔

KYE
With my faith and our samaya, I have called on you, ༔
Deity who reveals all that appears and exists. ༔
When I invite you from the open expanse of space, ༔
Respect your promise and come here now! ༔
When I, the yogin, is in such a need, ༔
If I don't ask you, father, who will I ask? ༔
If you don't tell me, your child, who will you tell? ༔

All space is filled with lights and rainbows, ༔
Songs and melodies resound beautifully—TRO LO LO! ༔
Dancers whirl with beautiful movements and expressions—
SHIK SE SHIK! ༔
Males blaze with magnificent splendor—YA LA LA! ༔
Females glow with beauty and dazzle with smiles—LHAP
SE LHAP! ༔
Bless the body, speech, and mind of the medium,* and
mine! ༔
Show us the illusory display of appearance and existence! ༔
Without delay, reveal the result of the divination! ༔

Offer a sang with this prayer. Raise aloft the ribboned arrow and
play music, show the mirror, and so on to the medium. Samaya. ༔

This text was written as it arose in the mind of the werma Seru
Öden Karpo. ༔ Ithi. Seal. ༔

---

*The medium is usually a child in whom the werma manifests.

12. The All-Clear Jewel Mirror

The Cleansing Sang Offering of the Luminous Werma[*]

Consecrate whatever offering substances you have.

HUM HRIH 𐅀
From space, the wisdom body of self-born insight, 𐅀
In the castle of werma, illuminating all phenomena, 𐅀
Is the Lord King Döndrup Norbu, 𐅀
The werma White Light A, along with his retinue. 𐅀
Just like a mother longing for her only child, 𐅀
Quickly approach this place with a loving mind 𐅀
And show me the wondrous signs and real marks. 𐅀

The samaya substances of the outer, inner, and secret
    offerings, 𐅀
Which are real or imagined by mind, fill the entire space. 𐅀
The clouds of jnana-amrita and mahasukha are of equal
    taste. 𐅀
Joyfully accept these and rouse miraculous power. 𐅀
Kindle the bliss-warmth in the realm of nadi, prana, and
    insight. 𐅀
Show me the essential vision of unerring auspicious
    coincidence. 𐅀
Open the miraculous gate, illuminating all phenomena. 𐅀
Open the single eye of wisdom 𐅀

[*]Translated by the Nalanda Translation Committee under the direction of
Vidyadhara the Venerable Chögyam Trungpa Rinpoche in June 1979.

And remove the veils that obscure the spotless penetrating
    space. ⁞
The power, ability, and strength of accomplishing great
    benefit for the teachings and beings— ⁞
Please promote this unobstructedly, fulfilling mind's
    desire. ⁞

You are the warrior Manjushri, the wisdom-illusion dance, ⁞
The great warrior who conquers the enemy troops of Mara. ⁞
With the mudras of bow, arrow, and sword of prajna, ⁞
You quell the warfare of klesha-ignorance. ⁞
King of the luminous werma and with your retinue, ⁞
From within equanimity, your self-existing power of
    kindness ⁞
Approaches in a web of miracles of blazing light, sharp and
    brilliant. ⁞
Please enter into my longing heart. ⁞
Please accomplish the two benefits, fulfilling mind's
    desire. ⁞
The time has come to fulfill your vow—samaya. ⁞

Thus, with this offering, expand beyond the limits of direction
your power of higher perception, which sees the nature of all
apparent phenomena without confusion. On the tenth day of the
sixth month of the Wood Monkey year (1884), Werma Seru Öden
Karpo wrote this down at the good tent Tashi Rangnang Chime
Ökyi Ding Gur (Auspicious Self-Appearance Deathless Light
Tent). May it be auspicious. Sarva mangalam.

13. Short Lhasang*

HRIH ༔
The virtuous mark, the great banner of the inspiring
    windhorse, ༔
And these clouds of offerings of all desirable things ༔
We offer to you, great being Gesar with your retinue. ༔
Fulfill all our wishes; be victorious in all directions. ༔

Thus, on the fifth day of the fifth month of the Wood Snake year
(1905), Mipham wrote this down. Sarva mangalam.

*Translated by the Nalanda Translation Committee under the direction of
Vidyadhara the Venerable Chögyam Trungpa Rinpoche in June 1979.

14. WINDHORSE SUPPLICATION*

HUM

The great banner of inspiring, auspicious windhorse,
The streaming out of great clouds of Samantabhadra
    offerings,
The three roots, protectors, dralas, and zodors,
The patron gods who protect us, and so on, are worthy
    offering guests,
Especially mighty Gesar Norbu Dradul
And the miraculous chestnut vajra stallion,
Along with warriors, maidens, kadös, and messengers—
Accept my offerings and spontaneously accomplish my
    aims.

This short windhorse supplication was composed by Mipham on
the auspicious tenth day of the ninth month at the upper retreat of
Rutam. Sarva mangalam. Virtue.

*Translated by the Nalanda Translation Committee under the direction of
Vidyadhara the Venerable Chögyam Trungpa Rinpoche in June 1979.

15. ৩৪ The Heart Essence of Good Fortune

*King Great Lion of Tibet: A Ritual to Raise Windhorse
and Increase Merit*

In this ritual, *The Heart Essence of Good Fortune*, for raising windhorse and increasing merit, we summon our confidence and courage by looking at the face of the self-arising Lotus King Guru Rinpoche—the wisdom of our own rigpa-awareness, unstained primordial purity, and Samantabhadra—and of spontaneous presence, Norbu Dradul. Chant the following prayer after the offering of praises to the dharma protectors and dralas.

HUM
Your spontaneously present form,
Born in a lotus and endowed with the marks and signs,
Is clothed in the dralas' resplendent armor,
While your wisdom mind
Is the wisdom mind of the lord of vidyadharas, Guru
  Rinpoche.

Triumphant and unchanging King Dondrup!
The power of your promise to ensure the well-being and
  happiness of all beings,
And your immeasurable love, grants all I wish for;
Remain in me in one taste with the bindu of pure mind
And grant me the two accomplishments!

Make the sugatas and their heirs who dwell in the ten
    directions,
The yidam and dakini deities and all the worthy objects of
    refuge
Shower me with the blessings of their enlightened body,
    speech, mind, qualities, and activities,
And raise the windhorse of power over the four aspects of
    well-being!

Grant a deluge of all the fiercely powerful dharma
    protectors and guardians—
Let them dissolve into my body, speech, and mind,
And through the power of their blessings,
May the windhorse of perfect power and strength rise!

Dralas and wermas of the universe,
Come and swarm inside the body of the great being Gesar
Like bees in a fragrant lotus
And raise the windhorse that grants me the power to
    accomplish everything I wish!

May spirits and elemental demons
Who roam the realms of the world
Protect me and be inspired by altruism, their minds as
    white as a full moon,
And raise the windhorse that powerfully grants positive
    circumstances!

Like the rays of sunlight that make the young lotus blossom,
Inspire the thoughts and actions of all beings
To support the positive circumstances I need
And raise the windhorse that grants the delight of a
    thousand celebrations!

Merit, like the moon that reigns over every excellence in all
buddha fields,
Has the power to make the kunda flower of "delight at
doing good" blossom;
May the excellence and qualities of the windhorse of
inexhaustible merit rise!

May my two feet perform the overpowering dance
On the heads of the proud leaders of the world,
And may I have the power to grab enemy factions from the
crowns of their heads and dominate them—
Raise the windhorse of the vajra endowed with fierce
strength!

May adverse circumstances be pacified and may my hopes
and wishes
Be accomplished as intended, without obstacles.
May I have the capacity to fulfill each task perfectly,
And by doing so, raise the windhorse of victory over all
adversity!

Within buddha nature, primordially present in all sentient
beings,
Everything is spontaneously accomplished,
Yet as soon as I think of you,
You accomplish what I need—O great being Dondrup,
Raise the windhorse that effortlessly achieves everything I
wish for!

Self-awareness, sole bindu, dharmakaya,
Ever inseparable from all the victorious ones,
Self-arising Padma, whose essence is utter purity,
Liberate all beings within the primordial ground!

> You who are all the victorious ones, you who are their heart,
> Accomplish all the activities of the sugatas
> For the benefit of all mother sentient beings.
> Lake-Born Vajra, one who successfully accomplishes the
>   buddhas' activities,
> May the flowers of auspiciousness of your glorious efforts be
>   scattered!

As you say these words, meditate on the king of the world, Gesar, visualized clearly in front of you. At the end, imagine that he dissolves into you and you become indivisible from him and maintain the recognition of stainless rigpa-awareness. Recite the *Sampa Lhundrupma*[5] and as many Vajra Guru mantras as you can.

By practicing in this way, the wind will move the sweet-sounding, inspiring, and auspicious flag of the windhorse, the virtuous banner, and it will be heard throughout the ten directions. Your actions will be sharp, fast, and seamless. You will encounter positive circumstances and good people. They will overcome the negative ones. You will triumph and be enthroned as the leader of humankind. You will become more powerful and so on, in life and in your experiences and visions. Extraordinary signs will appear in your dreams, such as riding a steed, hearing music, raising banners, climbing mountains, riding supreme thoroughbred horses, dragons, lions, tigers, and the like.

> This pith instruction from the secret depth of rigpa
> Arose in a pure vision
> As the magical display of the single bindu
> In which primordially pure awareness, King Lotus,
> And spontaneous presence, Norbu Dradul, are indivisible.

I wrote this prayer at the age of twenty, on the fifth day of the tenth month of the Wood Ox year (1865). Mangalam.

16. GREAT LION AKAR ÖKYI WERMA

Mirror Divination Practice

OM AH HUM HRIH
All phenomena are self-arisen, primordial wisdom.
In this great natural state, empty awareness is free from
elaboration.
Its manifesting power appears as the five lights of the utterly
pure universe and beings.
Within their expanse stands the blazing palace of great bliss
that reveals all things,
Where the executor of the enlightened activities of the
victorious ones and the three roots,
The great lion Akar Ökyi Werma, presides.
Brilliant white like crystal, he has one face and two hands
And holds a jeweled torch and a mirror.
Wearing white silks, he is adorned with rainbow-light
clouds of flowers.
The five delightful consorts hold a ribboned arrow and a
clear bright mirror.
The hundred thousand wermas who reveal clearly all that
appears and exists surround them,
Performing various vajra dances and singing songs—
As I think of you, grant me supreme clarity in mirror
divination!

When I invoke you and your entire retinue,
Marshal the forces of blessings, power, strength, and
capacity.

Direct your wisdom mind, the empty bliss devoid of
 impediment,
Sway and swirl in the delightful dance of your kayas—SHIK
 SE SHIK!
Cheerfully sing your songs—KYU RU RU!
Pour rains of flowers from your rainbow clouds—TO LO
 LO!
Let the manifestations of the wisdom of blissful heat sway
 and whirl—SHIK SE SHIK!
Bless us practitioners!
Never leave us apart from the all-illuminating wisdom light
 of the enlightened mind of great bliss,
Let it reside in the indestructible bindu of the five lights at
 the center my heart—
Grant me the supreme empowerment of clairvoyance!
Since the entire mandala of the wermas who reveal all that
 appears and exists
Are the body's nadi, prana, and awareness-bindu on the
 inner level,
And is one taste with bodhichitta on the secret level,
Stay here happily, one with great bliss,
And unlock the magic that reveals all that appears and
 exists.
Grant the excellent eye of wisdom that sees the three times
 unveiled,
Give me the knowledge of inevitable interdependence,
Grant me the siddhi of mirror divination!

Samaya seal. ༔ Virtue.

17. ཉྃ BOOSTING THE GOOD

A Practice to Raise the Windhorse of Circumstances,

Relying on King Vajra Great Lion

ཉྃ NAMO GURU PADMA MANJUSHRI VAJRA TIKSHNA YA
There is a relationship between the strength or weakness of the
power of good deeds and the fluctuations in the energies of the
"wind stallion" that results in either the success or failure of our
activities. Here is a method that relies on King Dradul of Tibet to
create the conditions that will raise the energies of the windhorse.
Since it is the ultimate method that is more profound than any
other, apply yourself with diligence.

Prepare flags of the five colors with more of the color of the year
element, of the relevant section of the eight trigrams, of the related
section of the nine mewas, or of the wind element. The flags should
be printed with drawings and inscriptions associated with raising
windhorse. The horse should be printed in yellow, the tiger in red,
the dragon in blue, the garuda in green, and the lion in white.
Add four silk streamers to the flag. On the flag, print the *Sampa
Lhundrupma*,[6] the Vajra Guru mantra, the prayer requesting
your wishes, mantras that raise the windhorse, and so on. For the
prayer requesting your wishes, the following supplication should
be printed on the flag; recite it as well.

HUM
The complete purity of all dharmas, the mind of
    Vajratikshna,
Spotless dharmata, the lotus-born buddha,
Unobstructed emanation, the great vajra warrior,

Vidyadhara Norbu Dradul, along with your retinue—
May you accept as the essence of the space of peaceful
    dharmata
This windhorse banner, which arises as the display of the
    virtuous mark,
An offering that displays its unceasing qualities.
Let the pleasing windhorse banner billow in the wind!
Bring forth the excellent activity of a hundred thousand
    virtues and great fame!

From your heart, which is the all-pervasive knot of eternity,
By the auspicious coincidence of the rippling, inexhaustible
    wonder
Of the miraculous horse, tiger, garuda, dragon, lion, and so
    on,
Increase the excellent windhorse's power of good fortune,
The highest among all the glorious virtues of existence,
The never-resting victory banner, adorned by a jewel finial
And imbued with the amrita essence
That is pleasing to the beings of the three levels.*

Write this supplication on the windhorse flags, soak them in fine
saffron water, and hoist them high. Look piercingly upward into
the expanse of the sky, shout "Ki ki so so ha ha!"[7] and recite the
Vajra Guru mantra. Say the heart-of-dependent-origination mantra. Then offer sang, as you beat the drum and sing beautifully.
Scatter blessed barley grains over the windhorse flags and chant
the following prayer about how to visualize:

HUM
Embodiment of the magical net that pervades the whole of
    space,

---

*This prayer was translated by the Vajravairochana Translation Committee.

Supreme kaya indivisible from wisdom, Lotus-Born,
Arising as the unstoppable champion of enlightened
    activities—
Supreme being, vidyadhara, Lord Norbu Dradul!
With the samaya of indivisibility with the ground, beyond
    parting and joining,
And heartfelt, unswerving faith and devotion,
Great treasure of wisdom and love, I remind you of your
    promise!
Arise from the expanse of Vidyadhara Padma's wisdom
    mind
With unimpeded movements within stainless
    dharmadhatu!
Dance the unconfined vajra steps,
Instantly fill the earth, the sky, and everywhere in between
    with your dance.
The dralas and wermas amass around you like rain clouds,
The most beautiful maidens sing joyful songs,
The vajra wind blows, caressing the skin and yet so
    powerful,
A shower of amrita, long-life nectar, and all that is desired
    rains down,
Fragrant incense sweetens the air,
Your skillful vajra steed gallops with all its might,
The multicolored silk ribbons tied to your head tossed high
    in the wind—PU RU RU!
The music of precious instruments resounds loudly—TRO
    LO LO!
And the dralas' flags flap and thrash—SHIK SE SHIK!
The voices of your legions of warriors fill the air with KI SO,
Supreme leader of the armies of haughty spirits from all
    three realms,
Vajra kaya surrounded by dakas and dakinis,
Perfectly splendid King Great Lion, and your retinue,

Please come to this place with the speed of lightning!

Accept this rippling flag of divine silk,
The pure virtuous sign of the rising windhorse.
The powerful vajra wind moves the flag of the supremely
    virtuous windhorse,
Sweet-sounding far and wide,
And glorious fame and renown fill the ten directions to the
    end of space.
This wondrous flag naturally brings joy to anyone who sees
    it.
The windhorse of activities resounds like the music of the
    gods.

Remain, full of delight, in the glorious knot of my heart,
And like divine clouds in a clear sky,
Reveal your dances—the play of most marvelous joy—
Which are indivisible from dharmadhatu's essence!
In the delight of a heart filled with nectar,
Increase my appetite for untainted bliss!
May an irresistible magnetizing power blaze forth
And its warmth attract the glorious partners I desire!

The powerful and skillful horse, propelled by the forceful
    vajra wind,
With unimpeded magic gallops freely across the sky,
His form more delightful than the most beautiful of clouds.
This vajra steed brings with him the conditions for swift,
    efficient action.
He can influence the power and potential of good actions
As he gallops through samsara to nirvana.
The vajra steed, wild and skillful, that you manifest to
    accomplish your activities—
Peerless man, Norbu Dradul, I offer it to you!

Accept it in the indivisible sphere of the expanse of peace
And within self-liberation, in the utterly pure lotus space of
　　dharmadhatu,
Let the flag of inspiring windhorse billow and snap!

The tiger, its unbearable roar so intimidating, so
　　overwhelming,
Fans the brilliance of the raging flames of wrath!
Awesome and splendid, he effortlessly bounds and leaps,
Embodying the might of the assembly of dralas
And granting us courage and strength of mind.
He is the vajra that overcomes mountains of malicious foes,
Emanated from the mind of the wrathful annihilator,
　　Dradul, "the Tamer of Enemies."
The tiger who moves through samsara and manifests from
　　the power of virtue,
Peerless man, Norbu Dradul, I offer it to you!

The lion's glorious form is of a great warrior, his stride
　　majestic!
He looks on contentedly as he dominates the world from
　　the summit of the mountain of meteoric iron!
He has manifested in the three realms from the magic elixir
　　of the gods
And overcomes all opponents in an instant!
This most majestic of lions radiates the light of increasing
　　virtue, abundance, and prosperity!
He destroys the strength of his opponents and supports the
　　victorious and the glorious!
This lion, your emanation,
Highest of the high and supreme leader of all humans,
O Great Lion's kaya who blazes with undefiled
　　magnificence,
Peerless man, Norbu Dradul, I offer it to you!

On top of the wish-granting tree,
The fabulous bird with wings so powerful that she can race
 against the wind,
Soars high in the sky that is her dominion.
Marvelous, flawless leader of the wermas,
She enhances qualities in people's minds.
Inexhaustible excellence of the jewel of joy,
She delights in astounding and enthralling bravery,
And manifests from the qualities of those who dwell in
 Manifest Joy!
Peerless man, Norbu Dradul, I offer it to you!

The womb of heavy, new rain clouds
Lit by beautiful flashes of red lightning
Gives birth to the roar of fame and virtuous words of praise.
The formidable thunder of the virtuous banner, the roar of
 the dralas' dragon,
And the clamor at the fulfillment of hope to be crowned
Descend into my heart as a shower of nectar of positive
 actions.
The dragon who proclaims universal fame and thunders
 renown
Emanated from Gesar's enlightened speech,
Peerless man, Norbu Dradul, I offer it to you!

In the primordially empty space of sheer simplicity,
All realms of existence, the universe and the beings it
 contains,
Is an endless dance of every kind of magical emanation and
 dissolution;
In an exhibition of displays beyond description,
Gods drink the nectar of joy that grants all desire,
Humans see the magical display of all manner of happiness
 and suffering,

Beings in subterranean hells experience unbearable
    suffering,
Noble residents of the pure celestial realms are forever
    peaceful, and so on,
While the many aspects of samsara and nirvana
Are one within the realization of primordial purity, the
    expanse of the dharmakaya.
These magical displays are the movement of my own mind,
Produced by its ceaseless interdependence with the wind of
    awareness:
The light bindu blazing with the essences of the five sensory
    stimulants
Of the five primary elements that make the three realms
Produces the secret, indestructible, vajra windhorse deities
From whom the interdependence of good and virtue arises.
They support the manifestation of magical displays of a
    multitude of positive circumstances
Within the unalterable, immutable expansive vase of space
And accomplish everything spontaneously the moment we
    think of it.
Natural radiance arising as the indestructible bindu, Great
    Lion,
Gather the energy of goodness and the virtue of positive
    aspirations!
On vajra wind, carry us wherever we wish to go!
May we enjoy everything we desire in the glory of samsara
    and nirvana—
Let the Great Lion flag of incomparable power fly high!

From the display of the lotus of primordial purity and
    spontaneous presence,
The magical emanation of the virtuous, supreme Great
    Lion's flag appears.
Like the alchemy of turning iron into gold, this flag can
    transform everything we do;

Our every positive endeavor will go well and the victory
drum of our fame resound,
And the glory of auspiciousness, abundance, and good
fortune
Will appear as the most excellent articles from the wealth of
existence and peace,
Such as the seven wish-fulfilling emblems of royalty,
The eight auspicious symbols and substances,
Sun, moon, wish-granting tree, bountiful cow,
Treasure vase, amrita, and so on.
Gather them all into a pleasing treasury of joy,
Pour their qualities into the heart of beings,
And make them an inexhaustible wish-fulfilling treasury of
happiness and well-being!

May the final jewel of the never-faltering victory banner rise
high!
May it blaze at the summit of the three realms of existence!
Hoist the victory banner of the ruler of three realms, King
Tamer of Maras,
High on the peak of existence!

The key points of the hidden meaning are implicit in the text.

First, prepare windhorse flags—five-colored flags that contain
the profound and secret key points of interdependence. Then offer
sang to the dralas.

If you say these words, you will dream of riding horses, tigers,
dragons, and so on. Acquire the flags, play music, and raise the flags
on top of a mountain that dominates in every direction. You will
see good omens, such as the sun or the moon rising in dreams, or
experience rigpa-awareness clearly, or feel joyful and develop courage. Everyone will pay homage to you and whatever you do will be
successful. I have heard it from the dakini Gaura herself.

In most cases these days, our windhorse is weak. The ordained
sangha destroys the discipline of the Vinaya, medicines are slow

and lack power, vows are treated with contempt, and beings engage in every possible kind of negative action. For such a corrupt time, when negative actions come from all directions, and the innocent are seen as enemies and are struck down, there is no method more profound than this, my child! Take this instruction into your hand and know how to use it.

Samaya. ༔ Gya gya gya. ༔

May the merit from composing this text be the cause of constant success,
May fame and praise resound everywhere,
May all actions have a positive outcome, even negative ones—
May this prayer be the jewel of humankind on earth!

This instruction, which has been covered in the bindu of awareness, appeared on the first day of the third month. It was on a day for hanging windhorse flags that I saw clearly and without doubt that it would increase the potential of our endeavors and bring about swift results, free from obstruction. This instruction will continuously create extremely virtuous and auspicious circumstances and will spread the glory of fame and renown throughout all of space. The vajra hero promised that this practice is undeceiving and its result would be timely.

Ithi. Mangalam.

18. Masang Practice

To invoke masang spirits to curse enemies, make a small man on a horse with willow shrub who carries a koruka and a shield of mushroom or grass, and an arrow and a bow of jagma grass. Place them in a fortress made from pieces of turf. Prepare a paper bag filled with salt, garlic, and sugar to put in front of the fortress. Lay white felt on an elevated, flat surface on which you place a ribboned arrow, chemar, and serkyem offering.

> SO
> Werma wrathful king, yogi Sharura—gather, gather!
> Finest masang warriors, form your armies—come, come!

Repeat this many times. Then say:

> Heed our war cry—SO!
> Gesar, tamer of enemies, lord of war—SO!
> Werma masangs of great might—SO!
> Powerful werma Nyi Nya—SO!
> Great Gungpa Kyatra—SO!
> The enemy is here! Help us kill him!
> ATSITSA! See the prodigious army of wermas!
> It spreads over the entire sky,
> It fills every inch of space between earth and sky,
> It gallops all over the earth,
> Its roar fills the whole country!
> It is here, in gold clouds in the sky!
> It is here, shaking the space between earth and sky with
>   thunder and lightning!

It is here, hitting the ground like thunderbolts and rain!
It will wage war against any enemy—
Set your armies on those who attack with their constant,
   inflaming invectives
The lineage holders of the Awe-Inspiring Land of Ling!
Unleash your hordes on those who threaten them with
   poisonous weapons in their evil hands!
Direct your troops on those who hold negative, hostile
   thoughts toward them!

A LA LA! Impressive army of wermas,
How wonderful you have come to protect us!
Enjoy this delicious chemar offered to please you!
We make you our protectors: please receive the investiture
   arrow and silken kata!
Here is the nectar drink of the warriors that instills
   fearlessness!
Now, kill the enemy and overcome this obstructing force!
Dralas, do not let your power and might weaken!
Wermas, do not forget your task!
Kill all enemies and destroy their stronghold,
Seize their wealth and quell their strength,
Raise high the great flags that please the father-gods,
Roar with the laughter of jubilant dralas,
Bring us and those around us
Victory against every adversity!

After you have said this, bring down the enemy's fortress, beat it to
destroy it completely, and dance on top of it, saying:

SO SO MASANG GESAR WERME MAK GI DRAWO
MARAYA P'ET P'ET
MIKHA MARAYA DRUB
SAM NGEN MARAYA CHING
JOR NGEN MARAYA NEN

Say this and send the effigy in the direction of the enemy.

Thanks to this practice, those who stand as enemies in front of you will quickly die or be defeated just as you want, of that there is no doubt.

I don't need to say too much, you'll see when you do this practice.
Don't tense up over details, it is easy to practice.
From awareness devoid of existence,
Unfolded these words devoid of nonexistence!

This practice is the special teaching of someone who understands interdependence well.

19. THE GREAT CLOUD

A Select Portion Offering for Prosperity and Abundance

Bless food, drink, mundane things, and the other offerings you have gathered. Offer them in your mind to the Great Lion Gesar and all the werma treasure guardians as follows:

OM AH HUM
A white cloud of nectar adorns the sky before me;
The wish-fulfilling jewel who satisfies all wants for
    prosperity and abundance,
Gesar, the great king of dralas,
Presides over Magyal Pomra and the wermas, guardians of
    treasures.

This gathering of offerings, all that one could ever need of
    food, drink, and wealth,
Is blessed and transformed into wisdom nectar, the source
    of all wants and needs—
This pure and sublime offering
I offer to you and your retinue, supreme being The Jewel!

You see clearly and distinctly the whole of phenomenal
    existence without exception.
Whether high or low or in between, you hold all beings
    with your love.
Like a wish-fulfilling jewel, you grant all our desires.
To the hosts of wermas, fulfillers of wishes, I offer praise!

Think of me with compassion, mighty lord of the dralas—
From the expanse of your infallible and steadfast jewel-like
  wisdom mind,
Rain down whatever I might desire of prosperity,
  abundance, food, and wealth,
And fill completely the chariot of my hopes and
  expectations!

Combine the recitation with offerings of tea and so on. Wherever you might be staying, whether at home or elsewhere, if you wish to obtain food or means through the auspicious connection of reciting this practice every day or on specific occasions, you will fasten your hands on the four treasures of longevity, excellent conditions, prosperity, and spirit of abundance. You will fulfill all your wishes and requirements, as there is good reason why these words have such power. I, who go by the name of Dhih, wrote this prayer spontaneously on the morning of the fourteenth day of the twelfth month of the Water Monkey year (1872). Mangalam.

20. Norbu Dradul's Heart Essence

AH

Your essence is Manjushri's vajra nature,
Yet you appear as the king who rules all the dralas of the
    universe.
In the past, the vidyadhara Padmasambhava,
Today, the great lion, Norbu Dradul Tsal,
In the future, Kalkin Rudra Chakrin,
Supreme deity of my heart, inseparable from me,
Indivisible from Vajrasarasvati and the four delightful
    consorts,
Accompanied by your contingent of mighty warriors,
    beautiful maidens, dralas, and wermas,
And the eight classes of haughty spirits of phenomenal
    existence who all obey your command,
I offer you wisdom nectar in clouds of outer, inner, and
    secret offerings—
With these supreme offerings that fulfill your wishes and
    restore samayas,
I supplicate you, I make offerings to you, I fulfill your
    wishes, I exalt you, I praise you, I reward you!

Armies of powerful dralas, bring forth the power of your
    compassion, might, strength, and ability!
Increase boundlessly my longevity, prosperity, and merit,
Good circumstances, renown, and windhorse!
Roar like thunder in the valley of the three planes of
    existence

And defeat resoundingly all my enemies and any adverse
circumstance!
Raise the inspiring and auspicious flag of victory in all
directions
On the summit of the three realms of existence!
Enthrone me in the center of the powerful wheel of activity,
Which holds the force of vajra wind, the magic that
accomplishes
Unimpededly whatever one desires just as it is wished,
And grant me the kingdom of the two accomplishments!

Dralas stirred my heart
With the roar of their eight laughters.
Then they said,
"Here is the thunder of universal victory
All enshrined in the bindu of bliss,
The DHI syllable of your heart."
Mangalam.

21. Inviting the Dralas Inside the Body

HUM HRIH

O wish-fulfilling jewel Gesar, embodiment of all three root
deities,

To behold your supreme wisdom body is a source of great
joy!

Remain happy and joyful on the milky lotus lake of my
heart

And transform my body into the impregnable fortress of the
dralas and wermas.

Irresistible, it ravishes the mind of whomsoever lays their
eyes upon me,

As it is endowed with the rarest qualities in the three
realms.

Its hundred thousand wondrous facets are a real nectar for
the eyes

And bring great satisfaction—a merriment of all manner of
appearances!

Let me swiftly accomplish the great majesty of vajra empty
bliss,

The source of the wondrous fortune of extraordinary
physical bliss,

And the glorious longevity and youthfulness of
indestructible wisdom!

Make me swiftly enhance the Buddha's teaching and the
welfare of beings,

And summon the vital essence of samsara and nirvana with
a profound might!
Let my extraordinary fame resound throughout the whole
world!
May my every intention be accomplished spontaneously
And the activities that bring me victory against every
adversity be performed!

This prayer was written by Seru Öden Karpo on the summit of Mount Senge Gingwa (Lion-Ready-to-Spring). Mangalam.

22. THE LOUD PEAL OF VAJRA LAUGHTER

A Practice to Entrust Gesar the Jewel with Activities

———

HUM

Supreme being, embodiment of all the three roots,
Ruler of the dralas, wish-fulfilling jewel,
Great Lion, whose power subdues all enemies,
The only guest in the lotus of my heart!

With unwavering faith, I serve you! With the purest
   samayas, I rely on you!
As I meditate on you in great nondual wisdom,
Remember to protect and care for me until enlightenment,
Look upon me with your wisdom eye! Unleash your power!

A beginner, suffering under a shroud of obscurations,
I confess my wrongdoing from the depth of my heart.
In you—who wields all power, hoists high the banners of
   victory,
And never disappoints—I place all my trust!

In this degenerate time, a thousand outer and inner
   misfortunes torment me.
I have no one else to turn to, and I long for you,
Like a child yearns for its mother;
Grant me your fatherly protection throughout the three
   times!

Even if all the beings of the three planes of existence rise
against me,
Make me victorious over my every foe and hoist high the
banner of my fame.
Place the precious jewels from the excellent vase of
immeasurable wealth
In the palms of my hands!

Raise me above humans—their universal monarch!
Raise me above animals, wielding the power of the lion!
May I be admired like the great sun
That outshines its competitors, the moon and all the stars!

May the glory of well-being and happiness forever fill the
whole of space,
May I accomplish omniscient wisdom,
And may the champion of the buddhas and bodhisattvas'
activities
Fulfill my every hope!

With a loud peal of laughter,
Accomplish all I wish for and envision, perfectly and
without obstacle!
Grant me Norbu Dradul's ultimate kaya, the self-arisen
primordial wisdom as vast as space,
Endowed with the brilliance of Gentle Splendor!

Jampal Dorje arranged this prayer on the eighth day of the fourth
month of the Fire Monkey year (1896) at Chime Chokdrup Ling.
Mangalam.

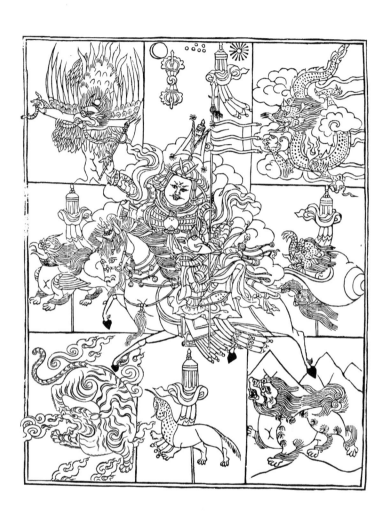

23. THE WINDHORSE FLAG IN NINE SECTIONS

The nine sections are as follows. The central part is yellow with a drawing of Gesar riding a horse. The four corners represent a garuda and a dragon in the two above, and a tiger and a lion in the two below. The four directions have drawings of white, red, green, and blue banners. The upper white banner has a five-pronged vajra next to it, and it is surrounded by the sun, the moon, and the stars on the right and left. The three other banners are associated with the combinations of lion and garuda, conch and makara, and fish and otter, on the right, the left, and below respectively.

A band of green cloth frames the prayer flag, inside the red line of the perimeter, the color of magnetizing activity.

Four streamers should be made with two pieces of cloth sewn together and be half the length of the flag—they are, from top to bottom, white, yellow, red, and green. At the top and the bottom of each streamer, write from the outside edge the windhorse mantra, and "Gather all, SARVA, gather, gather HOH!"[8] Add also a strip of cloth for each of the four activities on the streamer, according to the color of the streamer.

The nine-section grid is framed with four strips of cloth. On the upper part of the yellow belt that runs inside the green frame, write the Urna Jewel dharani.[9] Above, on the green frame, write the Vajra Guru mantra, the mantra for Avalokiteshvara as the Jewel of Windhorse[10] and the mantras of the other two protectors, mantras of Magön and so on, mantras of the eight classes of dharma protectors, Gesar's mantra, and "We place in their hands and entrust to the three jewels, the three roots and the dharmapalas, as well as the

Lotus-Born of Oddiyana and Gesar Norbu Dradul, this flag that raises the windhorse and makes our activities possible—now, draw the mu-cord!" On the green frame, on the side of the streamers, write this prayer to Gesar:

> EMAHO
> Essence of all the buddhas of the three times,
> Spontaneous Lotus-Born King of Oddiyana
> Taking the form of a drala, the supreme ornament of
> Jambudvipa,
> The great lion, King Gesar, we remember you from our
> hearts.
>
> Precious master of all siddhis,
> The glory of kindness and great bliss, eternal and pervasive,
> The sole lha of Tibet, Norbu Dradul,
> We respectfully supplicate you; please grant your blessings.
>
> In order to protect the teachings of the Victorious One, you
> manifest as king of the dralas,
> Displaying the supreme activity of the four ways of taming,
> Uniting with the secret consort of joy within bliss and
> emptiness.
> Bad circumstances, the maras and rakshasas of the four
> borders are liberated into space.
> You eternally show beings that their minds are dharmakaya.
> You open the gate of the inexhaustible jewel treasure of
> benefit and bliss.
> Undefiled, wish-fulfilling lha of life,
> Wish-fulfilling jewel, we supplicate you.
>
> Great warrior, who subdues the enemy, the hordes of Mara,
> By merely remembering you, opposing forces are destroyed.
> Subjugator, the great glorious one, possessing vajra power,
> Wrathful vidyadhara, we supplicate you.

Master of the lives of the vicious eight classes of arrogant
    demons,
Lord who commands phenomenal existence, dakinis, and
    dharmapalas,
Unerring protector, to whom we look with hope in this life
    and the next,
Dharmaraja of supreme bliss, we supplicate you.

Wisdom vajra body of all the buddhas,
Emissary of the buddha activity of the victorious ones of the
    three times,
Great vajra warrior, who grants whatever one desires
    without obstruction,
Supreme being who fulfills all purposes, we supplicate you.
In the jewel palace of supreme bliss, which fulfills one's
    wishes,
Please instantly establish all sentient beings
In the royal law of primordial indivisibility beyond meeting
    and parting
Of the kayas and wisdoms of the three root mudras.

Unequaled lord, embodiment of the three jewels and the
    three roots,
We supplicate you; please look upon us with eyes of
    kindness.
Be inseparable, of one taste with our hearts' essence.
Please grant your blessings; look on us with the mind of
    wisdom.

Please dispel outer, inner, and secret obstacles into space.
Having spontaneously accomplished all wishes without
    exception,
Until we attain enlightenment, protect us and grant your
    blessings.
Bestow the ordinary and supreme siddhis.[11]

Also draw the Kalachakra's "Powerful Ten Aspects" diagram on the green frame. At the bottom of the frame, write the heart-of-dependent-origination mantra. You can also write the prayer for raising windhorse and for the accomplishment of wishes that starts with the line, "The complete purity of all dharmas, the mind of Vajratikshna..."[12]

It is also good to add on the side nearest to the pole, behind the rider, drawings of a conch, a half vajra on lotus, and other symbols. You can also write the four lines that start with "Great warrior..."[13] on a white cloth sewn on the back of the flag, at the level of the rider.

Some people tie the flag to the pole with a green piece of cloth above and a red one below, but I think that is up to you.

Fix the final jewel of a victory banner at the top of the pole.

Dhih wrote this text on the eleventh day of the seventh month of the Water Tiger year (1902).

24. PRAYER TO GESAR*

HEH

Embodiment of the three families,
Through the compassionate light rays of Pema Tötreng, you
    arose as the splendor of the world—
Supreme being, Great Lion Norbu Dradul, to you we pray!
Grant us supreme and ordinary siddhis!

OM GURU MANI RADZA SIDDHI HUM

By Mipham, on the third day of the eleventh month of the Fire
Monkey year (1896).

*Translated by Adam Pearcey. Courtesy of Lotsawa House.

25. THE SWIFT FULFILLMENT OF WISHES

*A Brief Offering Prayer to King Gesar**

The offering prayer to King Gesar that swiftly fulfills wishes is as follows:

HUM
From out of all-pervading space, your compassion unwavering,
Great Lion, Lord Gesar,
You who embody all three roots, Jewel Who Subdues Foes,
Together with your assembly of protectors, dralas, and
    wermas,
Through the force of your compassionate pledge, come now
And accept these offerings of samaya substances, amrita,
    and torma;
Show us real signs of accomplishment,
And fulfill all our hopes and aspirations!
Grant us supreme and ordinary siddhis, we pray!
OM MAHA SINGHA MANI RADZA SAPARIWARA
    IDAM BALINGTA KHAHI

This prayer was composed during the ninth month of the Wood Monkey year (1884). There is nothing that cannot be accomplished by praying assiduously in this way. Blessings and accomplishment will follow thick and fast! Mangalam.

---

*Translated by Rigpa Translations. Courtesy of Lotsawa House.

26. GESAR'S PITH INSTRUCTION FOR WEALTH PRACTICE

Emanate rays of light that—like rain that nourishes ponds and plants, like butter that fuels a burning lamp, like a mirror struck by sunlight, like the moon free of clouds—increase the radiance of the universe and its inhabitants hundreds and thousands of times. Everything sparkles brightly with dazzling brilliant splendor. The universe becomes like a ripened fruit bursting with juice, completely filling the whole of space—as if it were too big for the space to hold. Then, like mercury that gathers without a speck of dust attaching to it, the entire quintessence of the universe and its inhabitants is collected and drawn into you like metal attracted by a magnet. Repeat the emanation of light and absorption of quintessential elixir many times over. This pith instruction is known as "the great cloud of jewels."

Also, consider that all the prosperity and abundance of the universe and its inhabitants is contained within the single tilaka of blazing five-colored light. Emanate rays of light that reach all the world systems as far as the farthest reaches of space, setting them ablaze with red and yellow light and melting them in blissful heat—CHI LI LI! At the same time, the natural self-resounding of your fame and renown echoes throughout the universe, as if the entire trichiliocosm was pulsing to the beat of a drum—WUR WUR TING TING—accompanied by the melodious sounds of thunder, cymbals, and other sounds in one great symphony—CHIL CHIL! The entire universe vibrates from every corner—SHIK SHIK YOM YOM! Think that every being within the universe is filled with intense physical pleasure and joy in their minds as they hear your name and contemplate your qualities; they dance in wild ecstatic frenzy as if completely drunk, and they are brought entirely under your power. This is the pith instruction for captivating the three worlds through intense pleasure and joy. Repeat the visualization many times over.

At the end, the whole universe and its inhabitants melt into light. The rainbow-colored lights, and all the brilliance and radiance are absorbed back into you and the practice articles. The light dissolves instantly into the indestructible bindu of your heart—rest in the equipoise of the vajra secret of suchness, the great original state of empty awareness, in which there is no change or dissipation. This is the vajra knot, the pith instruction to apply the seal of indestructibility.

These are Gesar's most profound pith instructions for wealth practice, and the quintessence of the dakinis' heart blood. Ithi. Seal.

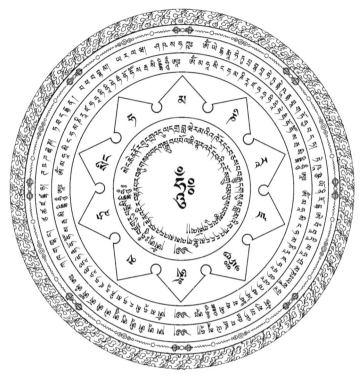

ༀ། །ཁ་བར་སྲོག་འཁོར་བཏགས་སོ།།

Gesar Life-Force Wheel

27. THE GESAR LIFE-FORCE WHEEL

Draw the syllable HUM at the center and, around it, the Vajra Guru mantra followed by: "For me, the practitioner who does not transgress your words and my samayas with you, Great Lion Jewel, Tamer of Enemies and your retinue of dralas and wermas, and the lamas of the three transmissions, please abide in this support and give me all accomplishments just as I want!"

On the ten surrounding spokes write: OM MA HA SING HA MA NI RA DZA HUM. Farther away from the center, on the ring that surrounds the ten spokes, write, beginning above the HUM, the ten-syllable mantra just mentioned followed by HA HAH HI HIH HE HEH HO HOH SARVA SIDDHI HUM AH.*

On the outer ring, write the vowel, consonant, and heart-of-dependent-origination mantras and the Supratishtha mantra. Around the outer ring, draw a vajra fence surrounded by mountains of fire.

Soak the diagram in amrita and saffron water. Draw a HUM syllable on a rock crystal with perfect natural shape and wrap it with the diagram in silks of different colors. If you wear it on you, the deities mentioned above will always be with you to help you just as if they were your shadow.

This instruction arose from Mipham's mind.

---

*You may repeat the sequence to fill the ring.

28. The Secret Practice of the Goddess

I am the Great Lion. I emanate lights that invite the chief dakini, Little White Vulture, in front of me. She has two hands, the right holding a noose made of sunrays, and the left a vase. She wears a gown of vulture feathers, and she rides a white vulture amidst her retinue of a hundred thousand dakinis. In her heart, on a moon, a syllable MAM appears with the mantra OM MAMA DAKINI GRIDHA BAKSHING SHITANI HARINISA PEM PEM DU DU DZA DZAH HUM HUM ABESHA A AH. The moment you burn a mix of mahamamsa and guggul as incense and recite the mantra, she will come. Offer her mahamamsa and a torma, and ask her to pledge to accomplish what you want. Samaya.

By Dhih. Mangalam.

Wangdu Gesar

29. KING GESAR: WANGDU PRACTICE

I am King Great Lion, brilliant red, full of bliss and desire, extremely handsome and blazing with a hundred beautiful expressions. My right hand forms the hook mudra, and the left pulls a garland of red lotuses toward me. I wear a brocade cloak and a head scarf of red silk and necklaces of red stones and pearls. I sit in the half-lotus posture in an expanse of red lights, surrounded by a host of magnetizing wermas and dakinis. In my heart, on a red lotus and a sun mandala, the red syllable HRIH is encircled by the syllables of the mantra. They emanate rays of light that summon the object of practice who is drawn, unable to resist.

OM MAHA SIDDHA MANI RADZA PADMA HASA BRAMO DAPARA HANA HANA [name of the object of practice] AKARSHAYA PASHAM KURU DZA DZAH

Reciting this mantra will quickly bring signs. With the mantra, bless a mixture of red salt, red langna flower, grape, and chang. If the object of practice eats or drinks them, touches them, or inhales the smoke when they are burned mixed with the smoke of other incense, they will throw any resistance to the wind and will surely come into your power. Samaya.

I wrote this practice in the evening of the nineteenth day of the tenth month of Parthiva, the Wood Bird year (1885).

30. WARRIOR SONG OF DRALA

*The Long Werma Lhasang**

KYE

LHA KI KI KI and SO SO SO!
Father Gesar the king, lha of war,
At the time when enemies fill the kingdom,
Lord Dradul, don't be idle, don't be idle.
I put my hope in no other protector but you.

A TSI TSI Your hosts of troops are awesome.
A LI LI They are youthful, wearing splendid accoutrements.
A YA YA The great men are very mighty.
The powerful father warriors are on the right.

The beautiful maidens, so lovely and perfumed,
Wherever you gaze at them, they are as if smiling.
Wherever I direct my mind, it goes to them.
The lovely mother warriors are on the left.

Above, the white clouds of the lha domain are brilliant.
In the middle, the stone houses of the human domain are
    dark and dignified.
Below, the mist of the lu domain rises and swirls.
Grasp the mu-cord and come here.

*This invocation for rousing confidence was translated by the Nalanda Trans-
lation Committee under the direction of Vidyadhara the Venerable Chögyam
Trungpa Rinpoche, June 14, 1979.

In the midst of this, O king, please take your seat of joy.
In this white country, the lha valley,
You are the lord of plentiful land and wealth—
King Gesar of Ling, fulfill this.

Hosts of clouds of cleansing amrita gather and gather.
Drums and melodious music of thunder reverberate.
Lakes of drink, white and sweet, abound.
Good fragrant incense billows.
Flags and banners flutter like flashing lightning.
With love and faith, mind yearns.
If a son does not rely on his father, on whom will he rely?
In the same way, a daughter must rely on her mother.
At this time, show the signs and marks.
Subdue the enemies of the eight directions.
Protect friends who are worthy of esteem.

Show your smiling face of deathless amrita.
O great White Light of A of the womb of space,
You soar on top of the great three worlds.
You play joyfully on a small seat of grass.

From within your mind of luminosity, look upon your
    child.
Please accept my offering of devotion.
From now onwards, until attaining the essence of
    enlightenment,
Be an unchanging protector and drala for me.
May your glorious mind and mine mix inseparably.
A LA LI LA LI LA MO LI

KYE
In the clear space of great emptiness,
Deities of the three roots, the nature of mercy and compassion,
Father Great Lion, on the troops of warriors

Bring down your blessings; be a protector and refuge.
By this cleansing sang offering of the tree of lha,
I offer up to the three jewels, the objects of refuge,
The lord gurus, yidams, and dakinis.

Lord Gesar of Jambudvipa,
He, at this time, is in the aspect of a general subjugating the
　　enemy.
With pennants on his helmet fluttering in the sky,
With swirling sparks of dharmapalas and protectors,
Pennants flapping with a cracking sound,
Mother dakinis dancing in concert,
His white helmet flashing forth rays of light,
Biting his lower lip in drala fashion, he menaces.
The lace of his armor of a hundred thousand flames is
　　impressive.
The armies of werma draw up in formation.
Their three weapons clasped at the waist shimmer.
The whistle of the blood drinkers shrills.
Horses gallop and canter, racing along.
The kadös march in formation.

If there is a warrior drala, it is Gesar.
If there is a werma, it is Gesar.
If there is a guru for the next life, it is Gesar.
If there is a leader for this life, it is Gesar.
Outwardly, he is the mighty general Norbu Dradul.
Inwardly, he is Avalokiteshvara.
His unchanging mind is Lord Padmasambhava.
I offer and praise the deities; may their wishes be fulfilled.

For me, your child, steadfast in samaya,
Today be refuge, protector, and helper.
Fulfill my wishes in accordance with dharma.
Now, on this very day,

Fulfill my aspiration.

May I be able to take the heart and lungs of my vindictive
enemies
And accomplish many good victories.
Leader of Jambudvipa, don't be idle, don't be idle.
A LA LA CHA CHA HE HE HO

His skillful chestnut steed
Outwardly manifests as a horse.
Inwardly, he arises as the mind of enlightenment.
He is the emanation of Hayagriva.
He is elegant, with a rainbow swirling about.
He has the treasure of the gait of swift wind
And the strength of the wings of birds.
He possesses the glorious strength of a snow lion.
His vajra mane flowing right and left
Magnetizes the dralas of White Conch Garuda.
The vulture down on the points of his ears
Magnetizes spies of luminous torches.
His forelegs of wheels of wind
Magnetize the dralas of lord of life.
The four hooves of the steed
Magnetize the dralas of swift wind.
On the tip of each hair, lhas reside.

If you do not protect me, your child, who will you protect?
Accept this purification and warrior drink; increase your
power of swiftness.
Miraculously lead me to the place that I desire.
Accomplish my desires.
Arouse the activity of windhorse.
O horse, PU PU SO SO CHA CHA, increase!

The minister is the leader of the activity of Great Lion.
He is the guide of arrows.
He is the renowned turquoise dragon in the sky.
He is the lha victorious in all directions.
He is the unassailable power of the vajra thunderbolt.
He is the general Denma Changtra.
He rides the steed Ngul Truk Dempa.
In his right hand he brandishes an arrow.
In his left he brandishes a bow.
He performs a vajra dance.
With troops of werma in formation,
He completely devastates the life of the vindictive enemies.
He cherishes dearly the child who holds samaya.
I offer to Denma, who brings long life into our home.
I offer to Denma, who provides a good journey while
    traveling.
I offer to Denma, who accomplishes purposes in commerce.
I offer to Denma, who is the good raider in disputes.
I offer to Denma, who is auspicious in everything.
I offer to Denma, who accomplishes whatever mind desires.
Be affectionate to this longing child.
Your arrow pierces the heart and lungs of the vindictive
    enemies.
I offer their heart's blood, which quenches the thirst of the
    wermas.

Accept my offering, King Great Lion.
Accept my offering, Minister Denma.
Arrange together the pennants of the king and minister.
Be not small in power against the vindictive enemies.
Be not weak in strength against the evil obstructing spirits.
Accept my offering, order of warriors.
Accept my offering, host of wermas.
Accept my offering, fierce assembly.

Don't be idle, don't be idle; perform these activities.
Bury the evil enemies upside down.
Glorify the good friends.
Proclaim fame like thunder throughout the kingdom.
Hold up the banner that is victorious in all directions.
It is time to hoist the drala banner.
It is time to sound the trumpet of werma.
Don't be idle, don't be idle, warrior of Ling.
Show the signs and marks right now.
Accomplish whatever mind desires
And grant me the supreme and ordinary siddhis.
E A TI MI BU LHA GYAL LO

In my heart there are many jewel treasures of supreme mind,
    profound and vast.
In the milk ocean of speech
Is this poetry, beautiful as a lovely garden of kumuda flowers.
This was not deliberately made pleasing to the ear and arranged
    properly.
It is the precious warrior song of werma,
Fully possessing thousands of blessings and great splendor.
In that way, these vajra words were composed.
This is the thunder that pleases the dralas and wermas.

Thus, on the twenty-fourth day of the third month of the Fire
Ox year (1877), this was spontaneously composed by lamplight.
Mangalam.

31. Spontaneous Success

Invocation to the Great Lion, Norbu Dradul, and Ritual to

Restore Harmony with the Father-Gods

KYE

In the self-appearing pure buddha field,

In the tent of the deep-blue sky,

In the celestial Awe-Inspiring Land of Ling,

In the expanse of the thick, rainbow-light clouds of Ma's
abundance,

In the Jewel Palace of supreme bliss,

The highest being who presides over all great beings,

The owner of the life force of the haughty spirits of
phenomenal existence,

The master of the vital essence of the dralas' and wermas'
hearts,

Who manifests as various, unstoppable jewels,

The deity victorious over all adversities,

All-Accomplishing White Werma,

Known in Tibet as Sengchen Norbu,

In China as Guan Loyen,

In Zhang Zhung as Drala Chenpo,

Is surrounded by a hundred thousand million of war gods—

All of you, come with your retinues,

KI SO CHA HE—we call you!

The nine eminent drala brothers,

The thirteen drala protectors,

The three drala brothers endowed with great power,

The thirteen changsengs expert in covering long distances,
and so on—
All the dralas and wermas who appear
In wisdom, activity, and worldly ways;
Some emanate as your display,
Some are integrated in your body,
But all are based on you.
You who are the mighty fortress of the dralas,
Thinking of you increases strength, power, and
resourcefulness!
May our hopes be fulfilled through the power
Of our unswerving faith and samayas
That make the inspiring victory banner of our forces heard
far and wide!
Reliable friends, long-serving protectors,
Father-gods, shoulder-gods, dralas,
I rely on you! I make offerings to you! Show your power!
I exalt you! I honor and praise you! May your wishes be
fulfilled!
I offer you the fermented nectar, the drink of the warriors!
I offer you all manner of banners and scarfs, tribute to your
valor!
I sing your praises to the tune of formidably intimidating
music!
I offer you clouds of sang and offerings of warriors' wealth!

Dralas of the Buddhadharma,[14]
And dralas of worldly existence,
Today, come to stay in these supports and remain steadfast!
Today I restore harmony with the father-gods!
Today I confess breakages of samaya!
Today I chant praises of the gods!
Today, give us victory over the maras!
Father-gods, come straight here!
Dralas, create no trouble, stir up no resentment!

Protect and guard us yogins and the people around us
Until enlightenment!
Accomplish spontaneously what we envision,
Indivisible in great self-arisen primordial wisdom!

KYE
When you soar in the realm of the firmament
Mounted on the turquoise dragon,
And taking the planets and the stars with you,
You seize the thick southern cloud, the source of wealth,[15]
Right from under the gaze of the sun and the moon.
Your breath gathers in billowing mists and clouds,
And you explode with the laughter of the dragon's roar.
In your right hand you hold a white banner,
And in the left a noose of lightning.
Powerful master of the three realms of existence,
Who enslaved into your service the eight classes of haughty
    spirits—
Enjoy this sang offering and the drink offering of nectar!

Gather at our call of KI! Rejoice at our SO!
Uphold the teachings of the Buddha,
Spread the fame of the fortunate ones with the right karma
Endowed with merit to the far reaches of space!

I make offerings to you, Akar Werma!
Owner of the inspiring, auspicious windhorse flags,
Great king of the wermas who subdues the maras,
Supreme being Gesar the Jewel, I make offerings to you!
I make offerings to you! I praise you, O most powerful one!

Fiercely powerful father-gods,
Show the power of your might, strength, and resourcefulness,
And do so for us, the practitioners who abide by the
    samayas.

Hoist our windhorse flags high in the sky,
Draw up the mu-cord of longevity,
Make the thunder of our extraordinary fame
As a peerless mighty lord,
Roar on the summit of the three realms!
Make all of phenomenal existence our servant!

Dralas of the Buddhadharma,
And dralas of worldly existence,
Today, come to stay in these supports and remain steadfast!
Today I restore harmony with the father-gods!
Today I confess breakages of samaya!
Today I chant praises of the gods!
Today, give us victory over the maras!
Father-gods, come straight here!
Dralas, create no trouble, stir up no resentment!
Protect and guard us yogins and the people around us
Until enlightenment!
Accomplish spontaneously what we envision,
Indivisible in great self-arisen primordial wisdom!

SO!
When you glide through the midair realm,
On the back of the magical chestnut steed of many skills
Garbed in the complete regalia of the dralas,
Together with the tiger, lion, garuda, and dragon, who move
    with dazzling splendor,
The eight classes of haughty spirits who mass in thick clouds,
And the dralas and wermas darting swift as lightning—
Delight in battle, rejoice in war!
You who are so powerful, conquer the hordes of enemies!

I make offerings to you, mighty Norbu Dradul,
Great being, King Great Lion, I make offerings to you!
I offer to you! I rely upon you, deity of my heart!

Fiercely powerful shoulder-gods, carry out our wishes,
Yogins, holders of awareness.
Hoist the inspiring flags of our windhorse!
Vanquish the armies of enemies who come up against us!
Level up all unevenness!
Make us stand out from our equals!
Make us victorious over every adversity
By giving us success in every beneficial circumstance,
And subdue those in positions of power!

Dralas of the Buddhadharma,
And dralas of worldly existence,
Today, come to stay in these supports and remain steadfast!
Today I restore harmony with the father-gods!
Today I confess breakages of samaya!
Today I chant praises of the gods!
Today, give us victory over the maras!
Father-gods, come straight here!
Dralas, create no trouble, stir up no resentment!
Protect and guard us yogins and the people around us
Until enlightenment!
Accomplish spontaneously what we envision,
Indivisible in great self-arisen primordial wisdom!

HE
When you range over the expanse of the earth,
You fan the flames of the destructive fire of the end of
    times,
And raise in your hands an iron bow and arrow
With which you pierce the life source of demonic enemies!

You who gather around you the eight classes of dharma
    protectors as your servants,
Fill the three planes of existence with your armies of
    emanations,

Each and every one raging with a terrifying wrath and fury!
KI SO CHA DRA DI RI RI!

Eat the flesh of our enemies! Drink their blood!
Devour their flesh and kill with dexterity!
To the forces that fall on the life force of samaya breakers,
I make offerings! I rely upon you, you who are so powerful!
For us who keep samaya, be our drala!
Spot in every cardinal and intermediary direction, above
   and below—in every corner—
Enemies and obstructing forces who have
Negative intentions toward us or try to harm us!
Bring them in front of you instantly!
Cut out the tongues of those who speak ill of us!
Rip out the heart of those who harbor evil intentions!
Sever the hands of those who prepare evil actions!
Gouge out the eyes of those who see us negatively!
Decapitate those who show us an ugly face!
Bring down the windhorse of protestors and critics!
Destroy their plans and change their minds!
Completely eradicate enemies and obstructing forces!

For us yogins, holders of awareness,
Remedy all obstacles to goodness and joy.
Let us never be apart from them,
Make them inseparable from us, like shadow and body!
Teach us what we don't know, summon our memory of all
   we have forgotten!
Vanquish those who want to compete with us—
Raise our triumph as high as the vajra top of the victory
   banner!
Plant the poles of the immutable windhorse flags
Of magnetizing and subjugating activities!
From the lotus grove in the heavens,
From the crowds of flying vidyadharas and siddhas,

And from the assemblies of those in positions of power
Extract the essence of strength, wealth, abundance, and
   prosperity!

In this auspicious Jewel Palace,
The dralas and wermas' castle,
Like a rain falling from above,
Like clouds gathering in the middle,
And like mist assembling on the ground,
Gather the vital essence of the abundance of Ma!

Kings, ministers, queens, subjects, Buddhist and Bönpo priests,
Servants, women, goddesses, and naginis
Who dwell above, below, and in all cardinal and
   intermediary directions—
Magnetize all beings of appearance and existence,
And make them our servants!

May the strong wind of the wermas
Carry to the far reaches of earth and space
Clouds pregnant with the sweet scent of our fame—
Make them pervade everywhere, and quickly!

Armies of dralas, manifestations
Of the single bindu of our own mind and of great equality,
Herukas of ultimate fruition—
Please appear and liberate beings!

On the sixth day of the ninth month of the Wood Pig year (1875).

———————

Place on the shrine the practice supports such as the ribboned
arrow and so on. Prepare offerings and a large sang. At the right
points in the practice, add:

Dralas of the Buddhadharma
And dralas of worldly existence,
Today, come to stay in these supports and remain steadfast!
Today I restore harmony with the father-gods!
Today I confess breakages of samaya!
Today I chant praises of the gods!
Today, give us victory over the maras!
Father-gods, come straight here!
Dralas, create no trouble, stir up no resentment!
Protect and guard us yogins and the people around us
Until enlightenment!
Accomplish spontaneously what we envision,
Indivisible, in great self-arisen primordial wisdom!

This extra prayer is to restore harmony with the father-gods. Practice it on an auspicious date. I remembered it on the twenty-fifth day of the fourth month of the Fire Monkey year (1896).

32. Prayer to Raise the Windhorse

Should you wish to raise your lungta, place a consecrated image of the king of dralas, Gesar, in front of you; raise windhorse flags in the sky and beautifully arrange offerings (chemar, sang, serkyem, and so on) in front of him. Then say:

HUM
The great play of appearance and emptiness
Unfolds in the display of Padma and the three families.
In the tent of the deep-blue sky,
The Jewel Palace of supreme bliss appears,
Where the mighty king of dralas,
Gesar Norbu Dradul Tsal resides,
Surrounded by mara-taming dralas and wermas
And all haughty spirits of the eight classes.

With faith and pure samaya
We make offerings to you and invoke your sacred pledge—
KI SO CHA'O, armies of dralas!
Move like a fearsome golden cloud!
Forces of wermas, do not forget your sacred vows!
We make offerings to you! We praise you! We pay homage
  to you!
Our multicolored banners move like lightning
Amidst the thundering clamor of drums, shawms, and
  cymbals, like the roar of a dragon!
All kinds of offerings are piled up like huge clouds—
With this nectar of primordial wisdom
Whose nature is great purity and equality,

I invoke the dralas and wermas and make offerings to you!
I exalt you! I honor and praise you! I offer you the drink of
warriors!

Raise for us yogins the victory banner of might
And marshal the power of the dralas' and wermas' sacred
pledge!
Accomplish your activities conspicuously!
Plant on the summit of the three realms of existence
The flagpole of the windhorse
Whose marvelous thundering sound
Roars with peerless might!
The supreme banner of victory over all adversity
Flies above the whole world!
Place in my hands
The wish-fulfilling jewel that beautifully adorns its crown!
Increase my power, strength, and capacity,
My majesty, grandeur, and dominance,
And the power to overcome enemies, obstructing forces,
evil intentions, and harmful actions,
Incinerating them like flies in the apocalyptic fire of the end
of times!
Swiftly bring to me,
Like rivers flowing into the ocean,
The strength of the armies of dralas and wermas
Who are as powerful as an intense blaze of vajra fire fanned
by wind!

If you want to ride toward the upper reaches of the sky of worldly
existence
On the back of the stallion Excellent Wind of Activities,
Plant posts of Sengchen Dorje's prayer flag
And take in your hands the wish-fulfilling jewel, the "king of
power."
If you do that, you will definitely see

Very clear signs and indications of the auspicious increase in the
    strength of your windhorse
In actuality, visions, or dreams,
And you'll hear the symphony of a hundred thousand praises of
    your virtuous qualities.
Samaya!

I wrote this supplication at the excellent time of the twenty-fifth
day of the sixth month of the Wood Dog year (1874). Virtue.

33. Sang Offering to the Dralas and Wermas

KYE

Clouds of smoke from aromatic woods,
Endowed with magnificent color, smell, and potency,
An ambrosia of primordial wisdom by nature,
I offer to the three Puwer brothers and their sisters,

The prescient Chau Yangkar,
The five great deities of Yungdrung and so on,
The factions of the three hundred and sixty dunglhas,
The armies of wermas in space, in the sky, and on the earth,

The wisdom, activity, and worldly
Divination deities and gods of the four knowledges and
    eight sights—
This cleansing sang offering is for all of you without
    exception!
Purify my veils, obscurations, and denseness within basic
    space!

Make the sun of clairvoyance shine brightly!
Grant me the siddhi of magical foreknowledge
That sees the three times without hindrance!
Wherever I go, wherever I stay, act as my drala.

Guide me on excellent and auspicious paths!
Stay as my drala, the one who arranges the interdependence

To manifest all the great things I want!
Accomplish all the activities I entrust to you!

Mipham wrote this sang offering at the place where the nine heads of Walse—one of the five great deities of Yungdrung Bön—show satisfied faces, in a perfect arrangement of virtuous place and time according to the excellent Chashen path of interdependence, when doing practice to increase abundance for the householder Kyalo. Virtue!

34. SWIFT ACCOMPLISHMENT OF ENLIGHTENED ACTIVITY

*An Offering to Great Lion Gesar Norbu**

Arrange tea, liquor, balim, and so forth. Having consecrated them, recite:

HUM HRIH
Within the land of terrifying rakshasas, on the Glorious
   Mountain,
Is the buddha field of the victorious ones of the three kayas,
   Lotus Light,
A wrathful realm of dark-red, roaring flames.
Inwardly, it is the home of the chitta-heart of the vajra body.
Within this palace of vidyadharas, viras, and dakinis
Is the equality of existence and peace, the wisdom vajrakaya,
Embodiment of infinite victorious ones, the Lake-Born Lord,
Along with emanations of compassion, forms of illusory play,
A host of male and female yogins and siddhas.
In order to grant your blessings to your devoted children,
You descend through the sky in the vajra dance of yogic
   discipline
And arise in the form of Mara-Taming Drala Werma.

Great vidyadhara, Powerful Supreme Ornament of
   Jambudvipa,
Masterfully wielding the sword of prajna and bow and arrow,

*Translated by the Vajravairochana Translation Committee.

Great powerful one, you conquer all possible enemies.
Great being, Great Lion Norbu, with your retinue and
　army,
All of you without exception,
Proclaim like thunder the KI and SO of the warrior
And raise to the sky the banner of the renowned virtuous
　mark.
Riding vajra steeds in a stomping dance,
You shatter the life essence of obstructing samaya demons.

From billowing clouds of blessings, you bring down a
　continuous rain of siddhi.
When we fortunate ones offer to you and honor you,
Come here by the power of your unobstructed compassion.
Accept this select offering of the warrior's drink of amrita.
Accept this nutritious and delicious torma offering.
Accept this argham offering of blood and intoxicating
　liquor.
Accept this fragrant smoke offering of luminosity.
Accept this offering of colorful banners and music.
Accept this secret offering of the experience of
　bliss-emptiness.
Accept this thread-cross offering of the phenomenal world
　arising as the primordial ground.
Accept this wisdom offering of the equality of all.

Precious Great Lion, consider us with compassion.
Emanation of the three families, don't forget your vow!
From now until enlightenment, remain inseparable from us,
Protect us, bless us, and accomplish our activities.

You have the nature of supreme compassion,
Always wielding the great weapon of great kindness.
Supreme in taming the hordes of maras,
Dispel all our fears of the four maras.

Drawing from the space of realization of supreme wisdom,
Bring down great blessings to the hearts of us fortunate ones.
Infuse our nadi, prana, and awareness-bindu with wisdom,
And transform whatever we do into the path of bodhi.

You majestically blaze with the wrathful mantra that tames
maras.
So that we may transform the interests and perceptions of
all beings into dharma,
Please bestow the siddhis of ability, strength, power,
And the mastery of the enlightened activities of destroying
and nurturing.

In the secret treasury of the glorious knot of eternity in the
heart center,
Open the gates to the treasure of jewels of perfect recall,
confidence, and intelligence.
With enlightened activity that benefits others as vast as space,
Please help us accomplish the two benefits just as we wish.

With bodhichitta and the conduct of Samantabhadra,
We abide in the supreme, profound vajrayana.
Greatly increase the clear realization of the bhumis and paths,
And quickly grant us the power of the completely liberated
victorious ones.

On the twenty-fourth day of the sixth month of the Iron Dragon
year (1880), Mipham wrote down whatever arose. May there be
virtue.

35. Brief Offering Prayer to King Gesar*

HUM HUM

From out of all-pervading space, your compassion
    unwavering,
Great Lion, Lord Gesar,
You who embody all three roots, Jewel Who Subdues Foes,
Together with your assembly of protectors, dralas, and
    wermas,
Through the force of your compassionate pledge, come now
And accept these offerings of samaya substances, amrita,
    and torma;
Show us real signs of accomplishment
And fulfill all our hopes and aspirations!
Grant us supreme and ordinary siddhis, we pray!

OM MAHA SINGHA MANI RADZA SAPARIWARA
IDAM BALINGTA KHAHI

Written by the one named Dhih.[16]

*Translated by Rigpa Translations. Courtesy of Lotsawa House.

36. Spontaneous Accomplishment of Wishes

*A Daily Offering to Gesar, King of Dralas**

OM AH HUM

We supplicate and offer to you, the embodiment of
the three roots, Great Lion Norbu Dradul, sovereign of mara-taming action, messenger of all yogins,
life pillar of all vidyadharas, great drala of all beings,
together with father, mother, and children retinues:
Elder Brother Bumpa Shelkar with the thirty brothers;
Glorious Chief of Dakinis with the eighteen dignified
ladies; hosts of armies of lha, nyen, and lu; allied troops
of dralas and wermas; and prideful ones of the phenomenal world who abide in the command. With this select
offering of samaya substances and vast offerings, both
real and imagined, we offer to you. We praise you. We
honor you.

From now until we attain the essence of enlightenment, may you be the father-god and drala for us yogins.
Be a protector, refuge, and army of allies. Protect us
from all types of harmful diseases, döns, and obstacles.
Increase and enrich all our desired goals of life, merit,
wealth, dominion, renown, majesty, confidence, and
family lineage. Magnetize whatever we wish for: gods,
spirits, and humans, as well as food, wealth, and enjoyments. Annihilate all the enemies and obstructing

*Translated by the Vajravairochana Translation Committee.

spirits who have evil thoughts and deeds that cause harm. May we quickly perfect the good qualities of the bhumis and paths, and attain unsurpassable enlightenment. May the power of the bodies of the ocean of dralas and wermas enter us. Bestow all the siddhis of complete victory in all directions.

At the behest of the royal son Jampal Dorje, this was written by Mipham Nampar Gyalwa on the slopes of Pal Lhundrup (Glorious Spontaneous Accomplishment), on the thirteenth day of the waxing moon of the first month of the Wood Sheep year (1895) of the fifteenth sixty-year cycle. Through this may the glory of the dharma king be supremely exalted, and may the benefit of the teachings and beings be spontaneously accomplished. Mangalam.

37. Sollo Chenmo[17]

The Swift Accomplishment of Enlightened Activity
*through Invocation and Offering**

Homage to the Glorious Heruka!

At any time of momentous significance—a life-or-death struggle, where a great prize is at stake, or something crucial could be achieved—focus on this important and urgent event[†] and gather as many offerings of serkyem (golden drink), first-portion offerings, tormas, multicolored pieces of silk, and so on as you can afford. Then concentrate strongly and invoke the dralas. If you do this, that you might fail or be cheated in your endeavor is impossible. Moreover, samaya commitments will be restored, and empowerments and siddhis will be obtained.

Hold up the drink and first-portion offering, and together with music at the appropriate intervals, recite the following:

> HO! Turn your attention towards us!
> HO! Turn your attention towards us!
> HO! Turn your attention towards us!
> From the unborn nature, the sphere of reality,
> The dynamic energy of compassion manifests in a ceaseless
>   display,

---

*Translated by Adam Pearcey with the kind assistance of Alak Zenkar Rinpoche, and edited by Ian Maxwell, 2003. Revised 2007, 2008, and 2021 with special thanks to Orgyen Tobgyal Rinpoche and Patrick Gaffney.
†*Sollo Chenmo* should only be recited on important occasions and not too frequently, because it is very powerful. (Alak Zenkar Rinpoche)

The victorious and powerful Guru Tsokye Dorje, the three
    families and the magical display of peaceful and wrathful
    deities, all gathered into a single form—
Great being Gesar, Vidyadhara Norbu Dradul—
You are the embodiment of all the buddhas
And all-pervading master of the peaceful and wrathful
    yidam deities,
Lord of all the gatherings of mamos and dakinis,
Chief of all the dharmapalas and guardians,
Heart-treasure of the ocean-like wealth deities,
King of all the dralas,
Vital heart of all the wermas,
Sovereign over all the eight classes,
Master of life for all the arrogant spirits,
Aid to all positive forces,
Drala for all that lives,
Glorious protector of all sentient beings,
Life pillar for all vidyadharas,
Support of Buddhist and Bönpo alike,
Mighty lord of activity, subduer of demons,
Vanquisher of all negative forces,
Stealer of the lives of all samaya breakers,
Great slayer of all maras and rakshasas,
Your body moves in a pleasing dance, subjugating the three
    planes of existence,
Your speech resounds with an awesome thunder,
    magnetizing the three realms,
Your mind generates the mandala of wisdom and love from
    the expanse of luminosity.
The mere thought of you brings cloudlike blessings and
    accomplishments.
Riding your vajra steed, wild and skillful, you move through
    the air.
You gather in KI and you delight in SO.
You are mighty in punishment and respect the dharma.

Your right hand holds the wish-granting cane, which brings
down a rain of gems and all that beings wish for and
require,
The spear in your left hand subdues all enemies throughout
the three realms and bears the flag of the dralas.
Your body is clad in full drala costume.
Emanating clouds of dralas and wermas,
You are surrounded by a retinue of virtuous dharma
protectors,
The glorious protectors of the pure abodes,
Your entire retinue of dralas and wermas
And all the great armies of tukkars and changses.
Although the clear light of your wisdom mind is free from
any trace of conceptualization,
Through the force of dependent origination and the
compassionate aspirations you have made, you determine
good and bad, and keep watch over the teachings.
You delight in all that is finest in this world, and journey
through peoples' lands.
You look after practitioners who keep the samaya, like a
parent caring for his children, and bring the longevity
and abundance of the dralas.
You reduce samaya breakers to misery and ferociously
consume their hearts.
You gather when offerings are made and support us when
practice is done.
You are swift when dispatched, and your might is unrivaled.
You never ignore those who depend on you.
You never turn away from the tasks entrusted to you.
You bring good fortune and are warmhearted.
Your blessings are great and your powers swift.
Your actions are positive and enduringly powerful.
You guide beings from happiness to happiness and to the
sanctuary of supreme enlightenment.

Great treasury of the two kinds of siddhi, Great Lion
  Norbu Dradul, we invoke you!
We invoke the great warrior spirit of the buddhadharma!
We invoke the vidyadhara and supreme ornament of this
  world!
We invoke the bearer of the sword of wisdom and the bow
  and arrow!
We invoke the one who averts battles and knows no
  afflictions!
We invoke the one who defeats hordes of brave enemy
  demons!
We invoke the one who dispels any fear of the four maras!
From now until we attain the essence of enlightenment,
With the great victory banner of faith and unchanging
  trust,
We rely on you, Great Lion-Like King of the Dharmapalas,
  as our wish-granting jewel.
On the ground of unchanging samaya,
We rely on you, Great Lion-like King of the Dralas, as our
  great cosmic mountain.
In the sky of pure approach and accomplishment,
We rely on you, Great Lion-like King of the Wermas, as our
  sun and moon.
There can be no error as to which dharma protector should
  be relied upon,
No mistaking the proper object of faith,
And no confusion about the offering deity.
Great Lion Wish-Fulfilling Jewel, together with your
  retinue—the armies of wisdom dralas and wermas,
Always remember the great vajra samaya free from uniting
  or separation,
And look upon us, your face lit up with joy!
Protect us, your eyes sparkling as you smile!
Reveal hidden meanings to us, your voice filled with
  laughter!

All of us, the master and the retinue of students, request
you: with a heart of joy, take charge of our environment,
our bodies, and our possessions!
Show us the actual signs of accomplishment!
Carry out the activities we request of you, just as we wish!
Be successful in the actions you have pledged to undertake!
Ensure that all the actions of our body, speech, and mind
remain virtuous and auspicious!
Cause our meditative experiences and realization to
increase!
Cause our wisdom and positive qualities to grow!
Grant us vast siddhis of long life, merit, glory, wealth, fame,
and good fortune, here and now!
Reveal to us the secret of awareness, the meaning of
intrinsic reality!
Empower us with your blessings and with primordial
wisdom!
Make whatever we do an expression of the dharma!
Make all our relationships and associations meaningful!
Let us accomplish, effortlessly and spontaneously, all
supreme and ordinary siddhis without exception!

i. Peaceful

HO! Great king of the dralas, at times you appear peaceful
with a bright complexion,
Your happy face shining in contentment like the moon,
Dancing with joy amidst clouds of all that is desirable.
The sight of you captivates our minds,
The thought of you increases our life span,
Through your practice, our splendor grows,
Master of deathlessness and longevity,
You bring down showers of amrita—the nectar of
immortality.

Great deliverer of abundance, you cause happiness, well-
being, and renown to increase.
Source of all that is auspicious,
You are the basis for all good fortune,
The support for all positive qualities,
The great embodiment of all that is glorious and magnificent,
A jewel to dispel poverty,
An elixir to overcome disease,
The great sound of victory from the battle drum of the gods
bringing new life to the weary.
King of indestructible vitality, good fortune and enjoyment,
together with your awesome armies of dralas and wermas,
we invoke you!
Your body of pure luminosity appears once again
In a tent of rainbow clouds in space,
With the youthful complexion of a sixteen-year-old,
Radiant and white, pure as crystal.
In your right hand, you hold a jeweled torch
To light up the three realms.
In your left hand, you hold a mirror of white silver
To reveal the three planes of existence.
You dance the dance of the viras of the male line,
And sing the songs of the dakinis of the female line.
Master of the divining mirror of clear appearance,
King of the all-illuminating wermas,
You reside in the castle of magical creation
And apply your powers of divination,
Revealing the good and the bad in apparent existence.
Great master of the four knowledges and eight visions,
You hold aloft the magical torch of wisdom,
Its flames of insight burning brightly.
You unlock the secret gateway to awareness and higher
perception
And bestow the great treasures of a clear and brilliant mind.
Magical king, Great Lion, radiant Akar Ökyi Werma,

together with the armies of all-illuminating dralas and
wermas, we invoke you!

An ocean of the three whites and three sweets,
Silk ribbons and banners that flutter in the wind,
The thundering sound of beating drums, melodious
chanting, and tuneful music,
Offering clouds containing all kinds of pleasant substances,
Food offerings and chemar piled as high as mountains,
Flowers and billowing clouds of fragrant incense smoke,
Fresh drinking water and streams to bathe the feet,
Orbs of light reflected in clear bright mirrors,
Sweet-smelling perfumes and rivers of nectar, and more
besides—
With these vast outer, inner, and secret offerings, both real
and imagined,
Great being Gesar Norbu, king of the dralas, Akar Ökyi
Werma, together with your retinue,
We make offerings to you!
We exalt you!
We honor and praise you!
We fulfill your noble wishes!
We offer the drink of warriors!
And confess our breakages of samaya!
We inspire great joy!
We invoke your solemn pledge!
For us vidyadhara yogins, dispel all misfortune and
adversity—illness, harmful influences, obstacles and
inauspiciousness—just like the sun banishing darkness!
When enemies arise, arouse us to action!
When poison appears, send us the antidote!
Show us the way through uncharted rocky terrain!
Build us bridges across unfordable rivers!
Convey us to the good and across mountain passes!
Deliver us from the bad and from remote valleys!
Avert scandal and malicious gossip!

Prevent adverse circumstances and obstacles!
Uplift us when we are low!
Prompt us when we forget!
Create mountains to flee to!
Make us forests to hide in!
Build secure fortresses to rely upon!
Fashion impenetrable armor!
And forge piercing weapons!
Teach us all that remains unknown!
Reveal all that is unseen!
Guard us during the day!
And watch over us at night!
Provide us with assistance at home!
And make us welcome abroad!
Open the gateways to insight and wisdom!
Reveal to our minds the signs of future dependent arising!
Make our self-assurance as vast as space!
Cause our strength and power to expand like the firestorm
at the end of an eon!
Sound the music of happiness, well-being, and renown!
Open the treasury of inexhaustible glorious qualities!
Illuminate the sun of our perceptions by day!
Make bright the moon of our dreams by night!
Inflame the light rays of experience in the interim!
Show us clearly the three planes of existence!
Vividly describe for us the three realms!
Show us nakedly all that is positive and negative in the three
worlds!
Bring all our hopes and aspirations to fruition!

ii. Enriching

HO! At times, you appear resplendent and content,
In your great palace that gathers the glorious qualities of
existence and peace,

In the form of the "king who transforms apparent existence
 into all that is desirable."
In your right hand you hold the "king of wish-fulfilling
 power,"
And in your left hand, the vase of inexhaustible treasure.
You revel in the pleasure grove of wish-granting trees,
Master of wish-fulfilling treasures,
King of precious gems,
Holder of the wealth of China and Tibet,
And hook to gather food and riches.
In space, you collect the prosperity of the gods as clouds of
 nectar;
In the sky, you draw in the prosperity of human beings as a
 mist of positive signs;
On the ground, you gather the prosperity of the nagas as the
 creamy ocean of the mu;
And let fall the prosperity of Ma as a rain of all that is
 desirable.
Great banner of renown,
Conveyor of a hundred thunderclaps of fame,
Master of the vital essence of existence and peace,
Basis of abundance, prosperity, and enjoyments,
Symphony of assorted wishes and desires,
The sight of you captivates our minds,
Your beauty increases our prosperity,
You take victory for all who are good
And journey at the crowns of all who are great.[*]
Magnificent turner of the wheel of activity, completely
 victorious over all,
You raise the standards of spiritual and secular authority
 higher than the very sky

---

[*]That is, you command respect everywhere, even from the great and important.
(Alak Zenkar Rinpoche)

And extend the range of our dominion beyond the limits of
    space—
To the Great Lion, Wish-Fulfilling Jewel, together with
    your armies of treasure-keeping dralas and wermas,
Mountains of food,
Oceans of drink,
Dances of seductive form,
Sweet music with a hundred melodies,
Clouds of fragrant incense,
Sumptuous banquets of delicious fare,
Festivals that inspire feelings of joy,
Offerings of things of wonder,
Billowing clouds of the six kinds of sensory delight,
Perfectly arrayed tokens of fortune and articles of
    prosperity—
In short, all the riches of existence and peace with nothing
    lacking,
Offering clouds of vajra bliss and emptiness in which all
    the positive signs of samsara, nirvana, and the path,
    and all the most essential glorious qualities are gathered
    together, crackling, vibrating, trembling, and shaking—
    with these sublime offering clouds in which apparent
    existence arises as all that is desirable,
We make offerings to you!
We exalt you!
We honor and praise you!
We fulfill your noble wishes!
We offer the drink of warriors!
We confess our breakages of samaya!
We inspire great joy!
We invoke your solemn pledge!
For us vidyadhara yogins,
Bestow the food of great vitality!
Provide the clothing of resplendence!
Confer the treasure of great abundance!

Hoist the flag of renown!
Sound the conch of fame!
Bring down a rain of all that is desirable!
Gather an ocean of good fortune!
Summon the vital essence of wealth and enjoyments!
Further increase our progeny, wealth, and influence!
Bring us profit in business dealings!
Ensure our success in games of chance!
Grant awards* to the successful!
Sound the conch in the assembly!
Bring us victory in debate and sport!
Help us to rival those who surpass us
And outshine those of equal standing!
Praise the victories of the good!
Create circumstances for every excellence!
Bring down powerful oppressors!
And eliminate thoughts of rivalry!

In short, empower us with the physical strength and might of the Great Lion Gesar and the dralas and wermas, and grant us all the siddhis of abundance here and now, this very instant!

iii. Magnetizing

HO! At times, you appear smiling and seductive,
Amidst an expanse of red light that pervades the whole
   animate and inanimate universe; and with your vajra
   hook and lasso, you magically activate and summon the
   vital essence of existence and peace.

---

*These awards—literally "bravery ribbons" (*dpa' dar*)—could include military honors, but also medals and accolades for sporting and academic prowess. (Alak Zenkar Rinpoche)

Your body sways in a dance of joy, stirring and captivating
the three planes of existence.
With the roar of your laughter, you summon the three
realms and bind them into service.
You take pleasure in the vital essence and magnificent
qualities of existence and peace, and glance about in
amusement.
You perform your dance of delight with radiant charm
And sing your song of joy in harmonious tones.
You dissolve the outer world and beings within it into red
light
And strike the animate and inanimate like cymbals.
You laugh with the thunderous roar of a drala
And unfurl the banner of the wermas.
Like lightning streaking through the sky, you playfully
assume a variety of expressions.
With your indestructible compassion born of bliss and
emptiness,
No one in apparent existence can resist your captivating
powers.
To the Great Lion Gesar, powerful wish-fulfilling king,
together with your armies of dralas and wermas who
carry out magnetizing activity,
An ocean of medicinal nectar,
A mountain of wish-fulfilling tormas,
Vast rivers of flowing red rakta,
Clouds of sweet-fragranced incense,
The movements of the vajra dance,
The melodies of harmonious song,
The dances of courageous warriors,
The beguiling chants of wisdom consorts,
Offerings of the bliss-emptiness experience,
The music of coemergent melting bliss,
The beautiful and seductive who gladly and smilingly
embrace—

With this sublime gift in which apparent existence becomes
a boundless symphony of indestructible bliss and
emptiness, we make offerings to you!
We exalt you!
We honor and praise you!
We fulfill your noble wishes!
We offer the drink of warriors!
We confess our breakages of samaya!
We inspire great joy!
We invoke your solemn pledge!
For us vidyadhara yogins, develop our powers of physical
attraction!
Grant us the capacity for prophetic speech!
Ignite the samadhi of bliss-emptiness in our minds!
Bring all that is visible under control!
Subjugate the three planes of existence!
Bind the three realms into service!
Stir people's hearts!
Move people's minds!
Magnetize appearances!
Bring us the vital essence of existence and peace!
Seat us upon the long hair* of the great!
Summon the wealth and splendor of the good!
Install us on the throne of great royal power!
Let whatever we desire fall into our hands!
In short, grant us, here and now, all the siddhis of
magnetizing great bliss, and the vajra of wielding power
over apparent existence!

---

*In other words, let us be the most powerful of all. The imagery here recalls King
Tri Ralpachen, who is said to have allowed monks to sit upon his long braided
hair.

iv. Wrathful

HO! At times, you appear fearsome and wrathful,
With your bow and arrow of means and wisdom, you stir
the brains of the maras and rakshasas.
With your sword of meteoric iron, you sever the heads of
untamed rakshasas.
With your vajra lance, you pierce the hearts of samaya
breakers.
With your iron hook of wrath, you gouge out the eyes of
adversaries.
With your blazing knife, you cut the main artery of the
enemy's life force.
You send out molten sparks of guardians
And press on the vital points of the gods and demons of the
eight classes.
You hurl down male protectors like an avalanche
And let fly female protectors like arrows.
You send forth wermas like shooting stars
And crash the cymbals of appearance and existence.
From the sun and moon of your eyes blaze fires like those at
the end of time.
The red lightning of your tongue lets fall the hail and
thunder of fierce mantras.
From the billow of your mouth stirs a churning ocean of
rakta.
From the "wind chamber" of your nose emerges a
devastating storm, black as an apocalyptic gale.
From the stronghold of your body swirl thick clouds of
drala battalions.
From the snowcaps of your teeth, poisoned arrows stream
down like hail and sleet.
From the clear light of your enlightened mind blazes the
great fire of vajra wrath.

In a ferocious rage, you feast on the flesh, blood, and life-
breath of your enemies.
To the wrathful Norbu Dradul Tsal whose might and
power are unrivaled throughout the whole of apparent
existence, together with an ocean of wermas who
subjugate enemies and obstacle-makers, we offer a
mountain of flesh from samaya-breaking enemies,
An ocean of blood,
Riverbanks of bones,
Forests made of hearts,
Thick swamps of marrow,
Fog and mist of steamy breath,
Smoky clouds of vast burnt offering,
Together with the flowers of the sense organs and all
our enemies' strength, power, abilities, life, glory and
riches—all this we offer to you, feeding it into your
blazing mouth,
We exalt you!
We honor and praise you!
We fulfill your noble wishes!
We offer the drink of warriors
And confess our breakages of samaya!
We inspire great joy!
We invoke your solemn pledge!
May all who would harm and injure us vidyadhara
practitioners
Or harbor evil intentions against us,
All hostile enemies
And harmful obstructing forces—wherever they may be—
be seen with your blazing eyes.
Let your summoning iron hook strike at their hearts,
Your tightening lasso bind fast their limbs,
Your cleaving sword slice off their heads,
Your piercing spear puncture their hearts,

And your swift arrows strike at their life force.

Burn their hearts in apocalyptic flames.

Hack apart their bodies with your vajra weapons.

Bring down a rain of poison with your weapon of sickness.

Subdue their sorcery and evil omens.

Tear off the genitals of the males,

Dry up the wombs of the females.

Crush the force of their intentions, strength, and capacity.

Cause the poisoned arrows of their evil schemes to fall back upon them.

Cause the weapons of their evil actions to bring their own destruction.

Do not put this off for years or even months; liberate them today—this very moment!

Avert all black magic, evil curses, malicious intentions, and violent behavior!

Bury evil enemies headfirst beneath the earth,

Praise and elevate friendly positive forces as high as the heavens!

Cause my own power, strength, and capacity to flare up like the fires at the end of time!

In short, carry out completely whatever wrathful direct actions we request of you, exactly as we desire!

v. Varied

HO! At times, you display miraculous, varied forms,

Traveling everywhere—through space, on earth, and in the sky,

With mastery over infinite enlightened actions.

Merely through our wishes, you bestow accomplishment.

Simply by calling upon you, you move like lightning.

Through practice alone, we forge a samaya connection.

By mere invocation, you hasten to act.

To the Great Vajra Lion and the armies of dralas and

wermas, we offer outer, inner, and secret offering clouds
and sacred wisdom nectar, all arisen from the display of
Samantabhadra.
We exalt you!
We honor and praise you!
We fulfill your noble wishes!
We offer the drink of warriors
And confess our breakages of samaya!
We inspire great joy!
We invoke your solemn pledge!
We invoke the vajra steed, wild and skillful!
We invoke the four secret bringers of delight!
We invoke the general Mikmar Chenpo!
We invoke Damchen Dorje Lekpa!
We invoke Mentsun Dorje Yudrönma!
We invoke Magyal Dorje Draktsal!
We invoke the elder brother Dungkhyung Karpo!
We invoke the armies of gods above!
We invoke the father Gerdzo Nyenpo!
We invoke the armies of nyens in between!
We invoke the younger brother Ludrul Öjung!
We invoke the armies of nagas below!
We invoke the aunt Gungmen Gyalmo!
We invoke the mandalas of mamos of appearance and
existence!
We invoke the younger sister Tale Ökar!
We invoke the goddesses of the five elements!
We invoke the four gods of the miraculous windhorse!
We invoke the thirteen Drönyak youths!
We invoke the nine chiefs of the dralas!
We invoke the thirteen dralas of Gönpo!
We invoke the three drala brothers and their sisters!
We invoke the dralas of the outer and inner world!
We invoke the dralas of varied activity!
We invoke the powerful protector patron gods!

We invoke the dralas who protect the forces of good!
We invoke the 360 tukkars!
We invoke the chongse, mighty gods of travel!
We invoke the wermas of the heavens, the earth, and in
    between!
We invoke the dralas and wermas of the retinue!
We invoke all the dakinis and maidens!
We invoke the legions of valiant warriors!
We invoke the armies of emanated gods of service!
We invoke the arrogant spirits of apparent existence who
    obey commands!
We invoke the dralas and wermas of all apparent existence!
In short, to all the armies of dharmapalas, dralas, and
    wermas in the mandala of the Great Lion Dradul Gyalpo,
    whether they appear in wisdom, activity, or worldly
    guise, we offer vast clouds of offering substances, both
    real and imagined!
We exalt you!
We honor and praise you!
We fulfill your noble wishes!
We offer the drink of warriors!
And confess our breakages of samaya!
We inspire great joy!
We invoke your solemn pledge!

KYE! Wisdom dharmapalas,
Mighty in action,
And powerful worldly guardians, all of you, consider us in
    your wisdom.
Look upon us with love, and through your great power,
    strength, and capacity, for us and those around us, from
    now until we reach the essence of enlightenment—
    without ever straying from your activity of guarding and
    protecting—help us to accomplish all that we desire,
    without obstacle and exactly as we wish!

SO! SO! Amidst thick clouds of the dralas and wermas of
   appearance and existence,
Whose cries of laughter resound like the thunderous roars
   of a dragon,
Is the one who has the majesty and brilliance of a dozen suns,
Gesar, Norbu Dradul, in his wisdom form,
Riding upon the one with the strength and speed of the
   seven apocalyptic storms,
The miraculous vajra steed, wild and skillful.
The armor of the various dralas gleams in the light.
Within the indestructible fortress of the vajra body,
Armies of dralas and wermas are dispatched and recalled.
At the mere thought of which, positivity bursts forth like a
   storm.
With a mind of unchanging faith and samaya,
And with various samaya substances and clouds of offering,
We invoke you; we offer to you—may your noble wishes be
   fulfilled!
We exalt you; we honor and praise you, and offer nectar,
   drink of the warriors.
Inseparably, from the state of the vajra mind of appearance
   and emptiness,
Look upon me, your devoted follower.
Lord over the haughty ones, emanation of Padma and the
   three families,
Great Lion Gesar and your retinue of dralas and warriors,
In this practitioner's body, speech, and mind,
Ignite your blessings, power, strength, and capacity.
Raise aloft the great banner of renown throughout the three
   planes of existence.
Let the great thunder of fame resound throughout the three
   worlds.
Outshine all who are hostile and antagonistic.
Let your enlightened activity reign victorious in all
   directions!

Thus, wheresoever is heard this dragon's roar
That brings joy to the minds of the dralas and wermas,
Bring down showers of prosperity, happiness, and fame,
And gather auspicious signs of impending fortune.
Whatever our focus, through a practice such as this,
Entrusting activity one-pointedly to the dralas and warriors,
Set aloft for all time the great victory banner of
Accomplishing whatever is desired, just as we wish!
Samaya!

This offering and invocation, as it arose in the mind of the werma Seru Öden Karpo, was first written down during the three years of the Fire Ox (1877), Earth Hare (1879), and Iron Dragon (1880) of the fifteenth calendrical cycle and completed on the eighteenth of the month of Saga Dawa in the Iron Dragon year. May it bring about the supreme auspicious circumstance for the precious teachings of the Buddha to become as exalted as the very summit of existence.

38. A Beautiful Vase of Nectar

Source Text and Practice Instructions for Gesar Dorje Tsegyal

---

REVEALED BY LHARIK DECHEN YESHE RÖLPA TSAL[18]

This upadesha from the visionary dharma cycle of the great being Gesar Dorje Tsegyal is called "the pure vision of the Great Lharik" and contains life-force entrustment, sadhana, and description of the life-force wheel. ༔

Homage to the lama, great powerful heruka Hayagriva! ༔

I, the worn-out fraud Trinle Rölpa Tsal, had, at dawn on the tenth day of the Monkey month in the Earth Dragon year,[19] a meditation experience within a dream, in which I was mostly dreaming. ༔

I arrived in the main shrine room of the Tradruk temple. There I met the Lord of Secret, Lama Shepe Dorje. Then I saw the mu-cord right in front of me. It looked like a white cloud piercing and entering the temple, the great being Gesar Dorje Tsegyal sitting at its tip. He looked vaguely the same as in the vision of the supreme refuge, Shepe Dorje, holding an arrow and a bow. The oathbound Dorje Lekpa was on his right, a young boy dressed in white with a dice in his hand. Mentsun Dorje Yudrönma stood to Dorje Tsegyal's left, while the general Mikmar Chenpo was in front of him, holding a six-foot-long magical noose, surrounded by the masang brothers and a myriad of young gods and menmos. I saw them before me with my own eyes. Then the vidyadhara Shepe Dorje transformed into the Lotus-Born of Oddiyana and I heard these words from the secret of his vajra speech: ༔

EMA! I bow before Hayagriva, the great and mighty deity of the Lotus-Speech. I, self-arisen Pema Tötreng Tsal, have bound the eight classes of gods and demons of Tibet in my service and have placed them in the great mandala of Jikten Chötö. Specifically, I have appointed the nyen Gerdzo and others as my kulhas. Manifesting every possible name and form, I am the great being Gesar Dorje Tsegyal. In essence, Dorje Tsegyal is Avalokiteshvara, the sublime treasury of compassion, in his wrathful form that subdues wrathful beings, the glorious Hayagriva. He is one of my specific manifestations for the future—the end of the twentyfold cycle—in the form of a haughty deity known as the great being Gesar. Externally, he is the courageous, strong, and swiftly acting king of dralas. Internally, he is loyal, brings good fortune, and is trustworthy. In particular, he is a powerful tamer of damsi and gyadre demons, and the yidam deity for these times. When you arrange the secret condition with Rinchen, the human emanation of a celestial menmo, this cycle of practice and related activities will progressively unfold. ⚬

Guru Rinpoche said this and other things and, after praising the teaching and encouraging me, at the end, he said the mantra HUM HUM HUM forcefully and my body transformed into the greatly powerful Hayagriva. As Guru Rinpoche directed his blessing, an inconceivable number of Hayagrivas, seed syllables, hand implements, and so on arose from basic space and showered down on me like a torrential rain. Then he entrusted the great being with helping me, and the samaya water was mixed. After that, my dream was just the ordinary dream delusion. ⚬

I didn't have the opportunity to arrange the secret condition with the supreme dakini named Rinchen. Only some defiled substance came, thanks to which the casket of the expanse of awareness opened to reveal the catalog of teachings, the lhasang and the secret thread-cross ritual that are based on the outward appearance of protector practices. I wrote them down on white paper. ⚇

Samaya. ⚇ Guhya. ⚇ Gya gya gya. ⚇

The steps for the conferral of the life-force empowerment of the great being Gesar, king of dralas, are as follows. In a secluded place, arrange the mandala. In the center, place the accomplishment torma for the yidam that needs to be practiced as a preliminary. Add the torma of the great being in front of it, with offerings and so on. Gather the necessary substances and articles. Visualize clearly the great being and his retinue in the torma. Perform the invocation and offering, the fulfillment, and recite his invocation mantra. ⚇

Disciples visualize themselves as the yidam deity and receive the descent of blessings. Bless them by placing on their heads the accomplishment torma of the preliminary yidam practice, and say: ⚇

> HRIH ⚇
> Receive the empowerment of the body ⚇
> Of the fierce and haughty deity, the Great Powerful
>   Hayagriva, ⚇
> Great subjugator of haughty spirits. ⚇
> Through this blessing, child, may you become the same as
>   the deity. ⚇
> HRIH PADMA TAKRITA HAYAGRIWA OM ⚇

Confer the empowerments while placing the torma at the disciple's throat and heart in the same way. ⚇

The actual empowerment to entrust with the life force of the haughty deity is as follows: ⚇

Invite the great being, make offerings, visualize once more the deity in the torma, and entrust it to the hand of the disciple. ⚇

HUM ஃ
Great being, king of dralas, ஃ
Lord Gesar and your army—main deity and retinue— ஃ
Abide by the command and samaya ஃ
Of the Lotus-Born and the heruka Hayagriva ஃ
And guard these disciples. ஃ
I appoint you to care for these children ஃ
With pure samaya and aspiration. ஃ
Always accompany them like their shadow, ஃ
And protect them until enlightenment. ஃ

Say this and entrust the torma into the hands of the disciples. Then, for the special disciples who will integrate the samayas, entrust the disciples with the life-force mantra and the la stone. ஃ

HUM ஃ
The wheel of the greatest, supreme glorious god of gods, ஃ
The great being, and the army of his retinue, ஃ
Which retains the entrustment with their life force ஃ
And is endowed with the syllables of their life-force mantra
    and their la stone, which emanate light, ஃ
I entrust to you—take them as supports. ஃ
Practice the recitation consistently, ஃ
Invoke, make offerings, offer praises without fail, ஃ
And make sure not to let any samaya deteriorate! ஃ

SAMAYA BENZA RAKSHAN TU ஃ OM TRI SHIM
KSHA MIMUTRA BARA HUM ALALI LAMO
TUNGWA KHYE A HO YE SIDDHI HUM KRAGSHE
RAKSHING ஃ BENZA SAMAYA DZA DZA ஃ DZA
HUM BAM HOH ஃ

Entrust his hand implements—the bow and arrow of strong metal and the blazing jewel—to the hands of the disciples: ஃ

HUM ⚬
I give you the bow and arrow that eliminate all hostile
    beings and influences ⚬
Such as enemies, obstructing forces, damsi and gyadre
    demons, and so on, ⚬
And the blazing jewel that gives you all you want. ⚬
I entrust you with these emblems of strength and
    confidence. ⚬

OM TRI SHIMKSHA MIMUTRA BARA HUM ALALI
LAMO TUNGWA KHYE A HO YE SIDDHI HUM
KRAGSHE RAKSHING ⚬ SARVA SAMAYA HUM
DZA ⚬

Once again, issue the command, remind the great being of his
pledges, and request him to protect the supreme outer, inner, and
secret supports. Recite sang, thread-cross, and fulfillment offerings, and urge the great being to perform the activities. ⚬

Tell the disciples to guard the samayas of avoiding the destruction of weapons, of avoiding production of foul smell by burning
impure objects, and so on; and of taking up the proclamation of
the great being's enlightened deeds, and so on. They will have to
do the practice, entrust the activities, and rely on the lama and the
deity with respect. ⚬

Then the disciples need to offer an elaborate mandala for giving
thanks. This concludes the section of entrustment with the life
force of the great being. ⚬

I prostrate to the lama, king of wrathful deities! ⚬
The steps of practice of the king of dralas, the great being Gesar,
are as follows. ⚬ Those who have received the empowerment for
this practice and maintain the samayas should go to an auspicious
and blessed hermitage, which can be a pure place at a high altitude,
on top of a fortress, and so on. On a shelf, draw a perfect square

with three rings around it, surrounded by a vajra fence and the five-colored ring of fire. In the center of the square, draw a sun disk marked with a white syllable A H. On top of the drawing, place an accomplishment torma adorned with a life-force wheel and a parasol. Arrange the amrita, rakta, outer and inner offerings, and especially two traditional Tibetan teacups on their stands filled with white tea and white beer. Add a torma that is the manifestation of the yidam, Hayagriva. ༔

After the mantra recitation of the preliminary Hayagriva practice and the recitation of his mantra, say slowly the sadhana of the great being. Then practice by dividing your time into sessions of recitation of the approach mantra. The direct experience of rigpa will become stronger, your body will blaze with blissful warmth, and you'll have goosebumps, all of the weapons of others will come into your hands; in dreams, you will see the deity's face, meet him as if he was in front of you, ride a white horse, wear armor, and be victorious in battle; at the very least you will see white clouds float and other similar signs. These are the best, middling, and lesser signs. This essential sadhana of the great being Gesar is the secret treasure of fortunate individuals. ༔

Samaya. Khatam. Hya. ༔

Homage to the supreme noble treasure of compassion! ༔

Herein, the explanation of the secret life-force wheel of the great being, Gesar Dorje Tsegyal. ༔

On silk, paper, birch bark, or some other material, in yellow, red, Indian ink, and so on, draw four concentric circles. In the center, write the syllable A H. Around the syllable and within the first circle, write the root mantra of the great being and the text of your request; within the second, draw four circles and write the syllables A, M A, T S A, and T R I inside; in the third, write the mantras of the lama and the yidam followed by "Do not transgress the command and samayas of the three root deities, and protect the

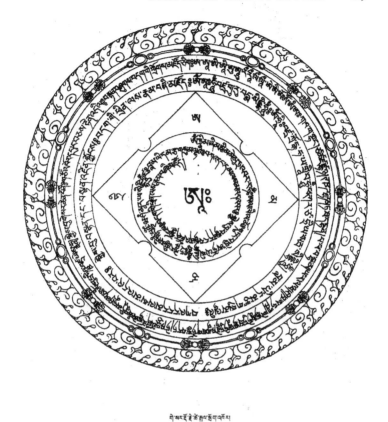

ཤེ་སར་རྡོ་རྗེ་ཚེ་རྒྱལ་སྲོག་གི་འཁོར་ལོ།

Gesar Dorje Tsegyal's Life-Force Wheel

practitioners, teachings, and holders of the teachings. Accomplish the four activities for me." In the fourth, write the vowel and consonant mantras, and add at the end, "Great being Gesar and the army of dralas and wermas who make up your retinue, remain firmly in this support, accompany me and help me." It is important not to make corrections by erasing superfluity or adding what was omitted. Soak the diagram in saffron water and the blessed samaya substance of amrita. Write a syllable A on the side of a rock crystal with eight facets and place it in the middle of the diagram. Do properly the usual practices—purification, washing ritual, generation, and absorption. Roll up the diagram in human hide and wrap it in silks of the five colors. Anyone with devotion who owns such a diagram should keep it constantly with them when moving around, like a captive bird caught in a snare. ༔

When the power of the interdependent connection between Mentsun Dorje Zulema in the form of a woman called Ratna, and the fortunate child who guards the samaya and is the owner of this teaching is roused by the sound of my name, Padma the Jewel, the heart essence sadhana of the great being Gesar who is the magical display of my and the peaceful and wrathful Avalokiteshvaras' compassion will be transmitted to him. Samaya. Gya gya gya. ༔

I wrote this text containing a few sections of the dharma teaching on the great being Gesar Dorje Tsegyal after the venerable Kalzang Norbu, the renunciate Lobu Rabgye from Upper Tibet, and Lama Dorje Palzang, also known as Wangchuk, kept requesting it in all sorts of ways. As the verses of vajra words from the pure vision were about to fade, I relied on contact with a dakini, smoke offering, washing ritual, and so on. Through their power, words that are not part of the pure vision vanished and omissions were rectified, and I wrote the text on white paper as it became clear in my mind. May it incinerate the damsi demons who have newly appeared, as well as the gyadre and gongpo demons. May it be the cause for the success of every intention that accords with the dharma. Virtue.

39. The Miraculous Fountain
A Method for Sewing a Gesar Wealth Pouch

The way to sew this wealth pouch arose in my mind on the twelfth
day of the fifth month of the Fire Monkey year (1896).

Fold a square twice to make four squares.
This square that you folded is the first piece.
Use another square to make eight triangles.
The lowest triangle should be larger, like a fang.
Use two squares to make the inside of the pouch.
For the eight triangles, fold a square into four small squares,
Then fold the cloth diagonally and you will obtain eight pieces.
Lift up the longer sides
Of the folded square
And cut to make the eight triangles.
For the larger triangle, sew the longest side at the bottom.
Inside, join the ends up to the aperture
And cut half a square to make the opening, and leave the other
    half.
When you do that, you have a small piece left.
Either use one-third above
Or below by extending it between two triangles.
The ones above should be red and yellow and adorned with
    rainbow patterns,
And the three below green and dark blue and adorned with
    rainbow patterns.
Decorate the opening with a cloth string.
Consecrate this pouch as an extraordinary treasury of abundance.

It looks like a six-sided jewel,
Which creates the auspicious interdependence for the six riches
to increase.
The three tips at the top are like three jewels laying against each
other,
This will create the auspicious interdependence for gathering the
abundance of the three planes of existence.
The open side is the glorious knot of eternity with six corners,
Which creates the auspicious interdependence for obtaining all
wants and needs.
The bottom is like the excellent vase.
Place it on a seat of grain;
This will create the auspicious interdependence for inexhaustible
vitality and merit.
They also look like the greatest masang sons,*
Which creates the auspicious interdependence for increasing the
vitality of the family lineage.
It also looks like the udders of the bountiful cow,
Which creates the auspicious interdependence for white food and
drink to increase.
From the top it looks like a blazing jewel,
Which creates the auspicious interdependence for the prospering
of wealth and increase in abundance.
It also looks like a whole rice grain,
Which creates the auspicious interdependence for grain to
increase in the storehouse.
It also looks like the great wish-granting tree,
Which creates the auspicious interdependence for both entourage
and servants to prosper.
It also looks like the great cloud of pure gold,
Which creates the auspicious interdependence for the acquisition
and growth of fame and good reputation.
It also looks like Mount Meru with surrounding mountains,

---

*The three lower triangles. (This note is from Mipham Rinpoche.)

Which creates auspicious circumstances for dharmic and secular
activities and the teachings.
The tree, the cloud, and Mount Meru representing prosperity,
abundance, and wealth—
All auspicious coincidence is complete with these three.
To simply hold this great treasury of abundance that creates
auspicious interdependence
Is enough to attract abundance.

Some have said this pouch conferred abundance and prosperity
on them.
The nine triangles are the places where abundance and prosperity
gather.
This pouch is like the dharmadhayo, the source of all things,
Or a large snake's hood pointing upward,
Which gathers an amount of prosperity and abundance that is as
vast as the whole of space.
The small root pointing downward
Is called the "firm root of the wish-granting tree."
This pouch is the source of everything we want and the
accomplishments of every objective,
The happiness of all beings and the fulfillment of their every
intention,
The gathering of everything good and the increase of what we
already have,
The growth of abundance and securing of wealth,
And the flourishing of the most excellent auspiciousness,
goodness, and well-being!

This text was written by Mipham.

Use five squares of cloth. Make eight triangles with one square, use
one full square for the greater triangle, which, with the three other
squares, add up to five.

40. Gesar Windhorse Flag

Sew together good-quality cloths and silks
Of appropriate size.
The middle is plain yellow and on it a drawing of a rider,
Gesar, in full regalia.
The upper right corner[20] is green and depicts a garuda,
The upper left corner is blue with the drawing of a turquoise
    dragon,
The lower left corner is white with the drawing of a lion,
And the lower right corner is vermilion with the red tiger.
The four directions—the apex, the side next to the pole on the
    left, the lower part, and the side opposite the pole—
Are respectively white, red, green, and blue,
With a banner drawn on each one.

In short, in the four corners are the four deities,
And the four directions are adorned with a banner
Drawn on white, red, blue, and green cloths,
All cut into squares and neatly sewn together.

The edge of the nine sections is yellow,
A quarter of the width of the inside corners.
It is surrounded by a green frame
Half the width of the inside corners,
All placed inside a perimeter in the form of a red line.

Sew white, yellow, red, and blue streamers
Down the outside edge, one below the other.
Divide the streamers into four parts—

One and a half parts from the top,
Write the mantra for raising windhorse.

Above, on the green frame, add the *Dusum Sangye* prayer and the
Vajra Guru mantra.
On the right side of the flag, write ཧྲཱིཿ,
On the left, draw a lotus, a golden vajra,
And a white conch that coils to the right.
At the bottom, write the heart-of-dependent-origination mantra
and the prayer of wishes.
You can add a white rectangle above the flag
Containing the drawing of a white victory banner
Topped by a blazing jewel that covers the tip of the spear.

Then imagine that from the bindu of the bliss of dharmadhatu,
The display of the Great Lion's unimpeded activities
Unfolds spontaneously and naturally.

When you raise these flags in the sky,
The windhorse also is bound to them.
So do the practice to raise the lungta
And attach the flag to practice supports.
Whenever you need, raise the beautiful flags in the sky and offer
a cleansing sang offering,
And, as it says on the windhorse flags, hoist them high up, on
mountaintops.

Since giving to everyone this most excellent and secret jewel,
Which is the source of increase in positive coincidence to
accomplish our activities by raising windhorse,
Would be a loss,
The terma text describes neither the windhorse deities
Nor the silk flag with four streamers,
But only alludes to them on a few occasions.
This is the innermost instruction, the tilaka of the lung

Of Great Lion the Jewel. ⚬
May the vajra steed who gallops wherever we wish ⚬
Bring us to the island of the Victorious One's three kayas! ⚬

Samaya. ⚬ Dhatim. ⚬

I put this text down on paper when an extremely auspicious coincidence manifested again on the ninth day of the first month of the Iron Horse year (1870). Strict seal of auspiciousness. ⚬ Mangalam. ⚬

Om padma cintamani jwala hung om mani raja ha ha hi hi hé hé ho ho sarwa vijaya siddhi hung om ah hung ho hé tak seng khyung druk di yar kyé "Gather all, sarva, gather, gather hoh!"

om maha senge mani radza ha ha hi hi hé hé ho ho pacify all illness, dön, negativity, obscuration, wrong view, negative intentions and actions shanting kuru ye soha

Om padma cintamani jwala hung om mani raja ha ha hi hi hé hé ho ho sarwa vijaya siddhi hung om ah hung ho hé tak seng khyung druk di yar kyé "Gather all, sarva, gather, gather hoh!"

om maha senge mani radza ha ha hi hi hé hé ho ho increase all longevity, merit, wealth, wisdom, qualities pushting kuru yé soha

Om padma cintamani jwala hung om mani raja ha ha hi hi hé hé ho ho sarwa vijaya siddhi hung om ah hung lo hé tak seng khyung druk di yar kyé "Gather all, sarva, gather, gather hoh!"

om maha senge mani radza ha ha hi hi hé hé ho ho magnetize all the three realms, the three planes of existence, and every god, demon and human washom kuru yé soha

Om padma cintamani jwala hung om mani raja ha ha hi hi hé hé ho ho sarwa vijaya siddhi hung om ah hung lo hé tak seng khyung druk di yar kyé "Gather all, sarva, gather, gather hoh!"

om maha senge mani radza ha ha hi hi hé hé ho ho all harmful influence, enemies, obstructing forces, five poisons, wrong views, curses, spells, negative intentions and actions maraya hung p'et

Om muné muné maha muné yé soha om hé hé tishtha tishtha bhandha bhandha dharaya dharaya nirundha nirundha amuka urna mani yé soha nama sarwa buddha bodhisattva bhyé apratishsané bhyé

Windhorse flag following Jamgön Mipham's instructions found in
Gesar Windhorse Flag (#40) and *Windhorse Flag in Nine Sections* (#23).
The supplication in the flag's left column and the verses at the bottom,
up through "three levels" at the beginning of line 5,
were translated by the Nalanda Translation Committee.
The rest was translated by Gyurme Avertin.

41. A Rain of Blessings from the Compassion of Great Lion, King of Jambudvipa

HRIH
Embodiment of the three roots
And manifestation of Pema Tötreng's compassion,
Great Lion, King of Jambudvipa,
With your retinue of dralas, wermas, mighty warriors, and
   beautiful maidens,
We invite you with heartfelt longing and devotion.
Look upon us with love and compassion, and come here this
   very instant!
In these bad times of the five degenerations,
We young shoots of dharma practitioners
Have no other hope or refuge than you!
To protect us, grant your compassionate blessing on your
   fortunate children
And show us clear signs of your powerful benediction!
Erect the fortress of the dralas and wermas in our body!
Bless our body, speech, and mind and transform them into the
   three vajras!
Arouse our intelligence, confidence, power, strength, and ability!
Grant us the siddhi of invincibility against every adversity
That can magnetize the three planes of existence!

Recite the mantra* and invoke the descent of blessings.

By Jampal Dorje.

*OM AH HUM BENZA MAHA GURU MANI RADZA SARVA SIDDHI PALA HUM

42. ༀ VAJRA STORM

A Practice of Bumpa Gyatsa Shelkar

This text called *Vajra Storm* is a practice of Dungda Karpo of Jambudvipa, who is also known as Gyatsa Shelkar of the Bumpa clan.

HUM HUM
Embodiment of the space-pervading magical net,
Nondual wisdom's supreme kaya born from a lotus
And appearing in the guise of the unstoppable champion of
enlightened activities,
The supreme being, the vidyadhara, Lord Norbu Dradul,
Who dwells in the indestructible bindu at the center of my
heart
And whose activities unfold as the natural, magical self-
manifestation of the warrior
Dungda Bumpa of Jambudvipa—
White-Face King Tamer of Enemies, arise from the
dharmadhatu!
Your wisdom mind pervades the whole of space,
Yet your activities overcome the most formidable evils
As you power onwards like the inferno of the end of time,
incinerator of the three realms!
King of dralas, endowed with the unswerving courage of
immutable basic space,
You who pierce enemies' hearts like the unstoppable
meteoritic head of an arrow
And have the power to accomplish your activities without
hindrance—

Stay here, and continue to be sharp-edged, swift, irresistible,
and fierce!

I praise you, great provider of siddhis and everything we
desire!
O bhagavan, peaceful in your immeasurable compassion,
You display the dance of wrath to eliminate the terrifying
armies of maras
In the form of the blazing kaya of the slayer, Yamantaka the
great—
I make offerings to you! I praise you! Accomplish your
activities!

As long as the relentless waves of grasping, thoughts, and
characteristics
Have not fainted into the Great Lion's ocean of
rigpa-dharmadhatu,
Hero who appears as the display of the magical net,
Always remain inseparable from the perfection of my rigpa.

On the spike of the camphor white warrior of pure
awareness,
The great flag of blazing meteorites you flap at every
opposition
And conquer them without resistance,
As you pierce the hearts of enemies with your unstoppable
arrow and feast on them!
Unleash an unbearable inferno
And burn to ashes our competitors, the dense thicket of dry
trees!
In this way, bring the might of others to our assistance,
O king of wermas, this I pray!

Let the laughter of your satisfaction thunder like a thousand
    dragons!
Place in my hands the banner that resounds with the
    unsurpassed fame
Of the peerless overlord who walks at will
On the crowns of the great rulers of gods, nagas, and
    humans,
And bring the three realms under my command!

Do not forget my wishes and needs
And all the good things that the spirits of prosperity and
    abundance attract—
Give me everything I want
And the treasury of every benefit and joy
That fills the vajra treasure vase of the unsurpassable Great
    Lion!
May I never be separated from the king and the minister
Within the expanse of Tötrengtsal's wisdom mind, the
    embodiment of all the victorious ones—
Take me to enlightenment!

This text arose from the ocean
Of the clear awareness of an unstained mind.
Like a temporary pond overflowing,
I could not help writing it.
The conditions created by this vajra storm
Will stir every banner of courage and strength,
Irrepressibly—
Wermas hold this practice closely!
You will know what is true and what is false when you practice it.
In the appearance of dreams and of reality,
You will see the magical dance of the warriors.
Like a fish in the ocean,
You will always find the place you need in this life

When you are under the protection of the dralas.
Free from obligations, you will enjoy the fruits of your desire
And swiftly accomplish the two siddhis.
Samaya. ༔ Mangalam.

These words came out of Mipham Jamyang Gyepa's mouth.

43. Crushing Malicious Forces

A Brief Invocation of Gabde

HUM HUM HUM
Incarnation of Mahakala and bodyguard of Great Lion
Who is the magical manifestation of the three protectors
    and the Lotus-Born,
You who arose in the form of a warrior, powerful, strong,
    and skilled,
Bernakchen, the great dharma protector from Gabde,
With your dark-red complexion, wrathful and roaring the
    maledictory fierce mantras,
Dressed in the garb of a mantrika, with black hat, gown,
    and so on,
You sling vajra stones at adversaries with both hands
And stamp ferociously on enemies, obstructing forces, and
    damsi demons.
Thanks to your superior powers you fly, devouring the three
    realms of existence.
Thanks to your superior strength, you smash Mount Meru
    to pieces.
Thanks to your superior miraculous abilities, you turn
    heaven and earth upside down.
Thanks to your superior speed, you crush enemy armies
    with a single thought.
You who turn the haughty dharma protectors into your
    servants and dispatch them,
Protector of the vidyadharas, great slayer of demons,
Arise from basic space, come here and take your seat!

With clouds of outer, inner, secret, and great-bliss offerings,
I invoke you and make offerings to you, Protector
Bernakchen!
With your slingshot, hurl indestructible, blazing meteoric
stones
At the enemies I am thinking of, and at the damsi and
gyalgong demons.
Annihilate any power and strength in their body, speech,
and mind,
Crush them to dust and leave not one trace of them behind.
Flatten black magic, curses, spells, malicious inscriptions,
and incantations of exorcists;
Eliminate sickness, epidemic, plague, and the degenerations
of the four elements;
Avert enemies of all kinds, thieves of all sorts, brigands of
all types, disputes of all classes,
And the weapons of words such as mikha, scandal, and all
other kinds of inimical words.
Lord of the assembly of wrathful dharma protectors and
your retinue,
Always remain in the pure bindu of my heart
And fill me with inextinguishable courage, spirit, power,
strength, ability, and resourcefulness—
Make me the leader of all, with natural power over
everything,
And bring me victory over all adversity! Accomplish these
activities, I pray!

Jampal Norbu wrote this supplication as it arose on the twenty-second day of the sixth month of the Earth Sheep year (1859). Virtue!

44. THE HOOK OF ABUNDANCE

A King Gesar Practice for Summoning Abundance
and Prosperity

Gather articles of auspiciousness and prosperity, supports for abundance, and copious beautiful offerings. Imbue them with magnificence through the practice of deity, mantra, and samadhi. Hold the ribboned arrow and say the following words to summon abundance and prosperity:

HUM
From the great display of empty appearances,
In the east, the land of Ma where good fortune arises,
At the summit of the auspicious white snow mountain,
Excellent clouds of nectar rise and billow—TA LA LA!
The red lightning of magnetizing flashes—KHYUK SE
    KHYUK!
The turquoise dragon's roar of fame thunders—WU RU RU!
The excellent rain of happiness and well-being falls—SHA
    RA RA!
The mist of abundance and prosperity rises thickly—TIP SE
    TIP!
The flowers of rainbow light rays fall like rain—TO LO LO!
And the sweet fragrance of medicinal incense perfumes the
    air—DUNG SE DUNG!
In this marvelous Land of Ling, a place desired by all who
    see it,
Stands the extraordinary Jewel Palace
Where the fearless king of Ling resides,

Endowed with the great spirit of abundance that increases
   abundance in everything.
While his mind is primordial wisdom, the equality of bliss
   and emptiness,
He appears as the magical dance of Padma and the three
   families,
In the form of Gesar, Masang Jewel of Abundance.
He has the appearance of a universal monarch.
His beautiful face is dazzling—YA LA LA!
He holds the golden wheel of royal rule and the wish-
   granting jewel,
Mighty warriors, beautiful maidens, and wermas all around
   him.
He leans against Magyal Pomra,
Who is surrounded by his three hundred and sixty brothers
   of the Ma clan.
Victory banners and flags are hoisted high in the sky,
And the warriors whirl in the beautiful dance of Ling
Amidst the glory of his astounding abundance and fortune.

On this very day, the yogins who keep samaya
Invite you to this offering ceremony—
Come without any hesitation!

We make offerings to you, we praise you, we invoke your
   sacred vows—
Pour a torrential rain of auspiciousness and abundance,
Heighten the blissful heat and the radiance of the universe
   and its inhabitants,
Encourage the samaya-bound dharma protectors to abide by
   their pledges,
Increase the power of the dralas and wermas forevermore,
And direct the activities of the yakshas who guard
   treasures.

Today, I call on you, deity of my heart—
With your unhindered magnetizing rays of light,
Bring the auspiciousness, happiness, well-being, prosperity,
    abundance,
Strength, wealth, resourcefulness, longevity, brilliance,
    radiance,
And the spirit of abundance that attracts victory against
    every adversity
And every speck of food, cloth, and possessions
That originate in any direction, including above and below!
Bring them here as orbs of bright five-colored light—
Draw them in! Gather them! Dissolve them
Into the articles of abundance and the substances of
    prosperity,
And into the yogins' body, speech, and mind,
So that they remain inseparable from them until
    enlightenment!
Like the excellent vase of jewels, the wish-fulfilling tree,
And the cloud of pure gold,
Always pour down a rain of every need and want!
Gather them in lakes of wealth made of everything desired!
Increase our strength, excellence, power, and ability!
Restore any deterioration in our family, physical
    constituents, nadi, and prana!
Increase the splendor of our prosperity, abundance, and
    good fortune!
Ripen the fruits of our hopes immediately!
Give us control over the vital essence of samsara and
    nirvana
So that our every need is fulfilled within the basic space of
    dharmadhatu
And we mature into wisdom kayas!
Shower down everywhere, at all times and spontaneously,
A rain of benefit and happiness on all beings who pervade
    space!

OM HE HE TISHTA TISHTA BHANDHA BHANDHA
 DHARAYA DHARAYA NIRUNDHA NIRUNDHA
URNA MANIYE SOHA
OM KHUYE KHUYE CHA KHUYE
KHUYE KHUYE YANG KHUYE
HUYE HUYE MAHA SHRI YE BIDZAYA DU
DEKYI PALJOR TAMCHE PUSHTIM KURUYE SOHA*

Sengchen Norbu Dradul
Enslaved the four border kingdoms
And became, thanks to interdependence, time, and aspirations,
The king of beneficent deities.
That is why I wrote down at this time, with the wish to do
    something positive,
This jewel of yangdrub practice
Called "The Natural Accomplishment of Every Desire,"
Which brings an abundance of all the most excellent things
And victory against every adversity.
Though it was born of the glorious knot—the treasury of the
    heart—
Of many learned and accomplished masters of the past,
It was kept sealed and was not revealed to others.
I wrote down these secret key points of interdependence
Thanks to the power of the lama and yidam's blessings
That brought me a little confidence.

This practice was written by Mipham at Dzongsar Tashi Lhatse
on the excellent date of the eleventh day of the sixth month of the
Water Bird year (1873). Mangalam. KAYA A RA ME. DU ME TI
PEN. Mangalam.

---

*Alternatively: All happiness, well-being, prosperity PUSHTIM KURUYE
SOHA.

PART THREE

EXTRA PRAYERS FROM THE REST OF THE *COLLECTED WORKS*

45. A Brief Protector Offering to Gesar*

KYE

Great powerful drala who accomplishes all that is desired,
Magical display of the three families and Padma,
King Great Lion, Norbu Dradul, along with your kadös and
    messengers,
We supplicate and make offerings to you: quickly
    accomplish our wishes.

In accordance with the request of the vidyadhara, a diligent practitioner and lord of yogins, I, Jampal Dorje, wrote this supplication in the retreat house of Dule Namgyal Ling (Place of Total Victory over the Maras) on the auspicious seventh day of the month of Pausha (the twelfth month). Through it, may the precious teachings of the practice lineage reign victorious in all directions.

*Translated by the Vajravairochana Translation Committee.

46. Gesar Sang

KYE
Great powerful dralha who accomplishes all that is desired,
Magical display of the three families and Padma,
King Great Lion, Norbu Dradul, along with your kadös and
 messengers,
To you, we offer sang! We give you offerings! Quickly
 accomplish our wishes!

Mipham wrote this prayer at the request of Doshul Drupwang Rigdzin, on the seventh day of the twelfth month of the Iron Hare year
(1891). Mangalam.

47. Short Sang

―――――

KYE ⁝

Mighty drala who accomplishes our every intention, ⁝
King Gesar, dralha of Jambudvipa and Tibet, ⁝
The thirty warriors and all the dralas, ⁝
We offer you this pure select portion—please accept it! ⁝
Accomplish everything we want ⁝
And grant the swift and effortless gathering of good
    circumstances, well-being, and prosperity! ⁝

You can add this prayer when you offer any amount of tea and
sang, as it possesses the key to bring you good fortune and positive
circumstances, and to foster a downpour of wealth. ⁝ By the tantric
monk Padma.

48. THE SWIFT FULFILLMENT
OF ALL WISHES
*Offering the Flag of Windhorse**

HO! Within the all-pervading purity of primordial wisdom,
Appearances arise, unceasing, as self-appearing ornaments;
And the great flag of the windhorse, auspicious,
    sweet-sounding far and wide,
Sends out, like Samantabhadra, vast clouds of exquisite
    offerings.

Miraculous and mighty is the king of horses, Balaha,
Adorned with the jewel of many kinds, he soars like the
    wind
And travels, unimpeded with his indestructible strength,
    wherever we so wish.
From his four miraculous limbs, there spread out

In the four directions, a tiger, lion, garuda, and dragon,
    taking flight and soaring in the sky.
Over the earth, in the air, and through the whole expanse of
    space
Sounds of happiness ring out, of goodness, victory, and
    accomplishment,
In songs of auspiciousness, with the resounding drumbeat
    of the gods,

*Translated by Rigpa Translations.

And melodious strains of music. While flowers fall like
  rain,
Clouds of divine offerings pervade every direction,
And all that is excellent throughout the three worlds—
Auspiciousness, glory, and riches—manifests spontaneously.

This vast offering treasure, containing all that could ever be
  wished for,
We offer to the root and lineage masters, the peaceful and
  wrathful yidam deities,
The dakinis of the three places, and oath-bound dharma
  protectors,
Dralas, wermas, wealth gods, and treasure-keepers,

Local deities, masters of the earth, all who safeguard what is
  beneficial and wholesome,
And all you guests who care for and protect us*—
We pray to you, make offerings, praise, and exalt you!
By offering you these supremely delightful and pleasing
  gifts,

Let the forceful vajra wind of your power and strength,
For us practitioners and those around us,
Increase our life, prosperity, merit, and the strength of our
  windhorse.
And with your actions, unimpeded in any way, make
  whatever we wish for come to be, just as we desire.

Transform everything that hinders and troubles us into an
  ally,
Hoist high the inspiring flag of auspiciousness and virtue,

---

*Mipham Rinpoche wrote that at this point you may insert verses such as the
ones he composed and placed at the end of the prayer if you wish to address
prayers to particular deities.

Overcome all that oppose and stand against us,
And with your enlightened activity, make us victorious over
all!

These verses, which are of an auspicious number, were written
in the Water Hare year (1903) on the auspicious occasion of the
tenth day of the ninth month, in the hermitage of Padma Samten
Deden Ling in Rutam, by Mipham Nampar Gyalwa. May virtue
and goodness abound!

Should you wish to address prayers to particular deities, you may
insert verses such as these:

GESAR

> Especially you, Gesar Norbu Dradul,
> With your miraculous, wild, and skillful vajra steed,
> Your fearless warriors, ladies, attendants, and envoys—
> We pray to you, make offerings, praise, and exalt you!
> Your awesome majesty we glorify as high as the
> dharmadhatu!

This is one verse you can add.

HAYAGRIVA

> You who magnetize all appearance and existence, deity of
> power,
> "Mighty Lotus" Hayagriva,
> With all the deities of your mandala, attendants, and
> emissaries—

We pray to you, make offerings, praise, and exalt you!
Your awesome majesty we glorify as high as the
dharmadhatu!

This is one verse you can add. And likewise:

GANAPATI

Glorious protector Ganapati, with your consort,
Protectors of body, speech, and mind, and protectors of the
eight classes in the ten directions,
Along with the drala Makpön Tsedzi Shuk—
We pray to you, make offerings, praise, and exalt you!
Your awesome majesty we glorify as high as the
dharmadhatu!

Say this and:

MAGYAL POMRA

Great guardian of the eastern lands of Dokham,
Magyal Pomra, with your entourage and attendants,
Masang wermas and dralas, with all your ladies—
We pray to you, make offerings, praise, and exalt you!
Your awesome majesty we glorify as high as the
dharmadhatu!

Insert verses such as these.

49. SHORT WINDHORSE SUPPLICATION*

HUM
The great banner of inspiring, auspicious windhorse,
The streaming out of great clouds of Samantabhadra
    offerings,
The three roots, protectors, dralas, and zodors,†
Accept my offerings and spontaneously accomplish my
    aims.

This short supplication was arranged by Mipham on the date mentioned above. Mangalam. Virtue. Virtue. Virtue.

---

*The Nalanda Translation Committee under the direction of Vidyadhara the Venerable Chögyam Trungpa Rinpoche translated the eight-line supplication in June 1979 (text #14 on page 115). In this verse, Mipham Rinpoche has used the first three lines and the last line of that supplication.
†Mipham Rinpoche says that you can change this line to invoke any deity of your choosing.

50. Short Lhasang[*]

HRIH

The virtuous mark, the great banner of inspiring windhorse,
And these clouds of offerings of all desirable things
We offer to you, assembly of the three roots, samaya-bound,
and dralas.
Fulfill all our wishes; be victorious in all directions.

Thus, on the fifth day of the fifth month of the Wood Snake year
(1905), Mipham wrote this down.

Change the third line to any deity you like, such as "We offer to
you, great being Gesar with your retinue." Mangalam.

51. Invocation for Raising Windhorse*

OM AH HUM

The assembly of the three jewels, the three roots, gods and
  sages,
The three protector-mahasattvas, Jayadevi,
Pema Tötreng, and the vidyadharas of India and Tibet,
The glorious protector Ganapati with the divine armies of
  dralas,
The five patron gods, the great being Gesar, and so on,
All those gods of the cosmic lineage who command
  coincidence—
To all of those I offer clouds of real and imagined good
  offerings.
I supplicate you:† with kindness, please grant your blessings.
Curses, spells, burial sorcery, döns, obstructing spirits,
  obstacles, and so on—
May all these signs of the weakening and corruption of
  windhorse be pacified.
Strife, enmity, scandal, warfare, lawsuits, recurrent
  calamity, and so on—
Pacify all such obstructing discord.

*Translated by the Nalanda Translation Committee under the direction of
Vidyadhara the Venerable Chögyam Trungpa Rinpoche. Chögyam Trungpa
Rinpoche chose not to include all the mantras, which have all been written here
as in Mipham Rinpoche's *Collected Works*.
†According to Chögyam Trungpa Rinpoche, when performing a lhasang, you
can replace "I supplicate you" with "I offer you this cleansing offering."

Multiply the power and strength of the virtuous windhorse,
The four-legged miracle.
Please accomplish the spiritual and temporal, supreme and
ordinary siddhis
And without exception whatever mind desires.

Mantra of Manjushri, buddha of wisdom:[21]

OM VAGISHVARA MUM[22]

Mantra of Avalokiteshvara, buddha of compassion:

OM MANI PADME HUM

Mantra of Vajrapani, buddha of power:

OM VAJRAPANI HUM

Mantra of Guru Rinpoche:

OM AH HUM VAJRA-GURU-PADMA-SIDDHI HUM

Mantra of the cycle of Kalachakra:

OM AH HUM HO HA KSHA-MA-LA-VA-RA-YAM
SVAHA

Mantra for windhorse:

OM SARVA-GRAHA NAKSHATRA DHYAMI
KARANI SVAHA

Mantra for controlling negative influences in the environment:

OM HE HE TISHTHA TISHTHA BHANDHA

BHANDHA DHARAYA DHARAYA NIRUNDHA
NIRUNDHA AMUKA URNA-MANIYE SVAHA

Mantra for Avalokiteshvara as the Jewel of Windhorse:

OM PADMA CHINTAMANI JVALA HUM

Invocation mantra for Gesar and his entourage of dralas and
wermas:

OM MANIRAJA HA HA HI HI HE HE HO HO
SARVAVIJAYA-SIDDHI HUM

Invocation mantra for the four gods of the windhorse:

OM AH HUM HO HE TAK SENG KHYUNG DRUK
DI YAR KYE
Gather all SARVA gather gather HOH*

Mantra for protecting longevity:

OM VAJRA-AYUSHE SVAHA
Rouse all our life, virtue, and glorious windhorse higher
and higher.†

Mantra of interdependent origination:

OM YE DHARMA HETU-PRABHAVA HETUM
TESHAM TATHAGATO HYAVADAT TESHAM CHA
YO NIRODHA EVAM VADI MAHASHRAMANAH
SVAHA

---

*The original Tibetan of the mantra is KUN DU SARVA DU DU HO.
†DAK CHAK GI TSE DANG SONAM PAL DANG LUNGTA TAMCHE GONG
NE GONG DU KYE CHIK

Mantra for enhancing the qualities of windhorse:

OM BHUR BHUVA SVAH SVASTI NAMA SVAHA

Mantra for all to be auspicious and good, and to create happiness:

OM SARVA TITHI NAKSHATRA GRAHE MAN-
GALE BHYOH SVAHA

Mantra to pacify obscuration in all directions, and particularly to prevent harm from the spirits who own the earth:

OM AKANI NIKANI ABHILA MANGALE MAN-
DALE SVAHA
NAMO BUDDHA DHARMA SANGHAYA MAMA
SHRIYE MANGALA BHAVATU SVAHA

If you recite this daily, there will always be auspiciousness. Whatever activity you undertake will be accomplished without obstacle, just as you wish. The merit and the power of windhorse will greatly expand, and fame and wealth will increase. All your goals that are in accord with dharma will perfectly increase, and you will quickly attain the supreme and ordinary siddhis. Mipham wrote this.

52. Perfect Satisfaction

An Invocation and Offering to the Gods of Travel
Relying on King Gesar

Assemble serkyem offering, select portion, torma, sang, chemar, gifts, and so on. Then say:

HUM
Magically manifesting wisdom kaya of the three families
    and Padma,
King of all the dralas and wermas of the universe,
Lord Great Lion, mighty Norbu Dradul,
All-Accomplishing White Werma and retinue,
Three jewels, lamas of the three lineages,
Yidams of the six classes of tantra, dakinis of the three
    abodes,
Three dharmapalas—Protectress of Mantras, Za, and Dorje
    Lekpa—and your assemblies,
Wealth gods, local deities, regional gods, treasure gods,
Tukkars, dralas, wermas, chongses, and the rest,
Powerful[23] gods of travel who protect at home, while
    traveling, when abroad, over long distances, and on the
    road,
I offer you these suitable samaya substances—
Sang, serkyem, chemar, silk ribbons, gifts,
Amrita, torma, flesh and blood, drumbeats, chants, music,
    and so on—
As well as offerings emanated by the mind in swelling
    clouds of wisdom nectar,

The empty bliss that pervades all the innumerable buddha
fields.

I offer them to you! Fulfill your powerful[24] pledge!

I exalt you, I honor and praise you! Since we have united our
vajra samayas,

From now until I reach enlightenment,

Protect me, bless me and grant me the siddhi

Of the unhindered accomplishment of my wishes, just as I
want.

Protect me from attackers, obstacles, and difficulties when
I travel,

And produce the positive circumstances I hope for, without
effort.

Accompany me from the start and all along the way

On the excellent highway to the supreme siddhi that bears
the two benefits—

Perform the activities I entrust to you!

May this prayer bring the effortless accomplishment of all wishes
and siddhis.

It was written by the werma Seru Öden Karpo on the ninth day
of the eleventh month of the Iron Dragon year (1880). Mangalam.

GLOSSARY OF TERMS

abundance or **spirit of abundance** (*g.yang*): Rather than abundance itself, *yang* refers to the capacity to attract abundance and well-being, as well as the ability to overcome difficulties and adversity. Chögyam Trungpa called it "enriching presence." It applies to people, but it can also be applied to the nourishing quality of food, to the warming quality of cloth, to cattle, places, roads, and the like. Tibetans keep in their houses yang dze (*g.yang rdzas*), articles that attract abundance. Abundance practices are performed to increase this capacity to attract abundance in people and consecrated articles.

authentic presence (*dbang thang*): In Tibetan, authentic presence is *wang-tang*, which literally means a "field of power." However, since this term refers to a human quality, Chögyam Trungpa Rinpoche loosely translated it as authentic presence. The basic idea of authentic presence, he explains, is that the merit or virtue that we achieve begins to be reflected in our being, our presence. It is a feeling of power that provides profound confidence, which radiates and puts us in direct contact with reality.

balim (*balim*): A Sanskrit term that means "offering." It is translated as *torma* in Tibetan, or sometimes referred to as *balingta*. In India, balim is usually a bloody offering from an animal sacrifice, although most people use nonviolent substitutes, like the Tibetan tormas. It comes from the words *bahuprakara*, which indicates that this offering is dear to all the different kinds of sentient beings, and *lipta*, indicating that it destroys negative karma.

chemar (*phye mar*): An offering of tsampa, mixed with small quantities of the three whites (milk, cheese, and butter) and the three sweets (honey, white sugar, and brown sugar).

chongse, changse, or **changseng** (*cong se* or *cang se[ng]*): Male and female Bönpo deities of travel. There are four types: those who protect soldiers going to war and traders on long journeys; those who mainly protect women and other members of the family who remain at home; the "thirteen changsengs expert in covering long distances"; and the "eight powerful deities of the road."

damsi (*dam sri*): Also called "samaya demon." *Si* refers to something negative that happened and has the tendency to repeat itself. This can manifest as spirits, and the damsi is one of many kinds of si (*sri*), who are animal-headed spirits. Damsi especially try to trouble the yogins who keep the samaya of Secret Mantra. They are seen as a major negative influence on practitioners, causing them to break their samaya. When practitioners commit a major samaya breakage, they become a damsi in this life as a human, and they will be reborn as a damsi demon in the next. Since as tantric practitioners, they accumulated a lot of merit before they turned against the dharma, they became very powerful enemies of the dharma. Gesar is particularly powerful in taming damsi demons.

dharmadhayo (*chos 'byung*): "Source of phenomena." It represents the source from which all dharmas, or phenomena, arise. In the tantras it is often depicted as a triangle or two triangles.

dön (*gdon*): Often translated as "negative" or "harmful influences." The term refers to spirits who harm people but also to a kind of pollution that can cause places or objects to have negative energy.

drala (*dgra/sgra lha/bla*): See Orgyen Tobgyal Rinpoche's comments on pages 26–27 and the translator's introduction on pages xxx–xxxi.

eight classes of gods and demons (*lha srin sde brgyad*): Also referred to as "eight classes," "eight classes of haughty spirits" or "of arrogant demons" (*dregs pa sde brgyad*), and "prideful ones" (*dregs pa*). There are different lists, sometimes of even nine or ten classes, and the majority of Tibetans understand the term to refer to all the gods, spirits, and demons that are present around human beings in the world. In this book, Mipham Rinpoche calls them "the eight classes," "masangs of the eight classes," "eight classes of gods and demons," "eight classes of haughty spirits," and even "eight classes of dharma protectors" as all these spirits have been bound under oath and have pledged to serve the dharma.

eight trigrams (*spar kha brgyad*): Also called "parkhas." According to the Chinese system of astrology, they represent the eight principal aspects of life. The advice of an astrologer is needed to determine which of the eight is the relevant one to draw on the windhorse flag page 123. They are constructed from a combination of broken and solid lines where the broken line represents yin (passive) and the solid line yang (active). Each trigram corresponds to a specific direction and element. There are year-of-birth parkhas; birth parkhas that depend on the age of the person, the age of the mother, and on the type of calculation; eight categories of changeable parkhas used to find good and bad directions for positioning furniture, direction of traveling, and medical treatment, for example; and day parkhas.

elemental demon (*'byung po*): Malignant spirits who belong to the preta, or hungry ghost, realm. They are not always malevolent and are not the most powerful of harmful spirits. They are called "elemental" because this class of spirits includes gods of fire, earth, wind, and so on. In English translations, they are sometimes simply called by their Tibetan name, jungpo or jungpo demons, or the Sanskrit *bhuta*.

expelling practice (*bzlog pa*): See **repelling practice**.

five patron gods (*'go ba'i lha lnga*): These "five deities of the individual" live with each person, follow them like a shadow, and increase their well-being. They are (1) the god of the maternal uncle (*zhang lha*) residing in the back of the head; (2) father-god (*pho lha*) in the right shoulder; (3) mother-goddess (*mo lha*) in the left shoulder; (4) drala (*dgra lha*) in front of the head; and (5) vitality-god (*srog lha*) in the head.

five secret goddesses (*gsang ba'i lha mo lnga*): The five female buddhas Dhatvishvari, Mamaki, Lochana, Pandaravasini, and Samayatara.

four aspects of well-being (*sde bzhi'i dpal*): Worldly dharmas and values, wealth, sensual enjoyment, and liberation.

four borders (*mtha' bzhi*): This term refers to Gesar's enemies in the four directions, who are also known as the maras of the four directions—China to the east, India to the south, Persia to the west, and Hor to the north. In the epic—which sometimes lists them as Düd, Hor, Mön, and Jang—they are the four principal anti-Buddhist kingdoms that Gesar must oppose. See also **mara**.

four gods of the windhorse (*rlung rta lha bzhi*): Garuda, dragon, tiger, and lion. On windhorse flags, the four supernatural guardian animals surround the flying horse with the flaming jewel of a universal monarch. They have their origin in the ancient Chinese astrological and geomantic tradition. The Tibetan tradition adopted three of these animals. The tortoise or "dark warrior," a national emblem of China, was replaced by the white snow lion, an emblem of Tibet. They are protective deities who always accompany an individual.

four ways of taming (*'dul ba rnam pa bzhi*): The four ways supreme nirmanakayas rely on to tame sentient beings' destructive emotions and lead them to enlightenment. They are the great merit of enlightened body, the direct perception of enlightened mind, their inconceivable miraculous abilities, and knowledge conveyed in speech.

gift (*brngan*): In this book, "gift" translates the Tibetan *ngen*. It refers to offerings assembled for a particular practice. Whereas sang and serkyem are offered universally, in ngen practices, a gift is offered individually, usually to a worldly protector such as Nyenchen Tanglha, Magyal Pomra, and so on.

gongpo (*gong po*): A spirit who instigates hatred, arrogance, jealousy, and disharmony in people's minds.

gya (*rgya*): Seal. Often placed at the end of termas and blessed by Guru Rinpoche, it protects the secrecy of the teachings it contains.

gyadre (*rgya 'dre*): A kind of gongpo who provokes fighting and conflict.

gyalgong (*rgyal 'gong*): Spirits who instigate sectarianism and rebellion. Tibetans say that the destructive behavior of the Red Guard during the Cultural Revolution was due to an attack of gyalgongs. Some people worship them, but many others see them as demons. It is said that people who believe that their teacher lacks kindness are reborn as gyalgongs.

gyalpo (*rgyal po*): A type of elemental demon often included in the eight classes of gods and demons. Gyalpos have very great power, and they rule the area that they inhabit, hence their name, which means "king." Some can be good, others are harmful. Many have been bound by great spiritual masters to work for the dharma, like Nyenchen Tanglha and Gyalpo Pehar, who is the chief of all gyalpos and was bound by Guru Padmasaṃbhava. Gyalpos are more powerful than tsens. Gyalpo protectors are particularly requested to look after temples and religious places. Gyalpo spirits are often the cause of madness. Note that the term also means "king," as in Great Lion Dradul Gyalpo, "King Tamer of Enemies."

haughty spirits (*dregs pa*): see **eight classes of gods and demons.**

ithi (*ithi*): Most profound meaning.

jagat (*dza gad*): See **warrior's drink.**

jutik (*ju thig*): Bönpo rope divination that uses sheep wool. The diviner places the longer ropes over his shoulders, and having tied the various rope ends together in a series of simple nooses, the ropes are collected into a bundle and cast on the ground. The diviner then refers to a divination manual to interpret the patterns formed as well as the location of the nooses.

Mipham Rinpoche wrote an important two-volume work that explains this ancient divination system.

kadö (*bka' 'dod*): Attendant; one who obeys Gesar's commands. They are all the haughty spirits of the world, also known as the eight classes of gods and demons.

khatam (*kha tham*): Secret and sealed.

koruka (*ko ru kha*): A three-dimensional cross made from three sticks and used in rituals. They intersect in the middle where they are bound by a rope that is used to make the cross spin.

kulha (*sku lha*): A deity who protects the body of a warrior.

kumuda: Sanskrit for "water lily."

kunda: Sanskrit for a kind of jasmine that blossoms by moonlight.

langna flower (*glang sna*): The scientific name of this Himalayan plant is *Pedicularis integrifolia*. The middle of the dark, mottled flower is shaped like an elephant's trunk, hence the name—*langna* in Tibetan means "elephant trunk."

la stone (*bla rdo*): Also called "life-stone" or "lado." A support, often a stone—in the case of Gesar, a naturally formed eight-faceted rock crystal—for the protectors to reside in. The connection between the life stone and a dharmapala comes about through ritual practices that link specific objects to various dharma protectors. It is as if the object becomes their favorite thing. Once that connection is made, the dharmapala will be attracted to wherever the object is kept. This principle does not only apply to protecting deities. When the la-vitality leaves a person, they will die soon after, so a portion of the la-vitality can be locked in a token stone, usually turquoise, which is then worn around the neck for security and protection.

lha (*lha*): A deity (Sanskrit, *deva*) or divine principle, sometimes translated as "god" when referring to a worldly spirit. The Nalanda Translation Committee leaves *lha* untranslated when referring to the triad of *lha*, *lu*, and *nyen*: heaven, on or below the ground, and everything in between. A *lhasang* is an invocation of the principle of heaven, inviting the awakened energy of drala and the principle of lha to descend. The column of smoke becomes a passageway through which positive spirits can descend. The descending lha lands on the body, speech, and mind of the practitioner—particularly on their body—and protects them from the loss of windhorse.

life-force wheel (*srog 'khor*): A circular diagram drawn on cloth or paper on which people write the mantra of their protector. Once it is consecrated, the protector constantly resides in it. The practitioners then always wear it.

lords of the three families (*rigs gsum mgon po*): See **three families**.

lu (*klu*): Tibetan for **naga**.

makara (*chu srin*): A mythical sea creature of Hindu mythology, similar to a crocodile.

mara (*bdud*): Often translated as "demon," it refers to negative influences, such as illnesses, that harm sentient beings; it can also refer to the "four maras," which trap beings in samsara (see **maras of the four directions**). In the Gesar epic, the evil demon king of the North, whom Gesar must destroy, is known as Düd, the Tibetan term for mara. See also the translator's introduction, page xxii.

maras of the four directions (*phyogs bzhi'i bdud bzhi*): The four anti-Buddhist principal kingdoms that are opposed to virtue and that Gesar must vanquish. See **four borders**.

mark of virtue (*dge mtshan*): See **virtuous mark**.

masang (*ma sang*): (1) Spirits who inhabited Tibet before the coming of Buddhism. Usually they are a group known as the nine masang brothers (*ma sang dpun dgu*). They are similar to the eight classes of gods and demons; in fact, they seem to refer to the same thing: all the gods, spirits, and demons. Indeed, Mipham Rinpoche uses the expression "masangs of the eight classes," probably equating masangs with the eight classes of gods and demons. (2) Name of an ancestral tribe of Ling. (3) One of the four types of nyen. (4) An epithet of Gesar, for example in the title Masang Jewel of Abundance (*ma sang g.yang gi nor bu*), as his father, Gerdzo, was a masang nyen.

menmo (*sman mo*): Feminine deities often paired with dralas, who can appear as beautiful women and can also be wrathful.

mikha (*mi kha*): Literally, "talking about a person" or "gossip," and it is generally translated as "scandal" in this book. There is an extraordinary variety of mikhas: people can say pleasant, unpleasant, or neutral things about someone. Mikha, or being talked about, has power. Mikhas are like weapons that can hurt and even kill humans, animals, and other beings when they are struck by them. When there are all sorts of mikhas or gossip about someone, then problems arise.

mirror divination (*pra*): A quite common form of divination in both Buddhist and Bön traditions. In order to acquire the ability to see the clues, the practitioner must have first obtained the power through the practice of the divination deity and the recitation of its mantra. The vision may appear in a mirror, in space, on the surface of a lake, on a fingernail, on the blade of a sword, and the like.

mu (*dmu* or *rmu*): Gods who reside in a heaven high above. In the Bönpo tradition, they are considered to be the ancestors of humans. The first king of Tibet, Nyatri Tsenpo, is a god from the heaven of the mu deities who descended along the mu-cord to lead the Tibetan people, who didn't have a king.

mu-cord (*dmu thag*): According to the Bön tradition, the mu-cord is a cord of light drawn from the heaven of the mu gods down to the human realm. The cord is like a ladder offering a pathway between heaven and earth, and a god can descend to rule and protect the Tibetan people. When a king died, his body dissolved gradually into light from the feet upward into the cord, which led him into the heaven of the mu gods. In Bön rituals, the mu-cord links man to heaven, and it plays an important role in popular rituals such as birth and marriage, as everyone, not only kings, is born with this cord attached to their head. In these practices, the mu-cord is used as an image of a pathway that Gesar and all the dralas and wermas can follow to come to help us.

naga (*klu*): Deities who live under the ground or in water (while the gods live in celestial realms and the nyens in between). Some nagas belong to the animal realm, while others are demigods. They generally live in the form of snakes, but many can change into human form. They are often depicted as human from the waist up with a serpent's tail below. They are supposed to control the weather, especially rain, and also wealth. Gesar's mother is a nagini (a female naga). The nagas figure prominently in the Indian epic tradition, but the word *lu* also refers to a native Tibetan deity associated with water.

nine mewas (*sme ba dgu*): A technical astrological term. *Mewa* means "mole" or "birthmark." Mewas are arranged in a magic square of three rows and three columns where all rows, columns, and diagonals form a count of fifteen. Each mewa has an association with a direction, a color, and an element. The position of the mewa changes every year, month, and day in the sequence 123456789. A complete mewa sign-element cycle takes one hundred and eighty years. The mewa of one's birth year is important as it is associated with vitality, but there are also specific life-force, power, wealth, body, and windhorse mewas, which are based on the birth mewa.

nyen (*gnyan*): Spirits who live in mountains, between the celestial gods and the underground nagas. Famous nyens are Machen Pomra and Nyenchen Tanglha, and Gesar's patron and father Gerdzo. Nyens are usually powerful gods who exercise a certain ownership over the lands where their mountain ranges lie and are thus also called "earth lords" (*sa bdag*).

patron gods (*'go ba'i lha*): See **five patron gods**.

prideful ones (*dregs pa*): See **eight classes of gods and demons**.

prosperity (*phywa*): A term from the Bönpo tradition referring to an individual's positive force that is the basis of prosperity. So it indicates more the cause of prosperity than actual prosperity, and this is what the prosperity rituals work on—the ability to attract prosperity and well-being. See also **abundance**.

protectors of the three families (*rigs gsum mgon po*): See **three families**.

repelling practice (*bzlog pa*): *Dokpa* in Tibetan, sometimes translated as "averting practice." A type of wrathful practice for repelling and dispersing negative forces such as enemies, obstacles, evil spirits, and so on.

ribboned arrow (*mda' dar*): An arrow adorned with silk bands of five colors representing the five elements, a small mirror, and other articles. It is a ritual implement required in practices that summon abundance or summon longevity. It is also used in traditional Tibetan marriage ceremonies. The vajra master wields the arrow slowly as it emanates rays of light of the five colors, which gather the vital essence of samsara and nirvana, all the abundance, and all the longevity and life force in the universe.

samaya demons (*dam sri*): See **damsi**.

sang (*bsang*): Tibetan smoke offering. There are different types of sangs, but as Jamyang Khyentse Wangpo explains, they are rituals during which offerings are given with cleansing substances—the smoke from the burnt aromatic woods—to purify all faults and problems for oneself and others while satisfying the recipients of the offerings. Orgyen Tobgyal Rinpoche explains sang from the Buddhist perspective in detail on pages 31–35.

select portion (*phud*): Literally, "the first part" of food, drink, and so forth, which is offered to the deities. It comes from the Asian tradition of reserving the first and best portion of something for the most honored guests—for example, the best piece of meat, food, or drink or simply the first portion before anyone else is served.

seven Cha deities (*phywa'i lha bdun*): The seven deities are the three Puwer brothers who are also known as the kings of the deities of divination, the three Tsamin sisters, and Chau Yangkar. According to the Jutik divination system, it is indispensable to propitiate them with mantras and invocations to the seven Cha deities before performing a divination. See also **Chashen** and **jutik**.

shoulder-god (*'phrag lha*): One of the thirteen dralhas. He rides a garuda and holds a victory banner and a flag on a spear. He is the constant personal guardian of people and resides in the shoulder. See also **five patron gods**.

sixty-year cycle (*rab byung*): The Tibetan calendar follows a sixty-year cycle system. In Tibetan astrology, years are identified by one of the sixty names formed by combining an element (earth, fire, water, wood, and iron) with an animal (hare, dragon, snake, horse, sheep, monkey, bird, dog, pig, mouse, ox, and tiger); for example, Fire Pig. Sixty-year cycles are also numbered. The first sixty-year cycle began in 1027 C.E., when this Tibetan dating system was established by Lotsawa Dawa Özer. We are currently in the seventeenth cycle. Mipham Rinpoche lived during the fifteenth cycle.

swastika (*g.yung drung*): In the Bön religion, it is equivalent to the Buddhist vajra, which often means "emptiness" and represents indestructibility. See also **yungdrung**.

thread-cross (*mdos*): A structure made from thin pieces of wood in a frame wrapped with threads of various colors into geometric patterns, such as circles, squares, and triangles. Thread-cross rituals are mostly practices for trapping demons, although thread-cross structures called "namkha" (*nam mkha'*) are also used in other practices such as ransoming of lives, offerings, or as a deity palace.

three aromatic woods (*bdud rtsi can gyi shing gsum*): Juniper, rhododendron, and tamarisk.

three families (*rigs gsum*): "Families" is a very loose translation of the Sanskrit *kula*, which has a wide range of meanings. Here it refers to the three enlightened qualities of wisdom, love, and power. These qualities can be concentrated in particular "physical" forms as Manjushri, Avalokiteshvara, and Vajrapani respectively, who are known collectively as the lords of the three families. Gesar is an incarnation of all three.

three planes of existence (*srid gsum*): Underground, on the ground, and in the air. Also referred to as "three levels" or "three worlds" (*sa gsum*).

three protector-mahasattvas (*rigs gsum mgon po*): See **three families**.

three weapons (*'khor gsum*): Bow, sword, and spear.

tsen (*btsan*): Deities associated with rocks and mountainsides. With the nyens, they stand between the heavens of the gods (*lha*) and the earth, the realm of the nagas. The tsens are mostly represented as ferocious red riders, wearing armor and riding red horses. In their right hand they usually brandish a red lance with a flag of the same color, while the left hand is used to throw their characteristic red noose.

tukkar (*thugs kar*): Bön deities who are specially dedicated to the protection and rule of a kingdom.

uniting the samayas (*dam tshig bsre ba*): In this expression, *samaya* refers to the fact that the practitioner holds Guru Rinpoche's command and can order the protector Gesar. *Uniting* means that the samayas of the protector Gesar and of the yogi practicing the dharma merge as one, indicating that they now support each other. And if Gesar is unable to help the practitioner, his samaya didn't "unite" with Guru Rinpoche's samaya that is asking Gesar to help the yogin—it is different from it. This process is detailed in the Samaya section in *Instant Fortune* (#4), pages 60–61.

vira (*dpa' bo*): Male counterpart of the dakini; they are realized beings who guard the charnel grounds and gather for tsok feast. They are usually called "daka" in English.

virtuous mark (*dge mtshan*): Also referred to as a "mark of virtue." An important phrase in Chögyam Trungpa's Shambhala teachings on lungta, in which it is described as the virtuous mark of windhorse (*dge mtshan rlung rta*), as in Mipham Rinpoche's Gesar texts. The windhorse is virtuous because it enables us to associate ourselves with the three kayas and to realize their nature. Trungpa Rinpoche explained that "virtuous here does not necessarily mean any old virtue. We are talking in terms of the one and only virtue—which is the great combination of primordial, unchanging, brave, gentleness, fearlessness, prajna, skillful means, daring, and patience. Those virtues are regarded as the mark of the good windhorse."

warrior's drink (*dpa' skyems*): A Secret Mantra term for alcohol, the drink that gives courage.

wermas (*wer ma*): An important category of protective deities. Sometimes they are said to be a particular type of drala, sometimes different from them. They are described as ferocious and fearless warriors who repel attacks and protect while traveling. They can also reside in weapons and enhance their power.

wisdom, activity, and worldly (*ye shes las 'jig rten gsum*): When applied to dakinis, the wisdom dakinis are the female deities such as Vajravarahi; the activity dakinis are the dharma protectresses such as Tseringma and Dutro Lhamo; and the worldly dakinis are the ones who help and support the accomplishment of positive actions. The same principle applies to wealth deities, treasure guardians, dralas, wermas, and so on.

yabdar (*g.yab dar*): A black or red silk streamer used to invite the protectors and for summoning maras before liberating them.

yaksha (*gnod sbyin*): Generally speaking, yakshas are a class of beings who assail and cause harm to humans. *Yaksha* can also refer to worldly wealth deities—gods of the desire realm who form the army of Vaishravana and are often supplicated as a means for obtaining wealth. In the practices collected in this book, it mostly refers to the latter meaning.

yama (*gshin rje*): A class of death-bringing demons. As a proper name, it is the Lord of Death and the ruler of all beings who are reborn in one of the cold or hot hells.

yungdrung (*g.yung drung*): Another name for Bön. *Yungdrung* is also the Tibetan translation of the Sanskrit *swastika*. See also **swastika**.

zodor (*zo dor*): Chief local deities. Many gods own and look after local areas, and in any given locality, the most important and most well-known are the zodors. They are local deities attached to a place, often a mountain. The main zodor in the Gesar epic is Magyal Pomra. In Gesar practices, zodors can also have a wider meaning and refer to all wermas.

GLOSSARY OF PROPER NAMES

Awe-Inspiring Land of Ling (*mthong ba kun smon*): An epithet of Ling that means it is a land such that anyone who sees it wishes to live there. Ling was an ancient kingdom of Tibet.

Balaha (*ba la ha*): Also Valaha; the Sanskrit name of the fabulous talking and flying white king of horses, who is an emanation of Avalokiteshvara. He was also one of the past incarnations of Buddha Shakyamuni, with his story told in the *Valahassa Jataka*. He bears a wish-fulfilling jewel on his back and is drawn at the center of windhorse flags.

Bernakchen (*ber nag can*): A form of Mahakala with two arms, famous for the power that comes from his mastery of mantra. His name refers to the fact that he has (*can*) a black (*nag*) cloak (*ber*). In the Gesar epic, he is Chökyong Bernak, one of the seven champion warriors of Ling, and a bodyguard of Rinchen Darlu. Mipham Rinpoche says that the emanation of Mahakala and the warrior of the epic are the same.

Chashen (*phywa gshen*): *Shen* means Bön. The Shen of the Cha is one of the four branches of Bön. The branch teaches methods of divination, astrological calculation, medicine, and Bön rites known as To.

Chau Yangkar (*phywa'u g.yang dkar*): See **seven Cha deities.**

Chime Chokdrup Ling (*'chi med mchog sgrub gling*): The hermitage at Junyung, Mipham Rinpoche's homeland. This is where in his late teens Jamgön Mipham had the vision of Manjushri that unleashed the power of his intelligence. He later lived there.

Denma or **Minister Denma Changtra** (*blon chen 'dan ma byang bra*): A clever strategist and tactical planner, and Gesar's chief minister. Also known for his archery skills and as a great and loyal warrior. Denma, or Den, is the name of the region he was from, which is located in Kham.

Dondrup (*don grub*): One of Gesar's names, sometimes translated as "All-Accomplishing," and is Siddhartha in Sanskrit. It means the one who accomplishes purposeful tasks. It was given to him when he was born in the god realm known as the Abode of the Thirty-Three, before transferring to the human world in Jambudvipa as Gesar.

Dorje Lekpa (*rdo rje legs pa*): One of the most important protector deities in Tibet and the main protector of Gesar.

Dorje Yundrönma (*rdo rje g.yu sgron ma*): Chief of the twelve Tenmas and the main protectress of Gesar.

Mentsun Dorje Zulema (*sman btsun rdo rje zu le ma*): One of the four menmos from among the twelve Tenmas, the protectresses of Tibet.

Elder brother Dungkhyung Karpo (*phu bo dung khyung dkar po*): See **White Conch Garuda**.

Gabde (*dga' bde*): The name of an area that some say is near Jyekundo. In the Gesar epic, Chökyong Bernakchen, one of the seven champion warriors of Ling, is from Gabde. So the name of his place of origin, Gabde, can also refer to him, as is often the custom in Tibet. Bernakchen is also a form of Mahakala with two arms. See **Bernakchen**.

Ganapati (*tshogs bdag*): An epithet for Ganesha, the elephant-headed deity with a baby's body who removes obstructions to practice. He sometimes appears in semi-wrathful form in the tantras, as a king of the dralas and as a local protector.

Gerdzo (*ger mdzo*): The nyen of the mountain Gerdzo Rimar Wangzhu, and Gesar's "biological father."

Guan Yu (*bkwan lo yen*): Guan Yu (d. 219) was a warrior of the late Han dynasty renowned for his courage and loyalty, who later became a saint venerated by Taoists. The Wanli emperor (r. 1573–1620) of the Ming dynasty elevated Guan to the rank of emperor (Ch. *-di*). Then called Guandi, he served as a protector of the Manchu rulers of the Qing dynasty, who erected numerous shrines in his honor throughout China.

Gungpa Kyatra (*gung pa skya khra*): A great warrior, one of the "thirty fathers and uncles" in the lesser lineage of Ling.

Gyatsa Shelkar of Bumpa (*'bum pa'i rgya tsha zhal dkar*): His name means "white-face Chinese grandson from the Bumpa clan." He is Gesar's elder half brother and a grandson of the emperor of China. After King Gesar, he was the second in line. He is the model of the perfect Tibetan warrior. So-called descendants of Gesar, such as the Mukpo family, actually originate from Gyatsa Shelkar, as Gesar didn't have children. Bumpa is the name of Gyatsa's clan and is another name for the Mukpo clan.

Jayadevi (*rnam rgyal lha mo*): Also known as Ushnishavijaya (All-Victorious Lady of the Ushnisha). An ushnisha is the special protuberance on the top of the head of a fully enlightened buddha. A popular deity who is considered an emanation of Buddha Vairochana, Jayadevi is a protector of the directions, especially of the upward direction. She is represented as peaceful, usually white or yellow in color, with two or three eyes and two to eight hands, and rich in ornaments. In Tibetan Buddhism, there are a number of ushnisha deities who protect the dharma or the household and, like Jayadevi, also protect various directions.

Kalkin Rudra Chakrin (*rigs ldan 'khor lo can*): He is, according to the Kalachakra, the kalkin, or king of Shambhala, who will lead the future armies of Shambhala against the barbarians, at the beginning of the Wood Male Monkey year in 2424.

Khamtrul Rinpoche Dongyu Nyima (1931–1980) (*khams sprul rin po che don brgyud nyi ma*): An important master of the Drukpa Kagyu lineage who was the eighth reincarnation of Khampa Karma Tenphel. He rebuilt Khampagar Monastery in Tashi Jong, Himachal Pradesh, India, in the late 1960s and played a leading role in reviving the Drukpa Kagyu lineage in exile. He also did much to preserve Gesar practices by publishing two volumes of Gesar practices from different masters. His teacher, Tsenyi Tulku Jampal Norbu, wrote extensively on Gesar. Khamtrul Rinpoche was one of Tulku Orgyen Tobgyal's main teachers.

Lelung Shepe Dorje (1687–1740) (*sle lung bzhad pa'i rdo rje*): See **Shepe Dorje**.

Ludrul Öjung (*klu sbrul 'od 'byung*): "Luminous Naga Snake" is Gesar's younger brother, one of the three dralas born to the same mother at the same time as him. *The Epic of Gesar* says that after Gesar's birth, an infant with a human body and a snake's head emerged from his mother's heart chakra within an egglike orb of blue light. As soon as he was born, he told his mother, "I am the third-born son, destined for kindness. I am without a physical body to accomplish the benefit of beings, but I will be the guardian on Gesar's white armor. I am his younger brother Ludrul Öjung. My retinue resides in the silken cape draped over his armor. When you are making an offering to me, offer the select portion of the three whites. I am a kulha who will never leave the great being's side."

Ma (*rma*): The valley around Machen Pomra, which is renowned for its rich pastures. In the Gesar epic and in the Gesar practices, it is considered a place of wealth where good fortune arises.

Machen Pomra (*rma chen spom ra*): A mountain range also known as Amnye Machen. It is located in eastern Tibet, in the heart of the Golok district, in what is now Qinghai Province.

Magyal Pomra (*rma rgyal spom ra*): A nyen, or mountain god, who is the deity of the Machen Pomra mountain range and a protector of Gesar. Magyal Pomra is a highly realized bodhisattva. He is one of the main treasure guardians and a deity who brings abundance.

Maheshvara (*dbang chen*): See **Padma Maheshvara**.

Ma's Upper Dil-yag Tiger Plain (*rma dil yag stag thang gong ma*): The place where the people of Ling used to assemble to discuss important affairs. This plain was one stage on the trade route between Tibet and China. Upper Tiger is surrounded by beautiful mountains.

Mikmar Chenpo (*mig dmar chen po*): The great warlord Mikmar (Red Eyes) is the chief of the nine masang brothers. He has a wrathful expression, wears a loose-sleeved red-and-green brocade cloak, and holds a six-foot magical noose.

Nyinya (*nyi nya*): The lord of the wermas.

Padma Maheshvara (*padma dbang chen*): An epithet of Hayagriva, who is the chief heruka of the lotus, or padma, family. *Maheshvara* means mighty one.

Palace of Lotus Light (*pad ma 'od kyi pho brang*): Guru Rinpoche's palace on the Copper-Colored Mountain.

Rutam (*ru dam*): A mountainous region to the northeast of Derge, in which Dzogchen Monastery is located.

Shepe Dorje (1687–1740) (*bzhad pa'i rdo rje*): Lelung Shepe Dorje was an incarnation of Vajrapani, the Lord of Secret. He is generally considered the first master to reveal termas related to Gesar, which happened in 1729 at Ölga in Lokha.

Sister Tale Ökar (*sring lcam tha le 'od dkar*): "Radiant White Light" is Gesar's younger sister, one of the three dralas born to the same mother at the same time as him. *The Epic of Gesar* reveals that after the birth of Gesar's younger brother, that same morning, rainbow rays of light emanated from their mother's navel chakra and a beautiful girl of white light emerged wearing clothing of vulture feathers. She said, "Mother, I am your fourth child. I do not have a body of flesh and blood. I am the drala who accompanies the noble steed. I will be Gesar's sister, Tale Ökar. When you make offerings to me, offer tea and turquoise. My retinue is at the ear tip of his chestnut steed, resembling the finest vulture feathers. I am the spy that sees or the lamp that illuminates circumstances and reveals what is hidden. I am the kulha who never parts from Gesar."

Thirteen changsengs expert in covering long distances (*cang seng mgron yag dar ma bcu gsum*): See **changseng**.

Three Puwer brothers and three Tsamin sisters (*phu wer mched gsum dang sring mo tsa min mched gsum*): see **seven Cha deities**.

Tradruk Temple (*khra 'brug gtsang khang*): In Yarlung, one of the geomantic temples built by Songtsen Gampo, and one of the three most important temples in Central Tibet, together with Samye and the Jokhang.

Vajratikshna (*rdo rje rnon po*): The Sharp Vajra; a slightly wrathful form of Manjushri who flattens the mountains of wrong views and rips apart the net of misunderstanding. This is the form of the all-accomplishing wisdom, which is jealousy in its natural pure manifestation and one of the five wisdoms.

White Conch Garuda (*phu bo dung khyung dkar po*): Gesar's elder brother, one of the three dralas born to the same mother at the same time as him. *The Epic of Gesar* says that on the day of Gesar's birth, as soon as the sun rose, a white light emerged from the chakra at the crown of his mother's head. It transformed into a man who was as white as a conch and with the head of a garuda, holding a spear with a white silken pennant. He told his mother, "I am your firstborn son. I will not achieve the benefit of beings with a physical body. I am the guardian who resides upon Gesar's white helmet and my retinue are in his garuda feather and pennants. When you make offerings to me, give me the three sweet substances. I am the elder brother White Conch Garuda. I will never be separate from Gesar."

White Little Vulture (*rgod chung dkar mo*): The eldest daughter of the naga king Tsugna Rinchen, and therefore the elder sister of Gesar's mother.

Yama (*gshin rje*): As a proper name, it is the name of the Lord of Death and the ruler of all beings who are reborn in one of the cold or hot hells. The term is also applied to a whole class of death-bringing demons.

Yudrönma (*g.yu sgron ma*): See **Dorje Yudrönma**.

Notes

Translator's Introduction

1. Robin Kornman, Sangye Khandro, and Lama Chönam, trans., *The Epic of Gesar of Ling: Gesar's Magical Birth, Early Years, and Coronation as King* (Boston: Shambhala, 2012), 501.

2. Dilgo Khyentse Rinpoche, *Pure Appearance: Development and Completion Stages in the Vajrayana Practice*, trans. Ane Jinba Palmo (Boulder: Shambhala Publications, 2016).

3. *Gling rje ge sar skyes bu'i mchod sgrub phyogs bsdus byin rlabs gter mdzod* (Zi ling: Mtsho sngon mi rigs dpe skrun khang, 2015). BDRC MW3CN7776.

4. Daniel J. Miller, *Drokpa: Nomads of the Tibetan Plateau and Himalaya* (Kathmandu: Vajra, 2008), 22.

5. René Thom and Robert E. Chumbley, "Stop Chance! Silence Noise!" *SubStance* 12, no. 3 (1983): 11.

6. Khenpo Ngawang Pelzang, *A Guide to the Words of My Perfect Teacher* (Boston: Shambhala, 2004), 245.

7. Another spelling of the first syllable is also found in old Bönpo texts. It does not impact the pronunciation but its meaning is different. If *dgra* means "enemy," *sgra* means "sound," as *bla* in this context refers to a particular type of vital energy. For the Bönpos, sound is the main agent of connection between a person and their la-vitality, and in this case too, *drala* refers to a protective being or energy. For more on this spelling, see Namkhai Norbu Rinpoche, *Drung, Deu, and Bön: Narrations, Symbolic Languages, and the Bön Tradition in Ancient Tibet* (Dharamsala: LTWA, 1995), 60–62.

8. "The Destroyer of the Teachings' Enemies—a Daily Sang Offering to the Omnipotent Being Gesar, the Ruler of the World," trans. G. Avertin (unpublished manuscript, 2020).

9. Sogyal Rinpoche, *The Tibetan Book of Living and Dying*, rev. and updated (San Francisco: HarperCollins, 2003), 36–37.

10. See page 139.

11. Dudjom Rinpoche, *The Nyingma School of Tibetan Buddhism* (Boston: Wisdom, 2002), 960.

12. Walpola Rahula, *What the Buddha Taught* (London: Gordon Fraser Gallery, 1959), 81.

13. Jamgön Kongtrul Lodrö Taye, *Bouquet of Red Lotuses: How to Practice the Outer, Inner, and Secret Sadhanas of the Lotus Dakini from the Three Roots of the Profound Cycle of Longevity* (Hong Kong: Namthar, 2020), 2.

14. Jamgön Kongtrul Lodrö Taye, *Bouquet of Red Lotuses*, 10.

15. See the foreword in Kornman, Khandro, and Lama Chönam, trans., *The Epic of Gesar of Ling*, x.

16. Orgyen Tobgyal, *The Life and Teaching of Chokgyur Lingpa*, 3rd ed. (Kathmandu: Rangjung Yeshe, 1988), 11.

17. Dzongsar Khyentse, *Not for Happiness: A Guide to the So-Called Preliminary Practices* (Boston: Shambhala, 2012), 98.

18. Jamyang Khyentse Wangpo et al., *Sublime Lady of Immortality: Teachings on Chimé Phakmé Nyingtik* (Hong Kong: Namthar, 2021), 228.

19. See Patrul Rinpoche, *The Words of My Perfect Teacher*, rev. ed. (New Haven, CT: Yale University Press, 2010), 210–12.

20. Alexandra David-Neel and Lama Yongden, *The Superhuman Life of Gesar of Ling*, trans. Violet Sydney (Boulder: Prajna, 1981).

21. Khandro Kornman and Lama Chönam, trans., *The Epic of Gesar of Ling*; and Jane Hawes, David Shapiro, and Lama Chönam, trans., *The Taming of the Demons: From the Epic of Gesar of Ling* (Boulder: Shambhala, 2021).

22. David Shapiro, *Gesar of Ling: A Bardic Tale from the Snow Land of Tibet* (Bloomington, IN: Balboa Press, 2019).

23. Dilgo Khyentse Rinpoche, *Mi pham 'jam dbyangs rnam rgyal rgya mtsho'i rnam thar snying po bsdus pa ngo mtshar bdud rtsi'i snang ba* (New Delhi: Shechen, 2012), 25. The English translation, however, says that Lharik was Rinchen Namgyal's immediately preceding incarnation. Dilgo Khyentse and Jamgön Mipham, *Lion of Speech: The Life of Mipham Rinpoche*, trans. Padmakara Translation Group (Boulder: Shambhala, 2020), 208n54.

24. John Whitney Pettit, "Essential Hagiography," in *Mipham's Beacon of Certainty: Illuminating the View of Dzogchen, the Great Perfection* (Somerville, MA: Wisdom, 1999), 23–29.

25. Dilgo Khyentse and Jamgön Mipham, *Lion of Speech: The Life of Mipham Rinpoche*, trans. Padmakara Translation Group; Khenpo Jigme Phuntsok, *Miracle Stories of Mipham Rinpoche* (Halifax, NS: Nalanda Translation Committee, 2008).

26. Khenpo Jigme Phuntsok, *Miracle Stories of Mipham Rinpoche*, 10.

27. Dilgo Khyentse, *Lion of Speech*, xi.

28. Dilgo Khyentse, *Lion of Speech*, 19.

29. Jamgon Mipham, *The Just King: The Tibetan Buddhist Classic on Leading an Ethical Life*, trans. Jose Ignacio Cabezon (Boulder: Snow Lion, 2017).

30. Dilgo Khyentse, *Lion of Speech*, 25.

31. Some people say that Mipham Rinpoche composed his first Gesar prayer in 1859, but *Crushing Malicious Forces* (#43) is a brief invocation of Gabde or Bernakchen, who is a form of Mahakala. Mipham Rinpoche included it as the last text of the Gesar section of his *Collected Works*, because Gabde is a protector of Gesar. This is where the confusion may come from. Most prayers in this collection begin with Padmasambhava (who manifested as Gesar), and yet they are not called "Guru Rinpoche prayers." *Crushing Malicious Forces* is not strictly speaking a Gesar prayer. Mipham Rinpoche composed his first practice to Gesar, *The Heart Essence of Good Fortune* (#15), toward the end of 1865, after having received the transmission of Lharik's terma from Lap Kyapgön

32. Rajiv Malhotra, *Being Different: An Indian Challenge to Western Universalism* (New Delhi: HarperCollins, 2011), 79–80.

33. We have compiled the Tibetan texts in the same order into one volume to make it easy for masters to give the reading transmission or to teach on a specific text, and published it on Tsadra Dharma Cloud, https://dharmacloud.tsadra.org.

34. Jamyang Khyentse Wangpo, "Bsang mchod kyi rnam gzhag," in *Gsar ma gtso bor ston pa'i zin bris*, in *Collected Works*, vol. nga (Gangtok: Gonpo Tseten, 1977–1980), 551–52. BDRC W21807.

35. Umberto Eco, *Experiences in Translation* (Toronto: University of Toronto Press, 2001), 50.

36. See note 1 above.

37. Jirí Levý, *The Art of Translation* (Amersterdam: John Benjamins, 2011), 81.

GESAR PRACTICES EXPLAINED

1. *Manjushrinamasamgiti* (*'Jam dpal mtshan brjod*): v. 141.

2. Jamgön Mipham, *A Garland of Jewels: The Eight Great Bodhisattvas* (Woodstock, NY: KTD, 2007).

3. See, for example, *Sollo Chenmo* (#37), page 211.

4. Dudjom Rinpoche wrote that when the second sixty-year cycle began (in 1087), Gesar, the king of Ling, born in the Earth Tiger year, was in his fiftieth year. The translators of his book then calculated his dates to be

1038–1124. Dudjom Rinpoche, *The Nyingma School of Tibetan Buddhism: Its Fundamentals and History*, trans. Gyurme Dorje and Matthew Kapstein (Boston: Wisdom, 2002), 952.

5. A monastery in Nangchen, Kham, that was established in 944 and later became the seat of the Yelpa Kagyu lineage.

6. This is mentioned in his biography, which lists the eight treasuries. See Dilgo Khyentse Rinpoche, *Lion of Speech: The Life of Mipham Rinpoche* (Boulder: Shambhala, 2020), 37.

7. See Dilgo Khyentse Rinpoche, *Lion of Speech*, 84.

8. *mgon po dgra bla bcu gsum gyi bsang mchod.*

9. In his guide to the *Sollo Chenmo* practice, Shechen Gyaltsap Rinpoche says that we can do the short daily practice of Hayagriva in the Tamdrin Yangsang Tröpa form, and he inserts the text of the practice from the Lama Sangdu terma cycle.

10. Rinpoche explains this in *Sublime Lady of Immortality*, 215–16.

GESAR PRACTICES AND CRAFTS

1. Reading *dpal*. Some editions of Mipham's *Collected Works* read *dpal* (glorious), while others have *dpa'* ("courageous" or "warrior"). The two spellings are extremely close in Tibetan which could explain the discrepancy in the different editions.

2. Master of the Seven Horses is a poetic epithet of the sun, whose chariot is drawn by seven horses. In ancient Indian thought, the larger the number of horses, the more prestigious the charioteer; this number of horses was an indication of the sun's power and rank.

3. Sanskrit, meaning "the whole world."

4. See text #38, *A Beautiful Vase of Nectar*, pages 218–19.

5. "The Prayer to Guru Rinpoche that Spontaneously Fulfils All Wishes." See https://www.lotsawahouse.org/tibetan-masters/tulku-zangpo-drakpa/leu-dunma-chapter-7.

6. See note 5.

7. During a sang practice in Lerab Ling, Orgyen Tobgyal Rinpoche explained this point: "You'll have to say 'Ki ki so so lha gyalo' loudly. At that time, according to Mipham Rinpoche's pith instruction, let your eyes gaze into the sky and put your awareness into your eyes one-pointedly. Stare straight into the middle of the sky, stare piercingly into the sky. Then bring your gaze higher and higher while merging your mind indivisibly with the sky. You have to really concentrate on that and not let ordinary conceptual

thoughts stain the mind. Consider that your windhorse rises limitlessly. If you do that, there is no doubt your lungta will increase."

8. OM MAHA SENGE MANI RADZA HA HA HI HI HE HE HO HO SARWA VIDZAYA SIDDHI HUM OM AH HUM HO TAK SENG KHYUNG DRUK DI YAR KYE gather all, SARVA, gather, gather HOH! OM BENZA AYUKHE SOHA rouse all our life, virtue, and glorious windhorse higher and higher!

9. OM MUNE MUNE MAHA MUNA YE SOHA.

10. OM PEMA TSINTA MANI DZOLA HUM. The other two protectors are Manjushri and Vajrapani.

11. This prayer was translated by the Vajravairochana Translation Committee.

12. This is the prayer for requesting wishes at the beginning of text #17, *Boosting the Good* on pages 123–24.

13. Great warrior, you subjugate the troops of inimical maras,
With your sword of prajna and bow and arrow,
And quell the warfare of negative emotions and ignorance—
Eliminate all fears of the four maras!

14. Concerning this prayer, which is inserted three times in the supplication, see the supplemental section at the end, page 178.

15. In Tibet, clouds coming from the south always bring rain, which allows the crops to grow; hence the clouds are "the source of wealth." These clouds may also protect from frost, unlike clouds from the north, which bring snow. This explains why "southern clouds" are seen positively by Tibetans and are often used as an image of wealth in poetic compositions.

16. This prayer appears above, #25, page 153. In the different editions of Mipham Rinpoche's *Collected Works*, the prayer is included in these two places. This time, it is without practice instructions at the beginning, and with a different colophon, probably an indication that Mipham Rinpoche wrote the exact same prayer on two separate occasions. Since we have chosen to follow the order of the *Collected Works* dictated by Jamgön Mipham himself, we have repeated it.

17. Commonly known as *Sollo Chenmo* (*gsol lo chen mo*). The term *gsol* here is rather difficult to translate into English, as it has at least three separate meanings when it occurs in practice texts: "to encourage," "to offer," and "to tell or command." It has the latter meaning in the Tibetan word *gsol ka*, or "protectors' practice," but here it mainly has the sense of offering. This type of practice is called *gsol mchod* (translated here as "invocation and offering").

18. Lharik Dechen Yeshe Rölpa Tsal is not yet another of Mipham Rinpoche's

numerous names but someone else, the tertön who revealed the terma that is the basis of Mipham Rinpoche's writings on Gesar, many of which—probably all—are further revelations of this terma that Lharik wasn't able to reveal fully. See translator's introduction, pages xliv–xlv.

19. Probably 1808. See translator's introduction, page xlv.

20. Tibetans traditionally indicate right and left from the perspective of the deity they are describing, which is the opposite of the perspective of the observer, the one we are used to. See the flag on pages 228-29.

21. We have added these titles indicating the purpose of each mantra.

22. To follow the approach of Chögyam Trungpa Rinpoche, who guided the translation of this text, the mantras here reflect the Sanskrit pronunciation, instead of the Tibetan that we have followed in the rest of the book. For consistency, the mantras in the Tibetan pronunciation are as follows.

OM WAGI SHWARI MUM

OM MANI PADMA HUM

OM VAJRAPANI HUM

OM AH HUM BENZA GURU PADMA SIDDHI HUM

OM AH HUM HO HANG KSHA MA LA WA RA YAM SOHA

OM SARVA GRAHA NAKSHATRA DHYAMI KARANI SOHA

OM HE HE TISHTHA TISHTHA BHANDHA BHANDHA
    DHARAYA DHARAYA NIRUNDHA NIRUNDHA AMUKA
    URNA MANI YE SOHA

OM PEMA TSINTAMANI DZOLA HUM

OM MANI RADZA HA HA HI HI HE HE HO HO SARVA
    VIDZAYA SIDDHI HUM

OM AH HUM HO HE TAK SENG KHYUNG DRUK DI YAR
    KYE | KUN DU SARVA DU DU HO

OM BENZA AYUKHE SOHA | DAK CHAK GI TSE DANG
    SONAM PAL DANG LUNGTA TAMCHE GONG NE GONG
    DU KYE CHIK

OM YE DHARMA HETU PRABHAWA HETUN TESHAN
    TATHAGATO HYAWADAT TESHAN TSA YO NIRODHA
    EWAM WADI MAHASHRAMANA SOHA

OM BHURA BHUWA SWAH SWASTI NAMA SOHA

OM SARVA TITHI NAKSHATRA GRAHE MANGALE JO
    SOHA

OM AKANI NIKANI ABHILA MANGALE MANDALE SOHA
    | NAMO BUDDHA DHARMA SANGHAYA MAMA SHRI YE
    MANGALA BHAVANTU SOHA

23. The word *gnyen po* (antidote) is probably a misspelling of *gnyan po* (powerful), a term often associated with the gods of travel.

24. See previous note.

BIBLIOGRAPHY

Tibetan

Dilgo Khyentse Rinpoche. *Mi pham 'jam dbyangs rnam rgyal rgya mtsho'i rnam thar snying po bsdus pa ngo mtshar bdud rtis'i snang ba*. New Delhi: Shechen, 2013. BDRC MW8LS20744.

Jamgön Mipham. *Gsung 'bum mi pham rgya mtsho*. 27 vols. Lama Ngodrup and Sherab Drimey: Paro, Bhutan: 1984–1993.

———. *Gsung 'bum mi pham rgya mtsho*. 32 vols. Khreng tu'u: Gangs can rig gzhung dpe rnying myur skyobs lhan tshogs, 2007. BDRC W2DB16631.

———. *Kun mkhyen mi pham rgya mtsho'i gsung 'bum*. 42 vols. Gser rta rdzong: Bla rung sgar, 2014.

Jamgön Mipham, et al., *Gling rje ge sar skyes bu'i mchod sgrub phyogs bsdus byin rlabs gter mdzod*. Zi ling: Mtsho sngon mi rigs dpe skrun khang, 2015. BDRC MW3CN7776.

Jamyang Khyentse Wangpo. "Bsang mchod kyi rnam gzhag." In *Gsar ma gtso bor ston pa'i zin bris*, 551–52. In *'Jam dbyangs mkhyen brtse'i dbang po'i bka' 'bum*, vol. nga, 1–713. Gangtok: Gonpo Tseten, 1977–1980. BDRC W21807.

Mañjuśrīnāmasaṃgīti. *'Jam dpal ye shes sems dpa'i don dam pa'i mtshan yang dag par brjod pa* (*'Jam dpal mtshan brjod*). Derge Tengyur (D 360), rgyud, *ka*, 1b1–13b7. BDRC W30532.

English

David-Neel, Alexandra, and Lama Yongden. *The Superhuman Life of Gesar of Ling*. Translated by Violet Sydney. Boulder: Prajna, 1981.

Dilgo Khyentse Rinpoche. *Pure Appearance: Development and Completion Stages in the Vajrayana Practice*. Translated by Ane Jinba Palmo. Boulder: Shambhala, 2016.

Dilgo Khyentse Rinpoche, and Jamgon Mipham. *Lion of Speech: The Life of Mipham Rinpoche.* Translated by The Padmakara Translation Group. Boulder: Shambhala, 2020.

Do Khyentse Yeshe Dorje. "The Destroyer of the Teachings' Enemies: A Daily Sang Offering to the Omnipotent Being Gesar, the Ruler of the World." Translated by G. Avertin. Unpublished manuscript, 2020.

Dudjom Rinpoche. *The Nyingma School of Tibetan Buddhism.* Boston: Wisdom, 2002.

Dzongsar Khyentse. *Not for Happiness: A Guide to the So-Called Preliminary Practices.* Boulder: Shambhala, 2012.

Eco, Umberto. *Experiences in Translation.* Translated by Alastair McEwen. Toronto: University of Toronto Press, 2001.

Hawes, Jane, David Shapiro, and Lama Chönam, trans. *The Taming of the Demons: From the Epic of Gesar of Ling.* Boulder: Shambhala, 2021.

Jamgön Kongtrul Lodrö Taye. *Bouquet of Red Lotuses: How to Practice the Outer, Inner and Secret Sadhanas of the Lotus Dakini from the Three Roots of the Profound Cycle of Longevity.* Translated by Gyurme Avertin. Hong Kong: Namthar, 2020.

Jamgön Mipham. *A Garland of Jewels: The Eight Great Bodhisattvas.* Woodstock, NY: KTD, 2007.

———. *The Just King: The Tibetan Buddhist Classic on Leading an Ethical Life.* Translated by Jose Ignacio Cabezon. Boulder: Snow Lion, 2017.

Jamyang Khyentse Wangpo, Jamgön Kongtrul Lodrö Taye, Dilgo Khyentse Rinpoche, Jamyang Khyentse Chökyi Lodrö, and Tulku Orgyen Tobgyal. *Sublime Lady of Immortality: Teachings on Chime Phakme Nyingtik.* Translated by Gyurme Avertin. Hong Kong: Namthar, 2021.

Jigme Phuntsok (Khenpo), and Ann Helm. *Miracle Stories of Mipham Rinpoche.* Halifax: Nalanda Translation Committee, 2008.

Kornman, Robin, Sangye Khandro, and Lama Chönam, trans. *The Epic of Gesar of Ling: Gesar's Magical Birth, Early Years, and Coronation as King.* Boston: Shambhala, 2012.

Levý, Jiří. *The Art of Translation.* Amsterdam: John Benjamins, 2011.

Malhotra, Rajiv. *Being Different: An Indian Challenge to Western Universalism.* New Delhi: Harper Collins, 2011.

Miller, Daniel J. *Drokpa: Nomads of the Tibetan Plateau and Himalaya.* Kathmandu: Vajra, 2008.

Namkhai Norbu Rinpoche. *Drung, Deu and Bon: Narrations, Symbolic Languages and the Bon Tradition in Ancient Tibet.* Dharamsala: Library of Tibetan Works and Archives, 1995.

Ngawang Pelzang (Khenpo). *A Guide to "The Words of My Perfect Teacher."* Shambhala, 2004.

Orgyen Tobgyal. *The Life and Teaching of Chokgyur Lingpa.* 3rd ed. Kathmandu: Rangjung Yeshe, 1988.

Patrul Rinpoche. *The Words of My Perfect Teacher.* Rev. ed. New Haven, CT: Yale University Press, 2010.

Pettit, John Whitney. "Essential Hagiography." In *Mipham's Beacon of Certainty: Illuminating the View of Dzogchen, the Great Perfection,* 23–29. Somerville, MA: Wisdom, 1999.

Rahula, Walpola. *What the Buddha Taught.* London: Gordon Fraser Gallery, 1959.

Shapiro, David. *Gesar of Ling: A Bardic Tale from the Snow Land of Tibet.* Bloomington, IN: Balboa, 2019.

Sogyal Rinpoche. *The Tibetan Book of Living and Dying.* Rev. ed. Edited by Patrick Gaffney and Andrew Harvey. San Francisco: Harper Collins, 2003.

Thom, René, and Robert E. Chumbley. "Stop Chance! Silence Noise!" *SubStance* 12, no. 3 (1983): 11–21. https://doi.org/10.2307/3684251.

DEDICATION

May this book reach all those who will benefit from it alone.
May it bring vast benefit to them, the dharma, and the world.
May it be a source of limitless benefit
And of the removal of obstacles to goodness,
Particularly for practitioners on the path.
May the lion's roar of the victorious ones fill the hearts of all
     beings
And may beings pass beyond sorrow and reach the citadel of
     boundless happiness.

CREDITS

Gesar the Warrior by Chögyam Trungpa first appeared as a foreword to Alexandra David-Neel and Lama Yongden, *The Superhuman Life of Gesar of Ling* (Boulder: Prajna Press, 1981). Printed with permission.

Prayer to Gesar (#24), *The Swift Fulfillment of Wishes: A Brief Offering Prayer to King Gesar* (#25), *Brief Offering Prayer to King Gesar* (#35), Sollo Chenmo: *The Swift Accomplishment of Enlightened Activity through Invocation and Offering* (#37) were translated by Adam Pearcey and are printed with permission from Lotsawa House (lotsawahouse.org).

The Swift Fulfillment of All Wishes: Offering the Flag of Windhorse (© 2010) was translated by Rigpa Translations and is printed with permission from Patrick Gaffney.

The Swift Entering of Blessings (#1), *The All-Clear Jewel Mirror: The Cleansing Sang Offering of the Luminous Werma* (#12), *Short Lhasang* (#13), *Windhorse Supplication* (#14), *Warrior Song of Drala: The Long Werma Lhasang* (#30), *Swift Accomplishment of Enlightened Activity: An Offering to Great Lion Gesar Norbu* (#34), *Spontaneous Accomplishment of Wishes: A Daily Offering to Gesar, King of Dralas* (#36), *Brief Protector Offering to Gesar* (#45), *Short Windhorse Supplication* (#49), *Short Lhasang* (#50), and *Invocation for Raising Windhorse* (#51) were all translated by and are printed with permission from the Nalanda/Vajravairocana Translation Committee.

Drawings of Gesar's various forms on pages 56, 74, 86, 106, and 162 by Tara di Gesu © 2022

Drawing of Gesar's wealth pouch on page 221 by Peter Fry © 2022

Gesar's prayer flag on page 228–29 Namthar Ltd © 2022